Biography and

Theory and History
Series Editor: Donald MacRaild

Published

Biography and History

2nd edition

Barbara Caine

First edition 2010
Second edition published 2019
by RED GLOBE PRESS

Red Globe Press in the UK is an imprint of Macmillan Publishers Limited, registered in England, company number 785998, of 4 Crinan Street, London, N1 9XW.

Red Globe Press® is a registered trademark in the United States, the United Kingdom, Europe and other countries.

ISBN 978–1–137–61116–1 hardback
ISBN 978–1–137–61119–2 paperback

This book is printed on paper suitable for recycling and made from fully managed and sustained forest sources. Logging, pulping and manufacturing processes are expected to conform to the environmental regulations of the country of origin.

A catalogue record for this book is available from the British Library.

A catalog record for this book is available from the Library of Congress.

Contents

Acknowledgements

Despite the growing interest in biography amongst historians, there has been little general discussion of the changing relationship between biography and history or of the changing ways in which historians and others interested in past lives have approached the writing of biography. It is these questions which this book attempts to address. As there is not as yet a substantial literature to refer to, I am more than usually indebted to the seminar groups to which I have given papers from the book and to the friends and colleagues who have discussed it with me. I owe particular thanks to Mark Salber Phillips for sharing with me his ideas on many of the questions that I have discussed here, for the challenging questions that he always asked, and for his immensely helpful critical comments on some earlier versions of the book. I would like to thank the convenors and participants of the staff –student research seminar in the School of Historical Studies at Monash University, the work-in-progress seminar at the Research School of Humanities at the Australian National University, the sociology seminar at the University of Essex, the life-writing seminars at Goldsmith's College, and the psychoanalysis and history Seminar at the Institute of Historical Research in London for the very valuable feedback I received from them. I would also like to thank a number of colleagues and friends for very helpful comments, and suggestions and for critical feedback on particular chapters of the book: Sally Alexander, Susan Foley, Michael Hau, Jim Hammerton, Katie Holmes, Rhys Isaacs, Carolyn James, Jim Mitchell, Clare Monagle, Pauline Nestor, Mark Peel, Ros Pesman, Chips Sowerwine, Alistair Thomson, Christina Twomey and Glenda Sluga. A fellowship from the Research School of Humanities at the Australian National University in 2007 provided an ideal environment in which to begin writing the book, and a similar fellowship from the history programme in the Research School of Social Sciences also at the Australian National University in 2009 enabled me to finish it, and I am profoundly grateful to them. James Cannon provided invaluable help in researching and completing the book. Finally, I want to thank my family, Larry, Tessa and Nicholas who, as always, coped with my preoccupation, kept my spirits up – and reminded me that there was a life outside my study.

Preface to Revised Edition

Interest in biography and in a variety of other forms of life writing has grown significantly amongst historians in the seven or eight years since this book was first published. One can see this very clearly in the number of lectures, special issues of journals and collections of essays that have been published in this period, exploring the relationship between biography and history, many of which stress the closeness and importance of this relationship. One can see it also in the number of distinguished social and intellectual historians who are turning to historical biography for the first time and who usually explain why this particular biographical project seems to them to offer new insights into an historical period with which they are already very familiar. This is a phenomenon that has been evident for some decades, but it is becoming ever more pronounced in many different fields of historical research.

But while the number of important new biographies grows and historians seem to be becoming more and more sympathetic to biographical approaches, the framework for discussing biography and history has not changed dramatically in the last few years. Hence I have not felt any need to change the structure of this book or to alter its approach and argument. Rather, while keeping this structure, I have sought to include some discussion of works published after 2010, indicating where it might extend or qualify arguments made in the first edition. As this new work does extend across all the issues that are raised in the book, I have made some revision to each chapter, although none has been completely rewritten.

As approaches to historical biography and arguments stressing the importance of the links between biography and history become more and more wide-ranging, it does seem to me important not only to interrogate and show the complexity in the concept of 'biography', but also to recognise that in this discussion there is not a single or uniform concept of 'history'. In the first edition of the book, I looked at the ways in which, since the 1970s, a traditional notion of biography has been both undermined and expanded by linking it to autobiography and life writing. New ideas about auto/biography and life writing have been accompanied not only by new approaches, but also by a massive expansion in the range of subjects now seen as both historically significant and warranting biographical treatment. Many of these new subjects have become very important in particular kinds of history: women's history stands out here, but so too does the history of sexuality and indeed much new imperial and postcolonial history, in contrast with political history. But not all of the biographical work on these subjects constitutes what would once have been seen as a full-scale biography – and there does seem to be a convergence between an increasingly flexible approach to biographical writing, on the one hand, and an increasing enthusiasm amongst historians to use biographical sketches or individual cases to illustrate or make their arguments, on the other. It seems to me that we are approaching the point where there is a more important question to be asked than that about whether and how biography and history either differ or resemble each other. This question centres on the importance of individual lives, however conceived and constructed, in the writing of history and the methodological questions that this growing reliance on individual lives raises. To make this argument more explicit, I have added a final short section called 'History and the Individual Life'.

Barbara Caine
Sydney 2018

Introduction

So great is the current interest in biography, not only amongst general readers but also amongst academics working in a number of different disciplines, that many scholars now talk of a 'biographical turn' in the humanities and social sciences.[1] The 'turn' that they describe involves a new preoccupation with individual lives and stories as a way of understanding both contemporary societies and the whole process of social and historical change. Biography has long been seen as part of history and as a way to enliven it by rendering the past 'more human, more vivid, more intimate, more accessible, more connected to ourselves'.[2] But its narrative form and its concern with individuals have often resulted in its relegation to the margins of historical study while political institutions or social and economic structures occupy the centre. Now, however, biography is coming to occupy more of this centre ground as it is seen to offer ways of throwing new light on a range of different historical periods and problems and of bringing individuals and groups who had previously been ignored into the framework of historical analysis.

For some, the most important contribution of biography to history is the insight that it offers into the lives and thought of significant individuals. It serves to remind us, Arthur M. Schlesinger argues, that political leaders, including American presidents, are not supermen, but human beings, 'worrying about decisions, attending to wives and children, juggling balls in the air, and putting on their pants one leg at a time'.[3] But for others, including social, feminist and some postcolonial historians, it is not the light shed on the lives of powerful individuals which is most important, but rather what can be learnt from the lives of less-exalted and ordinary people. Detailed study of the lives of individuals and of families and other groups offers extraordinary insights into the ways in which particular institutions and events and larger-scale social, economic and political developments were felt, experienced and understood by those who lived through them. A biographical approach in history, as in the social sciences, thus offers an important addition to the understanding of general developments by providing a way of accessing **subjective** understanding and experience.[4]

Although there have always been biographies written by historians, increasing numbers have turned to biography in the last two or three decades, including many who had never before contemplated researching or writing it. One reason for this decision may be the fact that biography is greatly prized by publishers and offers historians the opportunity to reach wide general audiences in a way that few other forms of history can do. But there are other important reasons why historians are directing more attention to it. Several of them explain their new interest in individual lives in terms of wider developments within contemporary historical analysis. The move away from structuralist approaches and explanations which has been so marked in all the social sciences over the past three or four decades is particularly important. The decline of Marxism both as a theoretical approach and as an intellectual influence, which began in the late 1960s and 1970s and became even more marked with the collapse of the Soviet bloc in the course of the 1980s, gave rise to a range of new historical questions.[5] As the pre-eminence of class division gave way to concerns about categories which often cut across class boundaries, including gender, ethnicity and sexual identity, so too the large-scale theories and analyses of historical and social change which had been widely accepted across the twentieth century were called into question and seen as 'grand narratives' that privileged the views and perspectives of particular dominant groups while silencing or suppressing those of subordinate ones. At a time when historians want to stress the need to encompass the many different historical narratives which could be produced at any one time, all of which are contingent on particular situations and locations, individual lives have come to appear more and more important because of the many ways in which they can illustrate how differences of wealth and power, of class and gender and of ethnicity and religion have affected historical experiences and understanding. Within this framework, biography can be seen as the archetypal 'contingent narrative' and the one best able to show the great importance of particular locations and circumstances and the multiple layers of historical change and experience.

This recognition of the illustrative capacity of biography reflects the very significant expansion in the range of biographical subjects that has been evident for the past few decades. Although once confined primarily to the discussion of individuals whose political, social, intellectual or literary contribution was deemed sufficiently important to entitle them to a biography, many ordinary people have now also become the subjects of biographical interest. It is not their exceptional nature or status which has been seen as most interesting about them, but rather their similarities to their peers. The life stories of ordinary folk are important because of their capacity to illustrate in detail how others who shared their class, gender, ethnicity, interests or problems understood or were affected by particular historical developments. The lives of individuals within this framework become significant because of what they show about the worlds in which they lived and their capacity to reveal facets of that world which are not available in other ways.

This new approach to biography accompanied the rise of the new histories that have become so prominent since the 1970s, including the 'new social history' microhistory, women's history, black history, and postcolonial history. All of these forms of history share a concern to explore the activities, experiences and historical agency of groups with relatively little political and economic power or social status and to locate and listen to the voices of those who had been silenced in earlier historical writing. They focus on marginal groups, including women, members of ethnic and religious minorities, and indigenous peoples, seeking to understand the nature of their experiences and the ways in which they understood the worlds in which they lived. As questions about the importance of gender, race and class and about experience and representation have come to the fore, so too has the recognition that the detailed analysis of individual or collective lives offers one of the best ways to explore them.

The lives of prominent individuals have not ceased to interest biographers, historians and readers. On the contrary, biographies of major political, religious and military leaders continue to attract a great deal of interest, as indeed do those of artists, writers and scientists. Many of these biographies continue to be written in a quite traditional way, seeking to show what was unique or significant about a particular individual, and often stressing the extent to which they stood out against others in terms of their particularly progressive views or unusual outlook and insight, or through their power and achievements. But even in some political biography and in studies of other eminent men and women, one can see new approaches, especially in the growing insistence on the need not only to understand the social and political contexts in which individuals lived but also to explore in much more detail the complex ways in which individuals relate to the worlds they inhabit. Thus in some biographical work on figures of great religious or political significance – Augustine and Charlemagne, for example, or Hitler and Mussolini – considerable emphasis has been placed on the ways in which even dominant figures serve in some circumstances to illuminate the social and political world in which they lived or, alternatively, on the need to have a very detailed understanding of the particular social, intellectual and political circumstances that enabled their rise to prominence and their exercise of power.[6]

One of the issues that has come to the fore as a result of this concern to show individuals within their own social worlds is a recognition of the ways in which traditional biography, with its intense focus on the life of one individual, imposes an artificial isolation on people whose lives were often lived enmeshed within close-knit familial and social networks. The desire to understand lives more fully as they were actually lived and to give proper weight to the relationships which many individuals had with 'significant others' or with wider networks and communities has also led to an increasing interest in biographical studies of couples, families and groups alongside those of individuals. This interest in group biography has appealed strongly to feminist scholars seeking to understand the impact of the legal, economic and social constraints and the ideals of feminine nature that women had to negotiate in particular societies and at particular times. By taking a family which included several daughters and analysing the similarities and differences in their domestic, sexual and social experiences, several historians have sought to question accepted ideas and to offer new insights into the general situation of women in particular societies.[7] Much of this work serves also to stress the significance of women's ties to one another both within familial groups and with friends outside. But this approach has not been confined to women and is evident also in studies of brothers and of cross-generational family groups which include both women and men. It is evident also in the growing list of biographical works that focus on friendships and on the shared and common experiences amongst people prominent in political and social activism or in the intellectual, literary and cultural world.

This interest in writing the lives of families, groups and intellectual coteries constitutes a new form of collective biography, a genre which in other forms has long been important for historians. Although most of those who write general works on biography deal mainly with the issue of how best to research, understand and write about individuals, the question of collective biography is a very important one in relation to history. Collective and comparative biographies of rulers have been written since classical times and have been augmented over several centuries by others devoted to the lives of artists and writers and now also to scientists and engineers. The encyclopaedias and dictionaries of biography that have been prominent at least since the late seventeenth century are particularly important. In some cases they stake a claim to historical significance for particular groups; in others they provide a major adjunct to nation-building and to the creation of a sense of a national past. What is notable at the present time is the simultaneous reassertion of the significance of dictionaries of biography, both national and selective or sectional, *and* the emergence of new forms of collective biography dealing with people in familial groups or within the framework of friends and colleagues. This latter approach serves both to position people more securely in their immediate social context and to expand the illustrative capacity of biography by showing both the common and uncommon features of particular lives.

Although the immense current popularity of biography gives the question of the relationship between it and history a particular cogency, debate and discussion about the relationship between biography and history is not new.

On the contrary, questions about the similarities and differences between biography and history have over many centuries played a significant part in defining and establishing what history is and how it is understood as a form of discourse. The similarities between them derive from their shared concern with narrating events and developments and with exploring and explaining human motivations, actions and experiences. Although the traditional concern of history with public and especially political events and actions separates it from biography with its focus on private life, from the time of Plutarch and Suetonius onwards historians and biographers have both concerned themselves with the actions, the motives and the impact of significant individuals – and often with the very same individuals. Over time, and indeed at any one particular time, historians have expressed very different views on this question of the similarities and differences between biography and history and the relationship between them, and the question has often been the subject of heated debate. Within this debate there have also been some significant shifts in focus. In the past three or four decades, for example, an earlier concern that biography paid too much attention to the role of the individual in history has given way to a newer one concerning the capacity of an individual life to illustrate or reflect broad historical change.

Although the writing of biography and the discussion of its relationship to history go back at least to classical times, this book focuses mainly on the period from the late seventeenth century to the present. It seeks to provide both a history of modern biography and an analysis of the changing ways in which the relationship between biography and history has been thought about and understood. Taking as its starting point the new interest in life writing associated with the rise of individualism and with the religious and political upheavals of the late seventeenth century, it explores the expanding range of biographical subjects that emerged at this time alongside the extensive new discussion about how lives should be written and understood. The word 'biography' first came into use in English in this period, and its introduction serves both to illustrate a growing interest in life stories and their increasingly important place not only in literary cultures but also in emerging ideas about the nation. The use of the term 'biography' and the discussion of it also show a new sense of how lives should be written. Concern with the presentation of a unique individual in such a way as to give a clear sense of what the person was actually like was one of the defining features of modern biography which served to differentiate it from its classical and medieval predecessors, which tended to work much more with established and exemplary character types. And, of course, this is also the start of the period in which history began to be seen and defined as a discipline – and in ways that made its relationship with biography a matter of particular importance. A series of new debates emerged about the relationship between biography and history: some argued for its superiority to any other form of historical writing; others set forth new methods and rules for historical writing in which biography apparently had little, if any, place.

The ideas about biography articulated by a number of different historians and the long-standing debate about the precise relationship between biography and history is the subject of Chapter 1, which includes some discussion about the ideas concerning the relationship between biography and history evident in the classical and medieval periods as a way of indicating the significant changes which occurred during the course of the seventeenth and eighteenth centuries and which establish the framework for the rest of the book. Chapters 2 and 3 focus on changing biographical practices. Chapter 2 explores the changes in how biography has been written and in the aspects of individual lives deemed appropriate for biographical treatment. Chapter 3 turns from the lives of individuals to the collective biographies that have been so important since the seventeenth century and to the group biographies that have become so prevalent today. Chapters 4, 5 and 6 discuss a range of contemporary developments in biographical writing. Chapter 4 explores the interest in life writing that has been evident amongst literary scholars since the 1970s and the tendency to link autobiography and biography within it, as well as the ways in which historians have taken this up. Chapter 5 moves beyond history to consider a range of other approaches to biography. It looks at the ideas of those approaching biography as a form of literature, at some of the arguments about the importance of psychoanalysis within biography and at the interest of some biographers in texts and in the question of performance. Chapter 6 surveys some of the new biographical practices that have become widespread amongst historians over the past few decades, focussing particularly on questions about gender and on new ways of thinking about the relationship of an individual to the society in which he or she lives.

1 Historians and the Question of Biography

▶ Introduction

Although debate on this subject continues, the central place that biography occupies in the writing and the study of history is accepted now in a way that has not been the case since the mid nineteenth century. One can see this very clearly in the numerous roundtables, lectures and symposia on biography that have been hosted by major journals, conferences and institutions like the London-based Institute for Historical Research in the last eight to ten years. To be sure some of these discussions have served to question rather then to recognise the place of biography in history. David Nasaw, in introducing the roundtable on biography in the *American Historical Review*, argued that biography 'remains the profession's unloved stepchild, occasionally but grudgingly let in the door, more often shut outside with the riffraff'. But the very fact that a roundtable on this subject was published in the *American Historical Review* testifies to the widespread interest in the subject amongst historians, as indeed do the subsequent ones with much more enthusiasm for biography in the *Journal of Women's History* and the *Journal of Interdisciplinary History*. What is particularly notable is that several of the participants in the *American Historical Review* roundtable refused to apply the term 'biography' to their work, even if that work was a lengthy reconstruction and discussion of the life of an individual. Instead, they insisted, they were using 'the medium of "life histories" of individuals and groups of individuals, to seek for evidence to probe many key historical issues',[1] or using an individual life to 'help us to see not only into particular events but into the larger cultural and social and even political processes of a moment in time'.[2] These, however, are precisely the things that other historians see as valuable in writing an historical biography. It does raise questions about the extent to which the concern amongst historians is focussed as much on the idea of biography as a particular literary form as it is on the related question of the role and importance of studying an individual life as a way to expand historical understanding and insight.

Discussion about the relationship between biography and history has been an important one for millennia. Beginning with a brief discussion of the contrast between biography and history established in the classical world, this chapter focuses on this debate over the past three centuries, the period in which the claim of biography to be seen as a significant part of history has been repeatedly asserted.

► Biography and history in the seventeenth and eighteenth centuries

Much of the modern debate about the relationship between biography and history begins with the differentiation between them established in the classical world. History was seen as something quite different from biography in the classical world and as having much greater quality, seriousness and importance. The high status of history came both from its concern with the important legal, political and military deeds and actions of any period and from its rigorous methods and concern with accuracy. This concern with the relations between different nations and peoples, and especially those involving wars, made history a form of knowledge that was of the utmost importance for anyone interested in political life.

To suggest that history had a higher status than biography is not to say that biography was unimportant in the classical world. On the contrary, it was considered one of the major ways in which to commemorate the life of a significant individual and to bring to mind noble characters or to evaluate the deeds and the lives of significant public men. Plutarch's *Parallel Lives*, for example, for many centuries the most widely read and influential of classical biographies, paired and contrasted Greek and Roman rulers, military leaders and philosophers in ways that showed both their strengths and their failings and allowed the scope for extended moral and philosophical reflections on their motives and conduct, and indeed on the civilisations that they served to represent. It was Plutarch who emphasised most strongly the differences between biography and history and who demanded freedoms for the biographer from the rigour that was so central to the writing of history. For the biographer, Plutarch insisted, it was not deeds that mattered so much as character, and the delineation of character often demanded that attention be paid to aspects of the private life or public figures that were not usually deemed significant in the writing of history. Plutarch refused either to confine himself exclusively to the political and military aspects of a person's life or to cover the public life of his subjects chronologically and comprehensively. On the contrary, he was deliberately selective, choosing those aspects of each person that he saw as most revealing of his character, accepting that these would not necessarily be the most significant episodes from an historical point of view. In a famous passage at the beginning of his life of Alexander, Plutarch pointed to the differences between biography and history, insisting that, unlike an historian, he would not deal comprehensively with everything Alexander had done.

> For I am writing biography, not history, and the truth is that the most brilliant exploits often tell us nothing of the virtues or vices of the men who performed them, while on the other hand a chance remark or a joke may reveal far more of a man's character than the mere feat of winning battles in which thousands fall, or of marshalling great armies, or laying siege to cities.[3]

The freedom to choose the incidents that reveal 'character and inclination' that Plutarch demanded for biography served further to underline its lower status. A biography might well offer a basis for private contemplation, and thus serve a moral purpose. But its stress on the individual and its concern with the private realm and with daily life meant that for many centuries it was regarded as a lower and less important form of writing than history.

This classical sense of the distinction between history and biography and the greater importance and seriousness accorded history in the Classical world was generally accepted up until the end of the sixteenth century. In the early seventeenth century, however, Francis Bacon challenged it, arguing that individual lives needed to be seen as a part of history, rather than as something quite distinct from it. For Bacon, there was not just one category or type of history, but several, of which biography was one. In his *The Advancement of Learning*, he suggests that

> history, which may be called just and perfect history, is of three kinds, according to the object which it propoundeth, or pretendeth to represent: for it either representeth a time, or a person, or an action. The first we call chronicles, the second lives, and the third narrations or relations. Of these, although the first be the most complete and absolute kind of history, and hath most estimation and glory, yet the second excelleth it in profit and use, and the third in verity and sincerity. For history of times representeth the magnitude of actions, and the public faces and deportments of persons, and passeth over in silence the smaller passages and motions of men and matters ... But lives, if they be well written, propounding to themselves a person to represent, in whom actions, both greater and smaller, public and private, have a commixture, must of necessity contain a more true, native, and lively representation.[4]

Bacon's insistence that individual lives might prove to be more useful and lively than chronicles of major political and military events anticipates the challenge to history that was offered much more extensively by biography in the eighteenth century.

This belief that biography was more lively and appealing than other forms of history was held strongly by many writers in the eighteenth century. Hugh Blair's widely read *Lectures on Rhetoric and Belles Lettres* (1783), for example, included a discussion of 'the inferior kinds of historical composition', in which he stressed the usefulness and importance of biography. It was less formal than history but often very instructive for readers to whom the small details of daily life would be appealing and instructive. Robert Bisset, who wrote a number of histories as well as a biography of Edmund Burke, made a similar point. 'No species of writing', he argued, 'combines in it a greater degree of interest and instruction than biography.'

> Our sympathy is most powerfully excited by the view of those situations, which, by a small effort of the imagination, we can approximate to ourselves. Hence Biography often engages our attention and affection more deeply than History. We are more concerned by the display of individual character than of political measures, of individual enjoyment or suffering, than of the prosperity or adversity of nations. Even in History the biographical part interests us more than any other.[5]

This emphasis on the capacity of biography to excite sympathy points to a concern with a new readership that emerged in the eighteenth century, making demands that traditional history could not satisfy. A significant part of this new readership was composed of middle-class women whose favourite genre was the novel. The rise and prominence of the novel, the emergence of sentimental poetry at the same time, and the extensive discussion of what women should read brought to the fore a recognition of the importance of the 'sentimental reader' and a new sense of the need to engage the emotions in all literary forms and for men as well as women.

In earlier times, the connection between history and public men assured its high status. The reader of history was generally assumed to be an educated man, interested in public matters and disciplined in his habits. To gain the greatest benefit from reading history, it was necessary that the reader 'be not confused, wandering and desultory in his reading. ... that he have a clear and good Judgement, that he may with dexterity apprehend what he reads and well discern what is to be selected'.[6] The increase in literacy amongst women and others not engaged in public life made many writers argue that if history spoke only to public men, it was 'meaningless to the largest part of mankind'. This was in marked contrast to biography, which spoke to everyone.[7]

The emergence of this new readership was accompanied by some new ideas about history. David Hume, for example, believed that women needed to study history, which was both more instructive and more entertaining than the novels that they read. History, he insisted, offered the best way 'of becoming acquainted with human affairs, without diminishing in the least from the most delicate sentiments of human virtue' and the only possible basis for women to be able converse sensibly with men 'of sense and reflection'. In part as a way of attracting this readership, Hume sought to introduce episodes and incidents into his histories that would affect his readers, and he deliberately experimented with sentimental approaches usually associated with fiction and designed specifically for a female readership. His account of the execution of Charles I, for example, was carefully written in a way that would move some to tears.[8] As David Wootton has argued, Hume offered a new approach to history in his concern to retell a story that had already been told. Prior to that, it had been assumed that those seeking a knowledge of history would do so through reading the works of great contemporary historians who had participated in the events that they depicted: Livy or Tacitus, if they wanted to know about Rome; Clarendon if they wanted to know about Elizabethan England. Hume argued that working with these original sources was both too time consuming and too confusing for most contemporary readers, who needed a concise and carefully composed account that would provide both instruction and pleasure. This approach involved a new sense of progress in historical knowledge, but it also involved a new way of incorporating individual lives into historical accounts.[9]

▶ Thomas Carlyle and the idea of biography as history

Interest in the nature of daily life in earlier times, and a sense, which had begun in the eighteenth century, that this was essential if there was to be a real understanding of the past, continued into the nineteenth century. Indeed, it formed the basis of a critique of earlier approaches to history that had placed political developments at the centre. In the early years of the nineteenth century, Francis Jeffery, the first editor of the influential *Edinburgh Review*, and a noted essayist and critic, insisted on the need to extend beyond the political realm of 'regular history' if one sought to understand even the forces shaping the character of the nation. For these forces consist of 'everything which affects the character of individuals: – manners, education, prevailing occupations, religion, taste, and above all the distribution of wealth, and the state of prejudice and opinions'.[10] Literature was particularly important because of what it revealed about the 'state of prejudice and opinion', but so too were individual memoirs and diaries, which provided an unparalleled insight into the lives, activities and opinions of particular individuals. Jeffery responded with great enthusiasm to works like Lucy Hutchinson's *Memoirs* or to Pepys's *Diary*, which was first published in 1825. Pepys's diaries, he insisted, 'fulfilled the desire of knowing, pretty minutely, the manners and habits of former times, – of understanding, in all their details, the character and ordinary way of life and conversation of our forefathers'.[11]

In Britain, the strongest cases for linking biography and history – indeed for seeing them as completely inseparable – was made by Thomas Carlyle. 'History is the essence of innumerable biographies,' Carlyle insisted, in his 1830 essay 'On History'. A study of the inner life, the changing nature of the conscious or half-conscious aims of man and of spiritual beliefs, he argued, might offer a more significant history than that evident in the study of political institutions or military episodes.[12] His work on Cromwell, with its emphasis on the importance of his religious beliefs, and through which a different way of understanding the seventeenth century was suggested, served to illustrate his approach.[13]

> We are always coming up with the emphatic facts of history in our private experience, and verifying them here. All history becomes subjective; in other words, there is properly no history; only biography. Every mind must know the whole lesson for itself, – must go over the whole ground. What it does not see, what it does not live, it will not know.[14]

Carlyle's belief in the importance of individual lives is evident throughout his *History of the French Revolution*, which continually refers to particular individuals in illustrating political developments or indeed the state of France itself and the pattern and process of the revolution. Following on from this, Carlyle used the terms 'history' and 'biography' interchangeably in his massive *History of Friedrich II of Prussia, Called Frederick the Great*. This focus on individual lives commended his way of presenting historical figures as 'real beings, which were once alive, beings of his own flesh and blood, not mere shadows and dim abstractions'.[15]

The illiberal and anti-democratic nature of Carlyle's thought, his strongly judgemental approach both to individuals and to historical events and his complete disregard for any wider analysis of economic or social or political conditions or developments, combined with the tortuousness of some of his prose, have led to a neglect of his writing and his ideas over the past few decades. Since the late 1990s, however, there has been a move to reconsider his work and to recognise the impact of some of his historical research. Blair Worden, for example, has argued that Carlyle's work on Oliver Cromwell served not only to rehabilitate Cromwell in the mid-nineteenth century but also quite markedly changed how the English Civil War was seen and understood.[16] In his discussions of Cromwell, Carlyle absolutely rejected the eighteenth-century view of him as a hypocrite and a manipulator, arguing that these interpretations of Cromwell illustrated the blindness and shallowness of eighteenth-century thought, rather than offering any insight into Cromwell. What stood out for Carlyle was the intensity and sincerity of Cromwell's religious beliefs. In his work on Cromwell, Carlyle began to describe the English Civil War as a Puritan Revolution in which moral questions and passionately held religious beliefs were at the fore, in place of the eighteenth-century concern with constitutional and legal issues. At the same time, he pointed to the insights biography could offer into the hidden conflicts of individuals, which had a profound impact on their actions.

Carlyle saw Cromwell as a tormented man who found it extremely difficult to deal with the public and political world, but who was driven to do so by his religious beliefs and his strong sense of the rightness of his cause. As Worden and others point out, Carlyle felt a great empathy, even a sense of kinship, with Cromwell, whose inner torment resembled his own. In his deep and in many ways personal involvement with Cromwell as a man and as a ruler, and in his writing about him, Carlyle used a biographical approach to offer a quite new interpretation of a major historical event – and one that has continued to dominate British historiography. At the same time, it is worth noting, as Fred Kaplan has done, that for all his obsession with and hard work on Cromwell, Carlyle was unable to write the biography of Cromwell that he spent years planning to write.[17]

Carlyle's approach to biography and its relationship to history was taken up in America by Ralph Waldo Emerson, for whom biography offered a better way of understanding the past than did history. Echoing Carlyle's belief that 'there is properly no history; only biography', Emerson insisted, 'Every mind must know the whole lesson for itself, – must go over the whole ground. What it does not see, what it does not live, it will not know.'[18] Emerson too insisted that history was essentially composed of the lives of significant individuals and that great men deserved particular veneration and attention. He wrote of essays on the men he saw as having the greatest universal significance, with an introductory essay on 'the uses of great men' in which he set out his general views.

> The world is upheld by the veracity of good men: they make the earth wholesome. They who lived with them found life glad and nutritious. Life is sweet and tolerable only in our belief in such society; and actually, or ideally, we manage to live with superiors. We call our children and our lands by their names. Their names are wrought into the verbs of language, their works and effigies are in our houses, and every circumstance of the day recalls an anecdote of them.

The title of Emerson's volume *Representative Men* emphasises his sense of the capacity of some notable individuals, in particular Plato, Montaigne, Swedenborg, Napoleon, Shakespeare and Goethe, to illustrate valuable human qualities that were widely shared and were particularly espoused by the American Republic.

Emerson's use of biography in developing and articulating ideas about the nation was followed by many others in America in the nineteenth century as many different authors sought to record the lives and activities of men (and very occasionally women) who had played a significant part in national or in local community life and to make clear the nature of their achievements. This noting of the lives of particular people was seen as important in itself, but also as showing the significance of America as a new nation staking its claim against the old world. Memoirs and biographies of eminent American men, the *American Law Journal* suggested, would serve to teach 'an envious world that *America* is not less the nurse of liberty than the cradle of glory'.[19] Biographies of presidents and military heroes played a particular part here, as figures like George Washington or Thomas Jefferson or Andrew Jackson were depicted in ways that helped define American character and values. James Parton, who became possibly the foremost American biographer of the nineteenth century, excelled at this. His *Life of Andrew Jackson* and *Life and Times of Benjamin Franklin* enabled him to illustrate two sides of the American character. Jackson served to embody the American frontier and the frontier spirit, whereas Franklin, with his many talents and interests, exemplified American ingenuity and the American belief in a person's capacity to determine his social standing by talent rather than birth.[20]

▶ The professionalisation of history

While Carlyle and Emerson stressed the close connection between history and biography, very different ideas about the nature of history and the way it should be approached were being discussed in Europe. This was particularly so in Germany. There is now some debate about precisely when the recognition of history as a discipline occurred in Germany – with increasing attention being paid to late eighteenth-century developments and to the establishment of the first German Chair of History in 1804. But the new emphasis on the importance of thorough archival research and the need for a critical analysis of historical sources, and the distinctive training seminars through which young men were taught how to become professional historians, were not evident until the 1820s and 1830s.

The establishment of history as a discipline and as a profession in Germany is closely linked to the work of Leopold von Ranke, who sought both to define a new scientific approach to history and to establish its proper method and forms of training. In the period from the 1820s to the 1840s, when Carlyle's influence was at its peak in Britain and was spreading through the ideas and approaches that he shared with Emerson in America, Ranke published his first book, *History of the Latin and Teutonic Nations from 1494 to 1514*, and began teaching his history seminars at the University of Berlin. At these seminars, students presented their research and were interrogated about their methods and especially about their approach to sources, which they were required to approach with great scepticism. The aim was to train them to the highest possible standards of rigorous inquiry. This approach was then introduced into other German universities by Ranke's students. All of Ranke's students were young men and this new training and the whole process of professionalising history served to exclude women from it in ways, which had not happened when history was written by amateurs.[21]

Nothing could have been more different from Carlyle's imaginative invocation of past events or his constant and often savage judgments on individuals and events than Ranke's careful approach to the dispassionate recording and documentation of the past. He explicitly eschewed any form of judgment in the 'Preface' to his first book.

'History has had assigned to it the task of judging the past, of instructing the present for the benefit of ages to come. To such lofty functions this work does not aspire. Its aim is merely to show what actually occurred.'[22] For Ranke, the questions that historians needed to deal with centred on political developments, especially those in Europe. He was interested also in the major religious conflicts of the sixteenth and seventeenth centuries, but there was little place for the study of individuals or for any form of biography in Ranke's

work. Some scholars have noted the impact of Ranke's Christian idealism and his search
for the guiding hand of God in history, and questioned the extent to which this theolog-
ical approach undermined his empiricism and demand for impartiality and objectivity.[23]
But none of this made him either more interested in or more sympathetic to biography or
to the question of the individual in history. There is a suggestion of a biographical interest in his history of the Catholic Church, which is entitled *History of the Popes*. And this
work did pose a number of problems for Ranke. His other works were structured around
the course of national political history, which could be discussed quite independently of
individuals.[24] The Catholic Church, however, could not be written about in this way. The
extent and the nature of papal influence at any given time was very much a consequence
of the personality and capacities of a particular pope and so individual popes had to be
analysed and indeed had to provide the structure of the work. However, this biographical framework served merely as a kind of scaffold as Ranke moved as quickly as possible
beyond the individuals in order to explore the development and impact of the institution
of the papacy on modern Europe.

Ranke's approach was quite well known in the Anglophone world in the nineteenth
century, but his concern with the need to professionalise history and to articulate precisely
its method were not taken up in Britain until the final decades of the nineteenth century.
History was introduced to university curricula in the course of the 1850s, but without any
of the insistence on rigorous method or on objectivity that had been so important for
Ranke. On the contrary, far from raising the status of history, its initial inclusion within
the university curriculum lowered it markedly. In 1852, Sir James Stephen, Regius Professor of Modern History at Cambridge, explained that history was being included in the
moral science tripos in order to cater for those young men who were incapable of reaching
high standards in classics or mathematics, but who were still 'men of whom it is unjust
to despond and who might thus be rescued from the temptations and the penalties of a
misspent youth'. The University Commissioners agreed that history might benefit aca-
demically limited but well-born young gentlemen through its capacity to develop 'larger
ideas and kindlier feelings'.[25] Biography, of course, played quite an important role here, as
individual figures provided the ideal focus for the moral questions and evaluations that
history was supposed to provide.

In subsequent decades, the introduction of honours degrees meant that more able young
men studied history, but until the end of the nineteenth century, history was considered
far more important as a training ground for men who would become active in public life
than for those who might seek to undertake research themselves. History, insisted J. R. Seeley, the Regius Professor of Modern History at Cambridge in the 1880s, was above all 'the
school of public feeling and patriotism'.[26] David Amigoni argues that biography was a stra-
tegic tool in Seeley's attempt to use history as a discipline that would help to reconstruct
public opinion as well as to educate future statesmen.[27] Even at the end of the nineteenth
century, when there was a new sense in Britain of the need for more rigorous historical

method, the moral importance of biography was still recognised. In his inaugural lecture 'The Study of History' in 1906, Lord Acton, while pointing to the need for history to deal primarily with political ideas and institutions, makes clear his sense of the moral importance of studying individual lives: 'We cannot afford wantonly to lose sight of great men and memorable lives, and are bound to store up objects for admiration as far as may be.'[28]

As the tone of his comment indicates, Acton was aware that he was fighting something of a rearguard action. Increasingly in the last few decades of the nineteenth century, academic historical writing had focussed on constitutional history and the development of English law and of legal, political and religious institutions. This is not to say that moral questions were ignored. On the contrary, history, especially at Oxford, was taught, in Reba Soffer's words, 'as a resurrected record of admirable development which accommodated simultaneously the transient **subjectivity** of time, place, thought and institutions and the absolute reality of moral, intellectual, material and political progress'.[29] There was still concern to understand not only the underlying causes of English progress but also the motivations and characters of the significant men who had been important in its unfolding. Nevertheless, the emphasis that was now being placed on the collecting and reading of the primary documents that explained legal and political developments meant that there was considerably less focus on individual lives than had been the case in earlier decades.

This point was made very clearly in the first issue of the *English Historical Review* in 1886. Explaining the reasons for their new venture, the editors of the review pointed out that, at this time, England stood alone among the great countries of Europe in not having a periodical devoted to the study of history which enabled those engaged in scholarly research to publish their work and to communicate regularly with one another. They wanted their new journal to cover a field that was broader than the political history concerned solely with states and governments, but not to attempt to offer a picture of the whole past, including everything man has either thought or wrought. They chose

> to regard history as the record of human action, and of thought only in its direct effect upon human action. States and politics will therefore be the chief part of its subject, because the acts of nations have usually been more important than the acts of private citizens. But when history finds a private citizen who, like Socrates or St Paul or Erasmus or Charles Darwin, profoundly influences other men from his purely private station, she is concerned with him as the source of such influence no less than with a legislator or general.[30]

It was assumed that the journal would contain 'articles on personages' in much the same way as it did on specific legislative developments or military events, but it was concerned only with the ways in which these 'personages' affected the public world – rather than with exploring the questions of character and personality that were so important in other forms of biography.

▶ Marxist history and the question of biography

The late eighteenth and the nineteenth centuries saw the development of a number of different theories concerning the underlying structures or the pattern or laws of development governing human history and demarcating the phases through which societies had passed. For those concerned with the writing of history, the most influential of these general theories was the **materialist** conception of history propounded by Marx and Engels, centring on the importance of class struggle within history. For Marx, it was the changing ways in which labour and resources were organised and controlled that explained the nature of social change and development. Opposing those who argued that one could define social stages and explain social change through changing ideas or systems of belief, Marx insisted that it was social existence that determined the nature of human thought rather than the other way around. As with any approach concerned primarily with questions of social structure and development, Marxism directed attention away from the study of individuals and from biography. What was of significance for Marxist historians was the question of economic and social processes – including above all the nature of feudalism, the transition to capitalism and the impact of industrialisation on social structures and social groups.

This is not to say that Marx himself or later Marxist scholars had no interest in biography. Marx rejected absolutely the kind of 'great men' approach to history articulated by Carlyle, as he did the idea that history ought to celebrate the achievements of notable leaders or inventors. However, Marx provided an alternative way of thinking about individual lives to that of Carlyle through his insistence that 'circumstances make men as much as men make circumstances'. Marx's statement, 'Men do make their own history, but they do not do it just as they please; they do not make it under circumstances chosen by themselves, but under circumstances directly given and transmitted in the past', both underlies Marx's own approach to individuals and has also been very influential for later and non-Marxist historical biographers.[31]

Questions about the role of the individual in history troubled many Marxist historians in the later nineteenth century as they sought ways to encompass their sense of the immense importance of rulers like Napoleon or Bismarck within a broader analysis of the transition to capitalism. This question was discussed at some length by the Russian historian and theorist G. V. Plekhanov in an essay titled *The Role of the Individual in History*. A great man is great, Plekhanov argues, 'not because his personal qualities give individual features to great historical events, but because he possesses qualities which make him most capable of serving the great social needs of his time, needs which arose as a result of general and particular causes'.[32]

In arguing his own position, Plekhanov applauded Carlyle's suggestion that great men could see further than others and desired things more strongly. A Carlylean hero, he argues, 'is not a hero in the sense that he can stop or change the natural course of things, but in the sense that his activities are the conscious and free expression of this inevitable and unconscious course'.[33]

Across the twentieth century, several Marxist historians have written major biographies. In some cases, this was a consequence of the popularity of biography – rather than an individual choice. Isaac Deutscher, for example, wrote his first biography, *Stalin: a Political Biography*, at the behest of his publisher, who persuaded him that a biography of Stalin would be far more widely read than the critical history of the Soviet Union that he had planned.[34] Subsequently, however, Deutscher chose to write a major biography of Trotsky as a way of offering a more sympathetic portrait of Trotsky, a man he admired profoundly, than he felt that Trotsky had offered in his autobiography, *My Life*. Deutscher sought to provide a picture of someone he considered to be 'one of the most outstanding revolutionary leaders of all times, outstanding as fighter, thinker and martyr'. In his discussion of Trotsky, he wanted also to suggest an alternative possible development of Russian communism to that which followed the rise to power of Stalin.[35] Deutscher's monumental biography has remained in print over several decades and is essential reading for anyone interested either in Trotsky or in the early decades of the Soviet Union. Ironically, despite its great scope and power, the close identification of Deutscher with Trotsky lessens its capacity to provide a critical analysis – and indeed there are some historians who see it as a work of hero worship that is not in accord with historical scholarship.

▶ Biography and history in the twentieth century

The question of how historians saw and thought about biography across the twentieth century is a complex one. There were always some historians who insisted on the importance of biography within history alongside a much larger number who disagreed, fearing the tendency of biography to place too much stress on individuals and to neglect wider historical processes. This view was often accompanied by a general sense that writing biography was an easier task than writing history because coming to terms with one individual did not require the complex and sophisticated analyses of political institutions and parties, or of economic and social structures and developments that was required in history. Hence, though often accepted as part of history, biography was generally looked down on as an inferior historical form. At the same time, many historians have written biography at some point in their careers, including those who have been most critical of it. The point at issue here is often a question of balance: few historians reject entirely the idea that biography is of some use, and most accept that it can at least offer insight into the motivations of particular individuals or the meanings of certain events. But many fear that the stress on individual motives and actions in biography directs attention away from broader and more important questions about underlying social and economic causes or about political developments. The balance has changed markedly over time and doubtless will do so again. But reading the record of this changing balance is itself sometimes rather difficult as past ideas and attitudes can be represented in different ways. We have seen this already in relation to Marxism. At the present time, when biography is both extremely popular and seen as very important, those engaged in explaining and assessing the nature and value of Marxist history stress the extent to which Marx himself thought about and offered ways of approaching biography. By contrast, books on Marxist history written in the mid-twentieth century, scarcely even mention Marx's approach to biography.

The same point can be made in regard to the *Annales* group in France, which was so important and influential in the first half of the twentieth century. Those connected to the *Annales* were concerned to extend the boundaries of history to include not only economic developments but also the insights that came from historical geography and anthropology. They rejected an emphasis on events, looking rather at longer patterns of social organisation, activity and beliefs. Their concern with *mentalités* (general outlooks and frames of mind) also meant that several of the *Annalistes* had a pronounced interest in psychology and the ways in which it might contribute to understanding the intellectual outlook and emotional make-up of people in earlier societies. But this was emphatically something that needed to be done in general rather than individual terms. 'Not the man, never the man, human societies, organized groups', Lucien Febvre argued in his book *La terre et l'evolution humaine*, a kind of slogan that was evident in much of the subsequent work done by himself, by Marc Bloch and by the others associated with them.

However, *Annalistes* have begun to rethink the question of biography, and more especially autobiography. The work of Pierre Nora has been central here, particularly his encouragement to historians to write autobiographical essays that linked their own lives with the historical research that they are undertaking – an approach that is discussed in more detail in Chapter 4. Several of these essays were published in his pioneering volume *Essais d' ego-histoire*, and in the years since then a number of other historians have written at greater length about the close connection between their lives and their work.[36]

This interest in biographical approaches among *Annalistes* has been accompanied by a new stress on the place of biography in the early work of the *Annales*. The exploration of *mentalités* that was so central to the *Annales* has thus been seen as leading the way into biographical work – as indeed is the case in some forms of **microhistory**. But some of the work produced by *Annalistes* is also now looked at through the frame of biography. This is the case with Lucien Febvre's work on Martin Luther. Febvre himself argued that his book *Un Destin, Martin Luther* was not a biography, but rather an analysis of the problem posed by the need to explore the relationship between an individual and the group. He offers very little by way of discussion of Luther's early, or indeed his later life, concentrating heavily on the crucial years 1517–1535 and on the issues of indulgences, Luther's conflict with the Catholic Church and with Charles V, the question of the peasantry and the establishment of Lutheranism. But later writers routinely describe it as a biography. This is done more easily at a time when an increasing number of biographies focus precisely on these questions of social and intellectual relationships, accepting that a biography does not need to deal in equal detail with every aspect of an individual's life.[37] Thus an approach to history that once eschewed biography in the interests of reorienting history around long-term patterns of economic, social, religious and intellectual life is now given a privileged place in the history of that very form which it sought to displace.

The rejection of individual stories evident amongst the *Annalistes* was typical of the attitude amongst many of those engaged in social and economic history as it became more and more widespread in the mid-twentieth century. The extent to which the advocacy of biography was a minority view is evident in the defensiveness of tone amongst those who saw themselves as defending biography and the role of the individual against those who accepted the idea that human behaviour was determined by external pressures and forces.[38] One can see it in the lectures and essays of Herbert Butterfield on 'The Role of the Individual in History', for example in Butterfield's suggestion that what he calls 'the primary interest in history', the ordinary human desire to know about our predecessors might now persist only in the hands of popularisers, while the enthusiasm for scientific techniques might transform academic history 'into something like a species of algebra'. In opposition to this, Butterfield stresses:

> The genesis of historical events lies in human beings. The real birth of ideas takes place in human brains. The reason why this happens is that human beings have vitality. From the historian's point of view it is this that makes the world go round ... Economic factors, financial situations, wars, political crises, do not cause anything, do not do anything, and do not exist except as abstract terms and convenient pieces of shorthand ... It is men who make history.[39]

It is not easy to find equally strong voices opposing the acceptance of biography as a part of history because, for the most part, those who did not see biography as having a significant role in historical writing or interpretation simply ignored it.[40] There was a pervasive sense that biography, in concentrating on one individual, was much simpler and less rigorous or demanding than history that is referred to by many of those who recall how strongly they were discouraged from undertaking it. And this general sense was so widely shared as to require little formal articulation. Thus no more than a couple of sentences were devoted to dismissing biography in two of the most widely read of the general discussions of the nature of history of the mid-twentieth century: E. H. Carr's *What is History* (1964) and Geoffrey Elton's *The Practice of History* (1967). Both Carr and Elton were amongst the large group of historians who wrote biographies. Nonetheless, Carr argued that a focus on the lives of individuals tended to exaggerate the role and significance of individuals as against the importance of structures and of people in the mass.[41] Elton acknowledged the importance of individuals but insisted that they have to yield first place to institutions. He was also concerned, moreover, that if one focussed on biography, there was the risk of bringing a literary approach to history that was inappropriate to the discipline.[42]

And yet, despite this hostility biography continued to be an integral part of history and particularly of the political history that often claimed pre-eminence. In both Britain and the United States, the detailed biographies of major political leaders were always required reading on history courses. And indeed, major political biographies often continue to be read and studied long after other historical works produced at the same time have been superseded. In British history, for example, John Morley's three-volume biography of Gladstone continued to be in print and required reading for students of nineteenth-century history well into the twentieth century, as did Moneypenny and Buckle's five-volume biography of Disraeli. Throughout the twentieth century, excellent biographies of political leaders appeared and continued to be essential reading for historians, such as John Griggs biography of Lloyd George, David Marquand's biography of Ramsay Macdonald and Jose Harris's biography of Beveridge.

The low status of biography was reinforced by the emphasis on language and on the need to understand cultural encoding which became so influential in the course of the 1960s and 1970s with the emergence of **poststructuralism**. What was important here was not so much an explicit attack on biography, which was not a subject of much interest, but rather the new ways of thinking about texts and reading which displaced the author and focussed on the various meanings in a text and the different kinds of reading that were possible. This new approach to reading was accompanied by a critique of earlier ideas of the self as a singular or coherent entity, and an insistence rather that this idea of an individual self as an autonomous being, able to act in accordance with its own will, was a fictitious construct. It was critiquing the idea of the author that was of most interest and concern within this framework, and a key text here was Barthes's 'The Death of the Author', which announced a metaphorical event: the 'death' of the author as an authentic source of meaning for a given text.[43] In any literary text that has multiple meanings, Barthes argued, the author was not the prime source of the work's semantic content. It was readers who made texts meaningful, drawing on both their own knowledge and cultural position, and their sense of the location of the text within a range of different forms of discourse, different forms of knowledge and different structures of power. Questions about individual lives were of no interest within this framework and appeared to become increasingly irrelevant and unimportant.

But even here, biography did not entirely disappear. On the contrary, Barthes himself engaged in a form of it, in his study of the nineteenth-century French historian Michelet. The book, Barthes insisted, was neither a history of Michelet's thought or of his life, but an attempt to restore his coherence and to recover the structure of his life 'or better still: an organized network of obsessions'. There was no suggestion of chronological narrative in this study, which consisted rather of a series of paragraphs which linked Michelet's writing of history with specific phases or episodes in his life or with other features of his personality and his physical health. But though not a biography in a conventional way, it was clearly a study of an individual life and one that stressed the importance of that life in the way in which Michelet had understood and written history.[44]

▶ Changing ideas about the role of biography in history

Although the idea of a 'biographical turn' in the humanities and social sciences has only been the subject of discussion for the past decade or so, one can see changes in approach to biography amongst historians from at least the early 1970s. It was in that decade that a number of historians began to insist on the capacity of individual lives to illuminate larger historical patterns and developments. Historians interested in this approach sought to bring individual lives and the wider historical context together by showing the impact of legal and social institutions or large-scale social, economic or political developments on the lives of particular individuals or groups. Like microhistorians, they argued that one often gained far greater understanding of particular institutions and forms of social change by analysing how they had been understood and negotiated by particular individuals. Hence for many historians, biography was increasingly seen to provide 'a unique lens through which one can assess the relative power of political, economic, cultural, social and generational processes on the life chances of individuals,' or to provide a prism which enabled later historians to see how particular individuals understood and constructed themselves and made sense of their lives and their society.[45]

The general historiographical works that expounded this view of biography did not appear until the 1990s. What appeared in the course of the 1970s and 1980s were, rather, discussions by particular historians of the way in which their own work linked biography and history and drew on an individual life in order to discern wider historical patterns. This approach was particularly significant in the new field of women's history. Kathryn Kish Sklar's widely acclaimed *Catharine Beecher: A Study in Domesticity* (1973), for example, was one of the pioneering works of this kind. Her book, she insisted, was a study of the middle decades of the nineteenth century through the life of one woman. 'It is also an effort to use the biographical density and motivational impulses of one person to uncover and isolate significant questions about the relationship between women and American society.'[46] Mary S. Hartman's *Victorian Murderesses* was another important pioneering work, developing this approach in a collective way through a series of biographical essays. While not wanting to ignore the particular characters or circumstances of her subjects, Hartman made it clear that she wanted to stress how the lives of these exceptional women were 'linked to those of their more typical female peers' and how they serve to throw light on some of the domestic and familial tensions and conflicts that many nineteenth century women faced.[47]

In the course of the 1980s and 1990s, a similar approach to that of Sklar, Hartman and Huggins was taken to the lives of workers, soldiers and craftsmen across several centuries. Much of this work bore a close affinity with, and can indeed be seen as part of, the microhistory that emerged in Italy in the course of the 1970s by Carlo Ginzburg and which was to be so very influential on much American and British history. Influenced in turn by the **ethnographic** approach of Clifford Geertz, those concerned with microhistory concentrated on the 'analysis, at extremely close range, of highly circumscribed phenomena – a village community, a group of families, even an individual person'.[48] The similarities between microhistory and new styles of biography were clearly evident in the ways in which an individual life came to be seen as able to shed light on whole groups who have tended to be ignored by historians in the past, and some historians argue that the lives of little-known individuals are better described as microhistories than as biographies.[49] But as I argue more fully in a later chapter, what seems more significant is the similarity in approach and concern of some forms of microhistory with that of biography, as both seek to show through an individual life the workings of a larger society. Just as this use of biography was evident in the early stages of women's history, so too it has become prominent in the last few years in post-colonial and transnational histories as historians have turned to particular individuals in their concern to explore the lives of marginal people who lived between cultures or who transgressed the racial, ethnic and religious expectations of their societies.[50]

It is scarcely surprising that this new approach was evident most clearly in works on women. The advent of women's history in the early 1970s brought a vast increase in interest and research into women's historical experiences, and the detailed study of individual lives offered one way to understand the nature of women's private and familial lives and the relationship between their private and public activities. And one can see over several decades that it is feminist historians and those concerned with women's history who have continued to deal most positively and effectively with questions about the value of biography in history and about how individual lives can best illuminate the writing of history. The difference between feminist approaches and that of some other historians can be seen if one contrasts the special roundtable on biography and history that has already been mentioned and that appeared in *The American Historical Review* with a similar roundtable in *The Journal of Women's History*. The unease with biography referred to by David Nasaw was echoed by almost all the contributors, several of whom refused to label their work biography, even if they were writing the life of an individual, preferring to say that they were using 'the medium of "life histories" of individuals and groups of individuals, to seek for evidence to probe many key historical issues',[51] or using an individual life to 'help us to see not only into particular events but into the larger cultural and social and even political processes of a moment in time'.[52] By contrast, Antoinette Burton and Jean Allman in their editorials for the two special issues on 'Critical Feminist Biography' published by the *Journal of Women's History* reflected the views of their contributors in stressing how important and innovative feminist approaches to biography have been and how closely linked to the development of women's history.[53] Women's history was concerned from the start with exploring the private and domestic world in which women were often thought to be confined – and with questioning the meaning of 'separate spheres', challenging accepted ideas about their separateness while looking at the links between the private and the public. Focussing on women's lives, they suggest, not only offered new historical insights but also challenged existing ideas about biography itself. Women's lives, they argue, in which public activity might be minimal and in which there is rarely a linear narrative or indeed the kind of 'linear self' that unfolds in a public life, require new ways of thinking about what biography is and how to do it. In their very capacity to explore decentred or fragmented subjects, they claim, feminist biographers are challenging and expanding biography as a form – and linking it ever more closely with history.

Biography has also played an important part in the emergence of other kinds of history concerned with marginal groups who had suffered both oppression and discrimination: in black and Afro-American history and in some areas of postcolonial history. In the case of Afro-American biography, Nathan Huggins contends that any black biography 'has a racial and social meaning larger than the life portrayed: the life comes to exemplify the need for reform,' and to raise broader questions about the impact of slavery and the Afro-American past on the ways in which individuals see and understand themselves.[54]

This suggestion that biographies and biographical approaches allow for and encourage the questioning of long-held assumptions about how particular institutions and established political forms actually worked has also been made in regard to imperial history. 'Biographical research', Achim von Oppen and Silke Strickrodt argue in a special issue of the *Journal of Imperial and Commonwealth History* devoted to 'Biographies between Spheres of Empire', 'offers a particularly useful approach to the examination of practices and experiences of boundary crossing in imperial and colonial history.'[55] Sharing with the practitioners of women's history an interest in the lives of 'ordinary' individuals and groups, they see biographies as offering insights into how individuals moved between the different spaces, jurisdictions, milieus, identities and even temporalities (e.g. traditional and modern, precolonial and colonial, past and future) into which the ideologies and rules of colonial worlds categorised them. This allows for a focus on how individuals living in complex and heterogeneous imperial spaces understood themselves and their own place. This approach through lives, they suggest, also points to the importance of understanding the British empire as made up of networks rather than being simply territorial.

In the course of the last decade, this new and expanded sense of the importance of biography within history has become evident in journals, symposia and in some general works seeking to define the nature and the practice of history. In her *History in Practice* (2000), for example, Ludmilla Jordanova suggests that biography is a distinctive and important form of history, which she terms 'holistic history' and sees as offering significant insights into the past. Taking a person 'as the unit of analysis', she suggests, 'is to adopt a quite particular historical approach, which emphasizes individual agency and sees the individual as a point at which diverse historical forces converge, while taking the span of life as a natural period of time'. In this way, biography has the capacity to cut across a number of different kinds of historical fields and approaches and to bring them together in ways that other historical approaches cannot match.[56] Making a slightly different, but even larger claim, Shirley A. Leckie sees biography as having an ever-larger role to play in a constantly changing world.

'As our globe becomes smaller and our communities more diverse', she argues, 'biography, which breathes life into dry census data and puts faces on demographic tables, will become the means by which to weave the stories of new groups into our national fabric.'[57]

An equally strong claim about the inseparable relationship between biography and history was made in Robert Rotberg's introductory essay to the symposium on this question in the *Journal of Interdisciplinary History* in 2010. Although far from asserting any change in approaches to either biography or history that brought a new kind of relationship, as Burton and Allman did, Rotberg insists that their inseparability is long-standing.

> Biography is history, depends on history, and strengthens and enriches history. In turn, all history is biography. History could hardly exist without biographical insights – without the texture of human endeavour that emanates from a full appreciation of human motivation, the real or perceived constraints on human action, and exogenous influences on human behaviour. Social forces are important, but they act on and through individuals. Structural and cultural variables are important, but individuals pull the levers of structure and act within or against cultural norms.[58]

Although Rotberg's extravagant statement underlines his sense of the importance of individuals in history, it does not address the qualms and concern expressed by many historians about biography as a particular kind of approach to and a form of writing about individuals or the view that in its concern to detail and interrogate a whole life, biography is antithetical to the concern of historians with structures or institutions or whole societies.

It is time now to recognise that we cannot assume that all biography is the same or that the general term 'biography' constitutes a uniform and undifferentiated category. Lucy Riall points this out in her very thoughtful and nuanced essay on 'the substance and future of political biography' in this special issue of the *Journal of Interdisciplinary History* that Rotberg edited and introduced.[59] There are considerable differences between literary and political biography and their acceptance by specialist readers, Riall insists, as indeed there are major differences between the assumptions and approaches found in most political biography and those evident in the biographies of little-known women that have become so important in women's history. Much political biography continues to work within a framework established in the nineteenth century that accepts the power, influence and importance of great (or bad) men. For Riall herself, this approach is not adequate, and there is a need to look at and to take on board some of the approaches developed in other kinds of biography if political biography is to have a serious place in the writing of history. What is needed now is a new kind of political biography that seeks to interrogate how an individual came to fill the position he (or occasionally she) did and what that reveals about the world in which he lived and the strategies or forms of representation that enabled his success within it. Addressing these questions allows for new ways of understanding the relationship between significant individuals and the times in which they lived.

In her discussion, Riall draws quite heavily on the work of Ian Kershaw as evident both in his important work on Adolf Hitler and his discussions of biography and history. In the book itself, however, Kershaw insists that he is not writing biography: that he passes over many of the details in which a biographer would be interested because he is interested 'solely and squarely in the nature and mechanics, the character and exercise of Hitler's dictatorial power'. He is more interested in the wider context that enabled Hitler to come to power and in theories of leadership, especially Weber's idea of 'charismatic domination' than in the features of Hitler's life.[60] But in Kershaw's subsequent general discussion of biography and history and of the role of the individual in history, he accepted that his work was biographical, although it was biography of a particular kind. Here Kershaw accepted the importance of biography in history but also stressed its limitations. Biography can 'help to illuminate the motivation behind actions, and how decisions, sometimes of momentous importance, were reached,' he argues, and it has something to offer in dealing with particular episodes or short-term developments where the actions of an individual may be crucial. But biography is for him only one small part of history, and it cannot help in understanding long-term processes of historical transformation – or even in illustrating them.[61] However, it is important to point out here that Kershaw is working with a different model of biography from that suggested by Jordanova or by Riall, and thus with a very different sense of relationship between biography and history. In both his general discussions of biography and in his work on Hitler, Kershaw stresses the need to see the close connection between individuals and the society in which they lived. Nonetheless, for him, the discussion of the importance of biography is directly connected to the question of the role of the significant and powerful individual in history and hence to the question of how much historical weight can be attributed to the views, motivations, actions and agency of significant and powerful people. He takes it for granted that the subjects of biography will be prominent men – or, occasionally, as he says, women. Although Riall too was dealing with a significant individual, her discussion of Garibaldi focuses as much on the myths that surrounded him and on the ways in which he established and embellished them as on his inner life. Hence for her, writing his life was a way into understanding not only the society in which he lived but also his skill in communicating with and his mastery both of contemporary ideas and values and of new technologies of communication.

All of this discussion, even that coming from those who continue to insist on the marginal and limited place of biography, makes it clear that biography is being given a larger place in historical research and writing than it has been accorded for much of the twentieth century. But what seems equally clear is the need to move beyond rigid ideas about or definitions of both 'biography' and 'history' and to engage in a wider discussion of the different ways in which individual lives can be and are being used to elucidate our understanding of the past.

2 A History of Biography

▶ Introduction

Any attempt to understand the relationship between history and biography needs to take into account not only changing ideas about the nature of history as a form of knowledge and understanding but also the changing ways in which biography has been understood, thought about and written. These changes can be seen in the ways in which lives were presented and, most particularly, in terms of the aspects of individuals' lives that biographers have either chosen to explore or deemed inappropriate for any kind of discussion. The question of how a life should be understood and depicted is important not only to those who write biography but also to those who read it. Their views have not always been the same. Thus, while one can see very marked changes in the areas of an individual life that biography might encompass from the late seventeenth century to the present, changing ideas have sometimes been signalled by an outcry from readers at a biography that seems to reveal too much or to lack appropriate discretion and decorum in dealing with the private or intimate life of its subject.

A notable feature of the history of modern biography has been the changing treatment of private life evident within it. One can see this not only in the aspects of an individual's life that are discussed but also, more broadly, in the shifts evident in the very meaning of the word 'private' in relation to biography. The link between biography and the private realm was emphasised strongly by the poet John Dryden in one of the earliest seventeenth-century discussions of the term 'biography' and what it involved. Whereas history dealt with many people and many public actions, Dryden argued, biography involved a descent into the 'minute actions and trivial circumstances' of an individual life. In history you are conducted into the rooms of state, but in biography

> you are led into the private lodgings of the Heroe: [sic] you see him in his undress and are made familiar with his most private actions and conversations ... The pageantry of life is taken away: you see the poor reasonable animal, as naked as ever nature made him; are made acquainted with his passions and his follies, and find the Demy-god [sic] a Man.[1]

Dryden's sense of the way that biography focussed on private life here involves seeing public figures, usually rulers or military leaders, in their more familiar domestic environment, when all the trappings of state or high office are set aside, and the individual can be seen for what he actually is. This sense of 'private' continued, but it was augmented by a slightly different one in the course of the eighteenth century as the focus of biographical interest shifted away from rulers and great men of state towards the lives of writers, artists, clergymen and others who were not fully engaged in public life. When Samuel Johnson stressed the importance of dealing with the 'domestick privacies [sic]' he tended to mean the social life of his subjects, rather than their working life. Under this rubric, although he mentioned their families, he devoted far more attention to exploring their friendships, their conversations and the forms of conviviality they enjoyed in their leisure hours. Sometimes this conviviality occurred at home, but it was equally likely to take place in inn, hotel or coffee house. Although families might be mentioned, marriage, sexual relationships and the actual tenor of domestic life were rarely discussed in any detail in eighteenth-century biography. In the course of the nineteenth century, the notion of 'private' changed again. Considerably more attention was now paid to early life and childhood, to the family of origin of a biographical subject, to the influence of parents and the importance of this early private and familial life on the formation of character. But though the relationship between an individual and his or her parents could be discussed, no such freedom was possible in relation to marital partners or children. On the contrary, a great deal of discretion was exercised with regard to the domestic life of an individual, and any hint of domestic unhappiness or sexual impropriety was deemed completely inappropriate for biographical treatment. In the twentieth century, entirely new ideas about the meaning of 'private' came to the fore as psychological questions, and issues of identity came to interest biographers. 'Private' thus came to refer to the intimate emotional life of an individual and to an interest in **interiority** and a person's sense of identity. For many contemporary readers, 'private' also involves a detailed depiction of an individual's sexual, emotional and domestic life. We are interested, above all, in the ways in which private and public lives are connected. But our understanding of 'private' has no place in the biographies of earlier centuries.

One can see similar changes in the ways in which the character and personality of a biographical subject have been understood and discussed. In the seventeenth and eighteenth centuries, the interest in presenting individuals as they actually were and in showing their character fully, so important to biography, usually meant that personal foibles and weaknesses were included alongside the generous or noble qualities that biographers extolled. In the nineteenth century, however, the protection of reputations came to be seen as far more important than revealing the whole. The revelations of an individual's indiscretions and failings came to be seen as something that biographers should ignore in the interests of presenting their subject in the most favourable way possible. In the twentieth century, foibles and failings returned with a vengeance. For some, like Lytton Strachey, they were almost the most interesting and important to reveal. But even for biographers less concerned to puncture Victorian ideas of respectability and to exhibit Victorian failings, it became impossible to contemplate writing a biography without being able to explore fully all aspects of an individual's life, character and behaviour. A new concern with people's hidden or unconscious motives, desires and conflicts involved a shift away from Victorian ideals of acceptable conduct and a rather less judgemental approach to human inconsistency and frailty.

This chapter looks at the history of modern biography, paying particular attention to the questions of how private life has been depicted and character revealed within it. It also looks at some of the newer approaches to biography which have become evident with an expanding range of biographical subjects across the twentieth century.

▶ The emergence of modern biography

Although the writing of biographies began many centuries ago and was undertaken in significant ways in the classical and the medieval periods, it has expanded greatly in the modern world. The emergence of modern biography has been seen as a development closely connected to the new approaches to science, sometimes referred to as the scientific revolution, which led to the sense of a life as a phenomenon which, like other natural phenomena, warranted close empirical observation and analysis.[2] It was connected also to the expanding interest in all forms of life writing during the course of the seventeenth century as autobiographies, journals and diaries providing a record of an individual's life, thoughts and feelings came to be written in increasing numbers. All of this life writing reflects not only the growing recognition of the importance of the individual, as distinct from the family or community, which emerged during the sixteenth and seventeenth centuries, but also the preoccupation with inner and spiritual life, and the encouragement to note and record its development accompanied Puritan revivals.

The introduction of the new term 'biography', meaning the history or written record of the life of an individual, in the late seventeenth century was a significant development. It was accompanied not only by increasing numbers of biographies but also by an expansion in the range of biographical subjects to include writers, theologians and religious figures of note.[3] Many of these biographies were written as a way to record the life, achievements and views of revered and beloved relatives and friends. There was also a new interest in researching and writing the lives of literary and religious figures not personally known to the author. William Roper's biography of his father-in-law, Sir Thomas More, first published early in the seventeenth century, was a noted example of the former group, with

Izaak Walton's eloquent and sympathetic Lives of John Donne, Henry Wotton, George Herbert and Richard Hooker serving as an example of the latter.

The range of biographical subjects expanded further in Britain in the aftermath of the Civil War and the Restoration. Large numbers of people who had been directly engaged in battle, or who had lost property or been imprisoned or exiled as a result of their religious and political loyalties, sought either to write their own story or to provide memorials for loved ones or patrons and teachers who had died or suffered grievously during the course of the war or in its aftermath. One of the first biographies to be written by a woman, Margaret Cavendish's *Life of the Thrice Noble, High and Puissant Prince William Cavendish* (1667), appeared at this time. It was intended as a tribute to her husband, seeking both to emphasise his honourable conduct and skill as a military commander of Royalist troops during the Civil War and to indicate the personal suffering and financial loss he had endured during the Commonwealth when he was forced into exile and had his estates sequestrated.

While the use of the term 'biography' signalled a new and growing interest in stories about people's lives, it also served as a way to link contemporary developments with earlier ones. Dryden, who is credited with the introduction of the term, used the word 'biography' to describe the life of the great classical writer Plutarch that he was writing as the reface to his translation of Plutarch's very influential biographical study, *Parallel Lives*.[4] Dryden paid tribute to the model of biography that Plutarch had established and especially to his treatment of the private as well as the public life of his subjects. Plutarch's insistence on the need to focus attention on private life and on the small domestic incidents that best revealed character was one also taken up in the eighteenth century by Samuel Johnson, one of the most important figures in the development of modern biography in Britain. Johnson was by no means the only important eighteenth-century British biographer, but he was the one who articulated most clearly a new form of biographical impulse and a new sense of the importance and role of biography.[5] The key concern of biography for Johnson was the delineation of an individual character, and he saw this as more likely to be made evident in social and domestic life than in public activities. Johnson echoed Plutarch closely in his insistence that the business of a biographer

> is often to pass slightly over those performances and incidents, which produce vulgar greatness, to lead the thoughts into domestick privacies [*sic*] and display the minute details of daily life, where exterior appendages are cast aside, and men excel each other only by prudence and by virtue.[6]

But, as suggested earlier, Johnson's understanding of privacy was very different from that of Plutarch. He was not interested, as Plutarch was, in showing a major public figure in a state of 'undress', or as he appeared when not engaged in public affairs, but rather in exploring the familial and social relationships of his subjects and particularly their ties to and behaviour towards their friends and, a matter of great importance in the eighteenth-century literary world, to their patrons. Johnson was not interested in the major public figures whose lives could be seen to embody and to represent the civilisation to which they belonged, as Plutarch was in his comparison of Greek and Roman lives. He was concerned rather with the lives of writers, exploring the struggles and conflicts that they faced in their daily lives and sometimes the 'invisible circumstances' which led them to questionable decisions and actions.

Sharing classical and Christian beliefs in the moral significance of depicting a life, Johnson saw this moral significance in a very different way. In his view, the moral benefit to be gained from biography derived not from the possibility of emulating an exemplary life, but rather from the special capacity that stories of actual lives had to expand people's sympathies and understanding of issues and questions that fell outside their own immediate experience: 'No species of writing', he insisted, 'seems more worthy of cultivation than biography, since none can be more delightful or more useful, none can more certainly enchain the heart by irresistible interest, or more widely diffuse instruction to every diversity of condition.'[7] The lessons to be found in such life stories depend on their truth. This emphasis on truth also made it important that all aspects of the life and character of a biographical subject be presented, including failures and vices. Like other biographers at the time, Johnson distinguished between accurate biography and **panegyric** – seeing the latter as something less valuable than a biography. 'If a man is to write A Panegyrick', he once explained, 'he may keep vices out of sight; but if he professes to write A Life, he must represent it really as it was.'[8] Detailed knowledge of a subject was, of course, imperative for a biographer – indeed, Johnson himself sometimes insisted that in order to write a man's life, one must have supped often with him and known him intimately.

The tenor of biography at any particular time clearly reflects contemporary tastes and developments in other literary forms. Hence, as Mark Salber Phillips has shown, this idea of the usefulness of biography and of its capacity to teach by evoking sympathy and emotion was similar to the claims then being made for fiction.[9] As with fiction, it allowed for and indeed encouraged the inclusion of a much wider range of people than had previously been seen as suitable biographical subjects. In addition to military, political and religious leaders, attention was now also paid to many whose lives had not been successful but had involved great struggles or difficulties and revealed the impact of personal failings and ill-fortune. Johnson was concerned also that a biography be recognised as a literary work, requiring care and skill in its organisation and presentation. He was very critical of the practices of contemporary biographers who

rarely afford any other account than might be collected from publick [sic] papers, but imagine themselves writing a life when they exhibit a chronological series of actions or preferments; and so little regard the manners or behaviour of their heroes, that more knowledge may be gained of a man's real character, by a short conversation with one of his servants, than from a formal and studied narrative, begun with his pedigree, and ended with his funeral.[10]

Johnson's approach can be seen in one of his earliest biographies, *The Life of Richard Savage* (1748). Savage had for a short time been a very close friend of Johnson's, and the biography was written shortly after Savage's death. It offers a very sympathetic portrait of a man better known for his profligacy, his excesses and his capacity to turn friends into enemies than for his poetry. Johnson began the book by pointing out that this would be a 'mournful narrative' like others dealing with the 'heroes of literary as well as civil history' who have often been as remarkable for their suffering as for their achievements. Savage was 'a man whose writings entitle him to an eminent rank in the classes of learning, and whose misfortunes claim a degree of compassion not always due to the unhappy, as they were often the consequences of the crimes of others rather than his own'. Johnson depicted Savage as a man whose misfortunes began in infancy when he was disowned by his mother and thus deprived of the comfort and family connections to which he was entitled. The truth of this depiction of Savage's childhood has been questioned: Johnson took it directly from Savage and made no attempts to verify it.[11] But what remains significant here is the way in which this illustrates Johnson's concern to expand the range of biographical subjects so that it included men, and occasionally women, who had not reached the first rank in any area but whose lives and painful personal struggles were sufficiently interesting and important to warrant their being recorded.[12]

Johnson's prominent place in the history of biography derives both from his own work as a biographer and from the fact that he was the subject of what many regard as the finest biography of the eighteenth century, James Boswell's *Life of Johnson*. Boswell's work remains one of the classic biographical studies, celebrated for the way in which it illustrates and brings to life Johnson's personality, his views and the tenor of his conversation. Boswell made great play of his own efforts in collecting the material for this work – in terms following Johnson's own injunctions. He was a friend of Johnson's for over twenty years, and during that time 'had the scheme of writing his life constantly in view'. He asked numerous questions of Johnson and also 'acquired a facility in recollecting, and was very assiduous in recording, his conversation, of which the extraordinary vigour and vivacity constituted one of the first features of his character'.[13]

As a very keen and assiduous diarist, Boswell kept an extensive and detailed journal of his own daily life and activities, paying particular attention in the years he knew Johnson to their meetings and to recording any conversations in which Johnson was involved. His biography drew extensively on the journals, although he took great care to verify information in the stories that he had been told and to ensure the accuracy of his accounts. Boswell's insistence that the biography was based on the very close intimacy between himself and Johnson helps to explain some of the curious features of his work: the two men met when Johnson was already in his mid-fifties, and hence the twenty years spanned by their friendship covered only the last two decades of Johnson's life. It is this period that features most heavily in Boswell's work. Boswell paid relatively little attention to Johnson's childhood and early life, or indeed to the earlier years of his adult life, focussing most of his attention on the period in which Johnson was a literary celebrity, renowned for his sparkling conversation as well as his writing.

It is worth noting here that, despite the sense of intimacy evident in Boswell's biography of Johnson, there is much that is omitted. Boswell provides detailed discussion of Johnson's friendships, manners, physical ailments, problems and some of his emotional weaknesses, as well as his ideas and his work. But he draws a veil over many aspects of his personal and emotional life. Although there are some small references to his susceptibility to women, most of these encounters and intimate episodes – including Johnson's plan to marry again after the death of his wife – are omitted.[14] For all the insistence on the importance of 'domestick privacies [sic]', therefore, by current standards eighteenth-century understandings of intimacy leave much still hidden.

▶ 'How delicate, decent is English biography, bless its mealy mouth!': the changing pattern of biography in the nineteenth century[15]

Throughout the nineteenth century, Boswell's *Life of Johnson* was widely regarded as the greatest biography ever written, although the approach that it embodied did not long survive. Even when it was first published, there were some who felt that it revealed more of Johnson's private life and personal weakness than was strictly necessary. And in the reactionary mood which came to dominate British politics and society in the immediate aftermath of the French Revolution, it became clear that the discussion of human frailty and failure, rather than increasing the sympathy of readers, invoked their censure and that lives needed to be written with greater care.

Intimate details and revelations of any form of sexual indiscretion or impropriety, in particular, were now met with harsh disapproval, especially in regard to women. When, shortly after Mary Wollstonecraft's tragically early death, William Godwin felt driven to write her story, *Memoirs of the Author of a Vindication of the Rights of Women* (1796), he produced a work which, although intended as a tribute and a memorial to Mary Wollstonecraft, served to destroy her reputation for nearly a century.[16] Godwin both loved and admired Wollstonecraft and sought, in depicting her life and ideas, to show her courage in flouting convention and in following her own wishes and desires. In so doing, he made public many facets of Wollstonecraft's life which had not previously been widely known. The most shocking of these concerned her relationship with the American merchant and adventurer Gilbert Imlay, with whom she had a child, though they were not married. Godwin described the state of suicidal despair into which Wollstonecraft fell when her relationship with Imlay ended. He also made clear the unusual way in which he and Wollstonecraft continued to live separately after they had married. The book unleashed a massive critical attack both on Wollstonecraft's life and on her ideas.[17] Godwin was accused of stripping 'his dead wife naked' and of mourning her with a heart of stone. Far from provoking sympathy for Wollstonecraft, his revelations confirmed the widespread belief amongst conservatives that sympathy for women's rights was inevitably accompanied by a threat to the family and to proper moral standards. The outcry occasioned by this book pointed to a new concern about the limits on what could be discussed in biography and the need for discretion, especially when it came to questions about personal and domestic life.

Throughout the nineteenth century, one can see the tensions and difficulties that many biographers faced in their attempts to combine the new sense of decorum, propriety and restraint with Johnson's insistence that a biography was different from a panegyric. Many biographers revealed anxiety about where exactly lines should be drawn. John Gibson Lockhart made this very clear in the biography of his father-in-law, Sir Walter Scott, which he wrote in the 1830s. Echoing Johnson, Lockhart felt it necessary that a biography encompass its subject's weaknesses as well as strengths. He despised 'the whole trickery of erecting an alabaster image and calling that a Man', he wrote in a letter to a friend; he added, however, in a comment which marks the differences in his approach from that of Johnson, that he trusted 'to the substantial goodness and greatness of the character' and thought that by showing a 'few specks' of weakness, he would make the portrait all the more effective. But Lockhart had considerable difficulty deciding how much detail about Scott's private life, and especially his acute financial difficulties, to include in what he saw as a memorial to Scott. One of Scott's early infatuations, for example, which led to an unsuccessful marriage proposal, produced acute unease as he felt that this discussion might seem to be 'trenching on delicacy' in the eyes of his readers. He would have preferred to say nothing about this matter, but felt impelled to do so because Scott's own sketch of his life, on which the biography was based, had dealt with it at length. '[I] considered it as my duty to tell the story truly and intelligibly', while trusting that 'I have avoided unnecessary disclosures.'[18]

Lockhart's sense that some criticism of an individual or the revealing of a 'few specks' was both acceptable and necessary and would ultimately add to a sense of the full humanity and the virtue or fundamental soundness of an individual was widely accepted in biographical writing throughout the nineteenth century. But, as this suggests, the primary concern was to show the achievements and merits of prominent and notable individuals, rather than their faults, often in the belief that their lives should be seen as exemplary and worthy of emulation. Recognition of the need to differentiate between biography and eulogy remained, but biographers were expected to exercise discretion and to omit those details or aspects of the life of their subject that were 'too painful' or best passed over.[19] The new emphasis on morality, propriety and respectability associated in Britain with the rise of evangelical religion and with an increasingly prominent and self-confident middle class meant that these 'painful' matters came to include habits such as drunkenness, gambling and any form of sexual indiscretion.

This concern to stress virtue also meant that harsh characteristics, including wit, were softened or omitted. Although often insisting that the truthfulness of their portraits could be seen in the extensive use that they made of the writings and especially of the letters of their subjects, most nineteenth-century biographers censored these letters heavily, cutting passages which seemed too satirical or showed a sharpness that was not in keeping with the image of the person they wanted to portray.

Not all Victorian writers accepted this ideal of propriety. Thomas Carlyle was scathing in his denunciation of these new developments:

> A Damocles' sword of *Respectability* hangs for ever over the poor English Life-writer ... and reduces him to the verge of paralysis ... The English biographer has long felt that if in writing his man's Biography, he wrote down anything that could possible offend any man, he had written wrong. The plain consequence was that, properly speaking, no biography whatever could be produced.[20]

Carlyle himself, however, while certainly prepared to offer critical analyses of the ideas and beliefs of his own biographical subjects, focussed on their religious doubts, their changing political affiliations, and their male friendships, but drew the line at any discussion of their marital or sexual lives. He wrote at length about the familial heritage of his friend, John Sterling, for example, but mentioned his marriage and his wife only briefly in a chapter entitled 'Marriage: Ill-health; West-Indies'.

Most of the biographies mentioned so far have been written by authors impelled to write in order to provide some form of memorial to a person to whom they felt a close personal tie. Many biographies were written for other reasons, including requests from publishers or from families to provide such a memorial and from individuals who wished that their biography be written after their death. Two of the most controversial nineteenth-century biographies were in response to such requests: Elizabeth Gaskell's *The Life of Charlotte Brontë*, written at the request of both Brontë's father and her widower, and J. A. Froude's *Life of Carlyle*, written at Carlyle's request.

In the nineteenth century, as in the eighteenth, there was a close connection between biography and other literary forms, especially fiction. The story of an individual life was the subject of a number of Victorian novels. In some notable cases, Charlotte Brontë's *Jane Eyre* and Charles Dickens's *David Copperfield*, the novel purports to be an autobiography, with the central character as its narrator. But the lives as depicted in these works are both shaped by biography and help to shape it. One can see this particularly in their strong interest in childhood and in the impact of childhood experiences on adult life. Although Victorian fiction was often more concerned with emotional states and an interior emotional life than biography, it shared many of the same restrictions in terms of the issues which could be discussed. Sexual propriety was usually maintained through the convention of ending the fictional life of a heroine at the time of her marriage – although occasionally marriage and even the trials and tribulations of a 'fallen woman' who had engaged in sexual relations outside marriage found their way into novels.

Mrs Gaskell had fallen foul of Victorian ideas of decorum in one of her novels, *Ruth*, which depicted a young girl who is seduced and abandoned by a wealthy lover. Although acting with a great deal of discretion, she fell foul of it again in *The Life of Charlotte Brontë*.[21] Gaskell's literary talent is evident throughout, and her descriptions of the Brontë home, of their neighbours in Yorkshire, of the family and the tragedies they faced as a result of disease and death all bear the distinctive sympathy and charm of her novels. Her sensitive and insightful characterisations of the Brontë sisters, although based on detailed knowledge, were also very discreet, omitting aspects of their lives which might have offended their father or laid them open to public criticism. Although she quoted from some of their letters, for example, she did not even hint at the emotional nature of Charlotte Brontë's relationship with her Belgian teacher, M. Heger. But Gaskell still managed to shock her readers. It was impossible to present the Brontë family in a way which accorded entirely with Victorian ideas of propriety – especially those expected of clerical families. Gaskell's depiction of Charlotte Brontë's father, the Reverend Patrick Branwell Brontë, and of the harsh life he imposed on his children was seen as distasteful. But her treatment of the life of Charlotte Brontë's brother, Branwell, especially her depiction of his sexual entanglement with the wife of his employer, his subsequent dismissal and then his descent into the alcoholism and drug addiction which led to his death exceeded all the boundaries of propriety. Indeed, the frank discussion of this issue in the first edition of the biography led to a threat of litigation. She was required both to apologise and to rewrite the book; in its rewritten form, the story of Branwell's sad final years is merely hinted at and is not discussed in any detail.[22]

But the storm provoked by Gaskell was nothing compared to the outcry occasioned by Froude's biography of Thomas Carlyle. Ironically, it was Carlyle's hostility to the 'mealy-mouthed' way in which nineteenth-century biographers censored the lives of their subjects and his insistence that, when it came to the writing of *his* life, this form of censorship not be practised which led to the scandal. As Carlyle's friends knew, he was an extremely difficult man, irascible, sardonic and frequently subject to ill health and physical discomfort, which did not improve his temper. These qualities, combined with his hatred of any form of noise and his absolute belief in male predominance and in the privilege of husbands to constant attendance from their wives, also made him a very difficult husband. He was forced to recognise this when, after his wife's death, he read her journals and saw how unhappy her life with him had been. In a spirit of remorse, Carlyle wrote about the sufferings he had imposed on his wife. He also appointed his friend J. A. Froude as his literary executor and gave him the task of both publishing these reminiscences and writing his biography, enjoining absolute honesty on him.[23] After Carlyle's death in 1881, Froude did as he was bid, first publishing Carlyle's *Reminiscences* and the *Letters and Memorials of Jane Welsh Carlyle*, which made clear both Jane Carlyle's unhappiness and Thomas Carlyle's remorse,[24] and following this with a massive four-volume biography in which he detailed the unhappy domestic life of the Carlyles and the many years of misery endured by Jane.

Froude's work was met with great hostility both by Carlyle's family and by the many members of the English and American literary establishments who had known and respected Carlyle and felt that it was an absolute travesty to have these details of his domestic life made public. The *Saturday Review* referred to Froude's work as 'a minute and hideous dissection, in which by a hideous process each of the subjects has been made to take part in demonstrating the morbid anatomy of the other' and commented that 'no deplorable or shameful detail has been spared'.[25] Others questioned his motives and expressed disgust at his treachery to his friend. As Trev Broughton has shown, this episode brought together two different concerns: questions about Victorian masculinity and the appropriate conduct and responsibilities of husbands were linked with those concerning biographical practices and the aspects of a life that it was acceptable to depict.[26] For many current readers, what is notable about Froude's biography of Carlyle is the extent to which he accepted some Victorian restraints, omitting any discussion of the sexual relationship between the Carlyles, for example, or any reference to the suggestion made by some of Jane Carlyle's friends that he was sexually impotent and that Jane Carlyle's consequent childlessness was another source of her misery. But for Froude's own contemporaries, such as Leslie Stephen, in revealing domestic secrets which he felt should have been left shrouded in decent obscurity, Froude had betrayed the biographer's office and broken the trust which should exist between a biographer and his subject.

▶ The 'new' biography and the inner life in the early twentieth century

If the biographical impulse in the nineteenth century was characterised by the concern to provide appropriate memorials and extol the virtues of significant people while passing over any aspects of their lives which might suggest personal failings, that of the early twentieth offered a very marked contrast. The Victorian belief in the need for restraint and decorum in dealing with personal failings and with private life had already been challenged at the end of the nineteenth century in a number of ways. One can see it most clearly in the novels dealing with the 'new woman' or the consequences of the prevailing double standard in sexual morality and even the issue of sexual incompatibility in marriage. But it was not these questions that were taken up in biographical writing so much as the appalling burden imposed on their children by the unquestioning religious faith and narrow and puritanical views and lives of some Victorian parents. This issue was dealt with in Samuel Butler's powerful autobiographical novel *The Way of All Flesh* (1903) and more directly in Edmund Gosse's *Father and Son: A Study of Two Temperaments* (1907), a work which broke the boundaries between autobiography and biography in ways which did not re-emerge until the 1980s.[27] Gosse's work offered a deeply moving picture of an unhappy childhood and of an impossible parent–child relationship. His depiction of the isolated and impoverished life he led as a consequence of his parents' intense religious beliefs and their devoted adherence to the Plymouth Brethren is remarkable for its clarity and lack of either sentimental indulgence or blame. The struggles he faced as a modern and educated young man having to deal with his father's denial of Darwinian evolution, and the ridicule which this engendered, are all described with acute insight and sensitivity. But most poignant of all is the extreme pain involved in his final break with his father when, after receiving daily letters which inquired into the state of his religious faith and which were interspersed with long and anguished conversations on this question whenever he went home, he made clear his own lack of religious faith and his need for an entirely different kind of life. This work anticipated later developments in its criticism of Victorian values and assumptions, especially those concerning the duties that children owed parents, however unreasonable parental demands might be. But it also added a new layer of complexity to biography through its depiction of the unintentional cruelty which could occur even in a very loving relationship as a result of incomprehension and incompatible differences.

The critique of Victorian values that Gosse offered became considerably more savage during the course of the First World War. For Lytton Strachey in particular, it brought a powerful sense of the destructiveness which accompanied Victorian ideas about religion, duty and Empire. Around 1910, Strachey had begun working on an extended series of biographical essays which would allow him to articulate his critical approach to the imperial world of the nineteenth century in which he had grown up. At the start, he envisaged a volume called *Victorian Silhouettes*, which would include essays on Henry Sidgwick, the painter George Watts, Darwin, Mill, Carlyle, Benjamin Jowett, Florence Nightingale, Cardinal Manning, General Gordon and Thomas Arnold. Strachey, who was a conscientious objector, became increasingly appalled as he watched the slaughter of young men in the including many of his friends, in the First World War, and he came more and more to see the war as a consequence of Victorian beliefs and assumptions, especially of Victorian hypocrisy and the refusal of the Victorians to face truths about themselves. He narrowed his selection of people down to the four – Florence Nightingale, Cardinal Manning, General Gordon and Thomas Arnold – who seemed best to illustrate the religious, educational and military approaches of which he was so critical and who to him encapsulated Victorianism. His essays exposed their foibles, questioned their motives and pointed to the significance of very personal factors in their major religious, political and professional activities. He offered an example of a new approach to biography in the brevity of his treatment, his crisp literary style and his often ironic tone, but also in his open criticism and his interest in hidden and sometimes unconscious motives.

For Strachey, the very form of Victorian biography itself served as a potent illustration of the worst Victorian values, and the impulse to critique and to show the dishonesty, hypocrisy and hidden flaws which underlay those values helped lead him to offer a new form of biography. What biography needed, he argued, was not the amassing of detail, but rather careful selection, critical analysis and interpretation. The duty of a biographer, in his view, required him 'to maintain his own freedom of spirit. It is not his business to be complimentary; it is his business to lay bare the facts of the case, as he understands them.'[28]

Eminent Victorians inaugurated extensive discussion about biography throughout the 1920s and 1930s as many writers sought to explore the relationship between biography and the modern tendencies in life and thought.[29] Virginia Woolf, one of the first to use the term 'new biography' and to attempt to define it, was particularly interested in this question.[30] The central problem of biography at the time, she suggested, was that of combining the hard granite of factual truth with the light of personality. In earlier periods, biographers had sought to illustrate the character of their subjects by focussing on their significant actions. But now, as people were coming to insist that 'true life' showed itself not in action, but instead in personality and 'in that inner life of thought and emotion which meanders darkly and obscurely through the hidden channels of the soul', the task of the biographer was rather different. This new emphasis on the interior life was accompanied by a changing sense of the appropriate relationship between the biographer and his or her subject. The Victorian biographer, Woolf argued, was 'dominated by the idea of goodness. Noble, upright, chaste, severe ... almost always above life-size in top-hat and frock-coat', and he or she toiled away, providing a heroic picture of an esteemed subject. The new biographer, by contrast, regarded those about whom he or she wrote as equals who could be interrogated, analysed and subjected to independent critical judgement. In this process, biographers also came more clearly into view as writers whose ideas, insights and judgements were seen as integral to their work.

▶ Biography and the quest for understanding

This preoccupation with what Woolf referred to as the 'inner life of thoughts and emotions' has been a driving force in the writing of biography across the twentieth century. In her widely read book on biography, Paula Backscheider has reformulated this slightly, suggesting that what the biographer really wants to do is to get below any surface or superficial impressions to 'the person beneath, the core of the human being'.[31] The question of how to access this 'core' has been answered in very different ways by various biographers: some look at an individual's writing; others turn to some form of depth psychology; still others turn to intimate domestic and familial relationships or to an analysis of sexual identities. Backscheider herself comments on the popularity of literary biography – especially on the numbers of literary biographies which have won major prizes. She suggests that this popularity is at least in part a reflection of the fascination with the inner life, something that is accessible in the case of writers because of the use that can be made of their own writings. Writers are usually believed to have secretive and creative imaginations. They are often free to explore feelings and issues that others feel the need to repress or deny. 'In contemplating the possible relationship between source and published work', she suggests, 'we see a fascinating variant on the flow from experience to interior life back to the life as it is lived and expressed.'[32]

Both in their reading of the published work of biographical subjects and in exploring other facets of their lives, some twentieth-century biographers have turned to the insights and suggestions which have come from depth psychology or **psychoanalysis**. 'Freudian psychology', Richard Altick suggested, offered a way to approach 'the seeming contradictions and anomalies of personality and of rationally accounting for "irrational" conduct; it gave the biographer a torch by which to move from the comparatively well-lighted territory of the manifest into the shadowy one of subliminal drama'.[33] As we shall see, the relationship between biography and psychoanalysis has always been a difficult one. Nonetheless, it is clear that most biographers now generally recognise the existence and importance of the unconscious and, with that, the need to gain access to intentions and meanings which are not easily evident. For many biographers, this has led to a particular interest in family dynamics, in repetitive patterns of behaviour set up in childhood and often evident in adult life, in aspects of individuals' lives and behaviours which seem self-destructive and more generally in those aspects of a life which suggest underlying tensions and conflicts.

One of the distinctive features of much contemporary biography is its concern to depict fully the personality of its subjects in ways which encompass their emotional make-up and interior lives as well as their public lives. This is in marked contrast to an earlier biographical interest in character, particularly the moral character in terms of both the strengths and the failings of an individual. The idea of character provided a framework for allocating praise or blame in accordance with the behaviour and the underlying characteristics of a person. It also suggested the possibility of emulation. Personality, by contrast, involves a far stronger emphasis on intellectual and emotional qualities and suggests the possibility of a psychological rather than a moral approach. Coming to terms with the nature of an individual, a subject of such interest in much current biography, replaces the possibility of emulation with a much stronger sense of the emotional and psychological complexity of an individual and of the challenge posed by the desire to understand. Obviously, this drive for understanding has brought a new sense of what aspects of the life of an individual it is either interesting or appropriate to investigate. Contemporary biographers, like most of their predecessors, stress the importance of an understanding of private life; however, the twentieth-century notion of 'private' focussed far more on the intimate relationships that individuals had with their parents and siblings, with sexual partners and with very close friends to whom they had deep emotional attachments than had previously been the case. Family of origin and education had been of great concern to nineteenth-century biographers. In the twentieth century, however, far more attention was focussed on the difficulties and tensions evident in parent–child relationships and the impact of those relationships and relationships with siblings on the formation of an adult personality. Leon Edel's massive five-volume biography of Henry James, for example, sees in James's childhood, and particularly in his relationships with his parents, the whole pattern of his future life.[34]

Entirely new territory was explored when it came to dealing with other aspects of emotional and sexual life as biographers sought to explore the full range of the erotic and sexual relationships of their subjects and to understand their sexual identities and desires. Although very interested in these questions, neither Lytton Strachey nor Virginia Woolf felt free to broach them in their biographies in the 1920s and 1930s, and it was only after the Second World War that discussions of an individual's sexual relationships began to appear. One can see the change from earlier practices particularly clearly in the biographies of political leaders, whose marriages and extramarital liaisons began openly to be discussed at this time. This was especially the case when an individual commanded little respect, and his or her private life became the focus of criticism. Within a decade of the death of the British prime minister David Lloyd George, for example, biographies made much of his long-standing liaison with his secretary, Frances Stevenson – with whom he maintained a household in London while his wife, Maggie, remained in the family home in Wales – and of his affairs with other women, often as a means of illustrating his shallowness and lack of integrity. It took rather longer for there to be open discussion of the extramarital relationships of men who were admired or revered: the extramarital affair of Franklin D. Roosevelt, for example, was not much discussed until the late 1960s and early 1970s, but it was certainly evident in the biographies of him and of Eleanor Roosevelt published in those decades. Those years also saw the first detailed discussions of the long-standing sexual relationship between Thomas Jefferson and his slave Sally Hemings, which had been hinted at but was categorically denied throughout most of the nineteenth century. Although it is clear that this concern to 'reveal all', and especially to divulge secrets of any kind, has encouraged a fascination with the scurrilous or potentially scandalous in the lives of public figures, it also reflects a sense amongst both biographers and their readers that one of the chief values of biography is precisely its capacity to link the private and the public.

It was not just the sexual relationships of public figures which came to preoccupy biographers in the 1960s and 1970s, but rather the whole question of sexuality and sexual identity as the underlying key to an individual's personality and life course. This centrality of sexuality as a way of understanding an individual's nature and behaviour was first discussed in the late nineteenth century, both by sexologists such as Havelock Ellis and also by Freud. However, it did not become a central feature of biography until much later. During the course of the 1970s, this approach could be seen in a number of different biographies. A couple of the most notable dealt with men whose homosexuality was seen as the dominating feature of their lives: Michael Holroyd's *Lytton Strachey* (1967–68),[35] followed a few years later by Phyllis Grosskurth's *John Addington Symonds: A Biography*.[36] These authors were well aware of the novelty of their own undertaking, as Holroyd particularly made clear: 'I was setting out to do something entirely new in biography', he pointed out, 'to give Lytton's love-life the same prominence in my book as it had in his career, and to treat the whole subject of homosexuality without any artificial veils of decorum.'[37] Both the importance and the problematic nature of sexuality for heterosexual men, especially Victorian men, were also explored in biographies in this decade. Derek Hudson's *Munby, Man of Two Worlds*, for example, explored the life of a middle-class man who had no sexual interest in women of his own class but was obsessed by the erotic possibilities offered by working-class women.[38] Susan Chitty looked, rather, at the difficulties that heterosexual desire posed for nineteenth-century clergymen. In her biography of Charles Kingsley, sub-titled *The Beast and the Monk*, Chitty made extensive use of Kingsley's erotic drawings of his wife, Fanny, to illustrate the problems that Kingsley's immense sexual passion for Fanny posed for him. As a Victorian clergyman, he was supposedly immune to bodily lust and was therefore forced to clothe his sexual passion in spiritual terms.[39]

When it came to writing about women, questions about sexuality tended to be dealt with in rather different ways from those evident in relation to men. Especially when dealing with nineteenth-century women, who rarely mentioned sex, biographers have instead looked at the overall patterns of women's emotional and domestic lives and at the ways in which women who chose to live with female companions often described their relationship in familial terms, likening their partner to a mother or beloved sister as a way of stressing the closeness and intimacy of a relationship, rather than using images from marriage or any more explicitly sexual bond.

▶ Feminist impulses

Over the last few decades, many women writers have become very interested in writing women's lives. This interest, which came to the fore with the re-emergence of **feminism** and of demands for 'women's liberation' in the later 1960s and early 1970s, focussed initially on the women who had once been well known as political activists or educators but were forgotten soon after their deaths. Many of them struggled to find publishers. Gerder Lerner, for example, has written eloquently about the difficulties she had placing her biography of the Grimke sisters, now the subject of many biographical and historical studies. Her book was rejected by 25 publishers, all of whom insisted that lives of women did not sell, before finally being accepted by Houghton-Mifflin in 1967.

Echoing many other feminist scholars, Lerner commented on the very strong tie she felt to her women subjects, with whom she shared a need to work out ways to combine her familial and domestic duties and responsibilities with a desire for a career and a public role. She 'identified with their outsider status':

> As the only Southern women of the planter class who became abolitionist agents in the North, they were not only emigrants but exiles from their own class. Angelina's struggles to

maintain an egalitarian marriage with a very active reformer husband spoke to me in a very personal way across the centuries. The complexities of combining social activism, innovative thought and the endless cares of household and children while living in near-poverty seemed as real to me as they must have seemed to them.[40]

This sense of identification with earlier women activists was articulated by a number of other feminist historians and biographers in the 1970s and 1980s who recognised that they were seeking new ways of understanding difficulties that they faced in their own lives through exploring the lives of other women. Some of them sought an idealised maternal figure or a role model as they researched the life of an older feminist leader. Belle Chevigny, for example, who wrote a biography of the nineteenth-century American feminist and transcendentalist Margaret Fuller, argued that the writing of women's biography involved women in seeking not only their own history but also an exploration of themselves in terms of another.[41] Elizabeth Kimmick suggested that the reciprocity of friendship offered the appropriate model for thinking about the ways in which feminist scholars wrote the lives of earlier feminists because it allowed for recognition of the place and ideas of the author and a clear sense that the work involved the establishment of a particularly close relationship between author and subject.[42]

Feminist concerns with the restrictions and limitations that women faced as a result of both legal and social constraints and the prevailing assumptions about and stereotypes of femininity can clearly be seen in many of the biographies of women published since the 1970s. In writing the lives of eighteenth- and nineteenth-century women, for example, considerable attention has been paid to the limited education that was available to them and the battles that they fought if they chose alternate pathways to marriage and motherhood or sought to combine these activities with a public life or a career. These issues are central themes in many collective and individual biographies of women, including those of Catharine Beecher, Elizabeth Cady Stanton and Eleanor Roosevelt in the United States and George Eliot, Virginia Woolf and Beatrice Webb in Britain.

Several of these biographies pay as much attention to the emotional conflicts, the familial relationships and the domestic lives of their subjects as they do to their public work or writing. This stress on the domestic and the private is important in itself, but it was also a way of exploring the significance of **gender**: the ways in which being born a girl affected or determined the nature of relationships with parents; of childhood, education and possible life choices; and of sexual relationships and marriage in a woman's life. This was a key question in Kathryn Kish Sklar's pioneering work *Catharine Beecher: A Study in American Domesticity*, see p. 22 for example, which stresses the importance to Catharine of her relationship with her father, the **charismatic** preacher Lyman Beecher. Catharine was devoted to her father and wanted to follow in his footsteps. However, the idea that his daughter should do so was inconceivable to Lyman Beecher, and he rejected any suggestion that this was possible. His response led to tension between them and intense suffering for Catharine as she sought to forge new directions for herself and to gain her father's love and support.

Blanche Cook's biography of Eleanor Roosevelt provides another very good illustration of many of these themes and of their centrality in writing the lives of women. Cook begins with a detailed depiction of Eleanor Roosevelt's painful late nineteenth-century childhood and of its impact on her. The beloved and loving but irresponsible and alcoholic father and the mother who died when she was only eight, but who had offered her little love or sympathy and made very clear her preference for Eleanor's brothers, left Eleanor extremely anxious and insecure. Cook explores her education, early social life and marriage and her development of a life of her own and an interest in women's education and other feminist issues in the 1920s after she discovered that her husband, Franklin D. Roosevelt, had been engaged in a passionate affair with another woman. At all times, as Cook makes clear, Eleanor Roosevelt's life required the negotiation of the claims and demands made on her as a wife, mother and daughter-in-law, and her own aims often took second place to these demands.

Although women who engaged in public life and activity were the first to claim the attention of feminist biographers, attention has also been paid to those women who, though active in feminist movements, philanthropy or imperial ventures, never attained the status of national leadership. Their lives are now seen as important not only in themselves but also because of the insights they offer into how important these various causes and issues were to the many women to whose lives they gave shape and meaning. The ready availability of material, and some degree of prominence, meant that middle-class women were the main subjects of biographical interest in the 1970s and 1980s. In the last couple of decades, however, interest has also been focussed on less privileged women, including African American women in the United States. Attention has thus been paid belatedly to major and iconic figures such as Sojourner Truth and Harriet Tubman, both freed slaves and very significant figures in abolitionism and feminism. As we shall see, attention is also increasingly being paid to women who did not have public lives, but who devoted themselves entirely to family and to the home.

3 Collective Biography

▶ Introduction

Despite the immense importance of collective biography for historians, until recently little has been written about it. The dominance of literary concerns in most theoretical discussions of biography has meant that attention has been almost exclusively focused on individual biography. In recent years, however, there has been a very considerable interest amongst social scientists and educationalists in the ways in which collective biographies allow new insights into the construction of subjectivities. In some cases, this has been inflected with a feminist concern to undertake such work collectively and to include reflection on the author's own experiences within the work.[1] For historians too, collective biography is immensely important. Many of those who have been engaged in writing it, moreover, have seen their own work as an essentially historical endeavour, either in itself or in terms of the resource it provides for other historians. In deciding who should be included in the British *Dictionary of National Biography* in the late nineteenth century, for example, Leslie Stephen, its first editor, insisted that pride of place needed to be given to details about the lives of those individuals in current standard British histories: the dictionary was clearly designed to augment historical knowledge and study.

One of the difficulties that one faces in dealing with collective biography, however, is the range of different kinds of work that come into this category. The term *collective biography* is used not only to refer to collections of biographical essays and all forms of biographical dictionary but also to any biographical study that has more than one subject, including works dealing with the lives of married couples, siblings, families and social, intellectual or political groups. In one of the few attempts to address this question of how to define or to differentiate between different forms of collective biography, Keith Thomas suggests that it has typically taken one of three forms: group biography, universal biography and national biography.[2] Thomas provides an excellent discussion of the links and the differences between universal and national biography but pays little attention to the immense differences between group biography and the kinds of biography found in almost all biographical dictionaries. For the most part, group biography focuses on people who are closely connected to each other through marriage, blood ties, friendship or involvement in a particular set of activities or ideas. The concern of these biographies is often to delineate the nature of this connection and to explore the relationships or the shared ideas and activities of the group, paying much less attention to those aspects of the lives of each member of the group which occur outside its ambit. This is markedly different from the series of individual biographical essays which usually make up a national or universal collection. The idea of 'collective biography' here refers to the ways in which the individual studies are selected and combined in order to make up some representation of the nation, of a professional group or of a kind of activism. One is, nonetheless, always dealing with individual biographies which are designed to be read alongside others.

As we shall see, there are now a number of ways in which the individual biographies in dictionaries of biography can be read and organised in order to give a greater sense of the groups into which individuals might fit. All of this makes it difficult to offer any hard-and-fast definition of collective biography or of the subgroups of which it is composed. On the whole, it is more helpful to think of collective biography as a continuum, extending from individual studies which are grouped together to make up a collective whole (like dictionaries of national biography), at one end, to those works in which the primary subject is a group of people and which focus on the interactions and shared experiences of its members, at the other end. In between, there are a number of different ways of linking individual stories or of looking at people in pairs, couples or families.

This chapter explores the history of collective biography, looking first at the different forms of collected lives to be found in the past, and especially since the eighteenth century, and then at the emergence and growing interest in group biography during the course of the twentieth century. It will also look at the changes evident in questions about the kinds of people seen as appropriate subjects for these works and at the kinds of histories that many of their authors sought to construct through their biographical studies.

▶ Encyclopaedias and universal biography

Collective biography has quite as long a history as individual biography, stretching back at least to classical times. From its earliest appearance, it has taken different forms: Plutarch's *Parallel Lives* was essentially a form of comparative biography in which pairs of Greek and Roman rulers, military leaders and writers were compared in order to explore their characters, contrast their qualities and establish their moral calibre and failings; by contrast, Suetonius' *Lives of the Caesars*, which follows the line of succession from Julius Caesar through the first twelve emperors of the Roman Empire, also provides a history of the Roman principate. This form of collective biography, in which individual lives are ordered chronologically so that they provide some insight into the history of particular institutions or historical periods, continued to appear over many centuries. One can see it very clearly in Bede's *Lives of the Abbots*, dealing with the abbots of Wearmoth and Jarrow.[3] During the Renaissance, this idea of writing a broader history through a series of individual biographies was taken up by Vasari, for example, in his *Lives of the Artists*, which was intended to show how the different arts 'like human beings themselves, are born, grow up, become old and die'.[4]

The vogue for this form of collective biography continued and indeed expanded throughout the seventeenth and eighteenth centuries. Just as Vasari wrote his *Lives of the Artists* as a way of demonstrating the importance of the arts, so too those seeking to stress the importance of (or to demand recognition for) the professional, scholarly or spiritual standing of other groups did so through the writing of collective biography. Religious figures were important here, particularly in America. Writers also featured prominently, especially in Britain, and a number of collected lives of English poets were published before the appearance of the best known of these works, Samuel Johnson's *Lives of the Poets*, in the 1780s. But alongside these works focused on particular groups, there was a growing fascination with the lives and life stories of many different kinds of people, including not only writers, philosophers and scholars but also a range of other 'worthies' and eccentrics. The earliest works of this kind were Thomas Fuller's *History of the Worthies of England* (1662) and John Aubrey's *Brief Lives*. But by the end of the eighteenth century, to borrow Keith Thomas's engaging list, one could find collected biographies of 'actors, admirals, bishops, botanists, dramatists, Gresham professors, learned women, physicians, poets, or regicides'.[5]

Although these limited and clearly focused collective biographies continued to be written, they were joined and in some ways surpassed during the course of the seventeenth and eighteenth centuries by much larger collections of lives which were altogether more ambitious in terms of their scope and coverage. Indeed, some of these new works sought to encompass every significant life ever lived. The rise of antiquarian interest encouraged this desire to establish accurate information about significant individuals in the past as extensively and comprehensively as possible. Many antiquarians shared the desire to encompass and to order all knowledge in a single major work, and this was evident amongst those groups seeking to produce the massive encyclopaedias of scientific knowledge or of the sciences and arts which were a feature of the Enlightenment, especially in France.

The most ambitious and successful encyclopaedia of universal biography was Pierre Bayle's *Dictionnaire Critique et Historique* (1697). Originally intended as a response to the errors in an earlier biographical dictionary, Louis Moréri's *Grand Dictionnaire Historique*, Bayle's dictionary was significant because of both its vast array of information and its critical methodology. He provided detailed information about his own sources and compared different versions of stories in a thorough and painstaking way. His work saw eight French editions in the fifty years after its first publication and was translated into English twice: in 1709 and again across the years 1734–41.[6] Its coverage extended from eminent men and women of ancient times through to the present and included stories of gods and mythological figures. Alphabetically arranged, it combined narratives about all of these individuals, with many different kinds of information about their religious beliefs and doctrines, artistic and scientific ideas and political involvements. The emphasis on documentation was evident in the footnotes, which often greatly exceeded the text in length. Portrait heads were also used, adding a visual dimension to the antiquarian and biographical concern with accuracy.

Bayle's dictionary encouraged the production of a British equivalent. Initially, English translators sought to satisfy their own nationalist concerns by adding more British lives to their editions of Bayle's work. Indeed, one of the two rival English translations of this work (published in 1734–41) included an additional 900 British lives.[7]

▶ National biography in the nineteenth century

During the course of the eighteenth century, a new focus on patriotic and national biography emerged. Although the lives of great figures from earlier times, especially Greek and Roman rulers and philosophers, continued to be important, they were seen to be of less direct and immediate concern than the heroic figures taken from one's own people and especially from the recent, rather than the distant, past. France was one of the earliest countries to seek to establish a canon of 'great men'. While borrowing from classical models such as that of Plutarch, this French canon was intended to demonstrate France's worth as a successor to Greece and Rome and, of course, its superiority to other European countries.[8] A similar concern was evident in the *Biographia Britannica* that appeared across the second half of the eighteenth century and was intended to be 'a British Temple of honour, sacred to the piety, learning, valour, publick [sic] spirit, loyalty and every other glorious virtue of our ancestors'.[9] Similar work was attempted for Scotland and Ireland.

This concern with national heroes became even more important during the course of the nineteenth century. Ernest Renan's lecture 'What is a Nation?', delivered in the early 1880s and widely disseminated both at the time and subsequently, emphasised the importance of ancestors and heroic figures in the making of a nation. 'The nation, like the individual', Renan argued, 'is the culmination of a long past of endeavours, sacrifice, and devotion. Of all cults, that of the ancestors is the most legitimate, for the ancestors have made us what we are.'[10] Within this framework, collections of national biography became 'an obligatory accompaniment to the process of European state formation'.[11]

Britain lagged behind other European nations when it came to producing a major collected national biography. By the 1880s, when planning for the *Dictionary of National Biography* began, many other nations, including France, Germany, Italy, Austria, Denmark, Belgium, Sweden and the Netherlands, had already published their collections of significant national lives.[12] Leslie Stephen, who undertook this task, was a literary critic and an intellectual historian with a special interest in the eighteenth century. Stephen was well versed in this history of earlier biographical encyclopaedias and dictionaries, and he worked very closely with the *Biographia Britannica* as a model. But he had to deal with major questions about what additional biographies ought to be included in such a diction- ary by the late nineteenth century.[13] The needs of historians were paramount in Stephen's planning of the *DNB*, and he insisted that at least one major criterion in selecting people for inclusion was their presence in the general histories of the period in which they lived. Particular attention needed to be paid to people who were not of the first importance, but who might be considered as second or third rank and would only be written about in a work of this magnitude. The *DNB*, he insisted, was not the place one needed to go for biographies of major literary and political figures, and it did not seek to supplant the standard biographies which already existed; its aim should rather be to fill in the details of lesser individuals who had nonetheless been significant in some area of political, social, economic or cultural life. Stephen was renowned also for his strict editorial guidelines and his firm approach to how such lives should be written.

Stephen stressed the importance of context in the writing of biographical essays, insist- ing that the ideas of each individual included in the *DNB* be placed within the appropriate intellectual framework. But his task was also to produce a *national* dictionary, and this nec- essarily involved some definition of the nation. As in all dictionaries of national biography, there were difficult decisions to make about how best to bring together disparate groups and individuals in order to produce something that was sufficiently unified to make it into a nation. One of the big issues here was how to deal with Scotland, Wales and particularly Ireland in order to incorporate them adequately into *British* history. But there was also a question of national characteristics and, in seeking to encompass the national character in all of its dimensions, Stephen also included a number of notable criminals and eccentrics, in addition to those who had been prominent in literature, art and intellectual life or pol- itics as well as the law, the Church and the army.

This discussion of who should be included in the *Dictionary of National Biography* was continued at some length by Leslie Stephen's successor, Sidney Lee, who edited the work from 1896 until 1912. Harking back to Tacitus and Plutarch, Lee insisted that a published biography offered the longest-lasting form of commemoration of distinguished ances- tors.[14] When it came to defining the nation and determining who should be encompassed within the dictionary, however, Lee's definition was somewhat circular and not very help- ful: he insisted that a dictionary of national biography should include all those whose lives and achievements in any department of national life excited amongst their fellow countrymen a desire to commemorate them. There was no question that this included 'every statesman, divine, painter, author, inventor, actor, physician, man of science, trav- eller, musician, soldier, sailor, who has commanded the widespread regard of his coun- trymen'. But as one descends 'from the heights of this Parnassus', who else should be included? Excellence in carrying out a profession as a doctor or priest, or indeed any meritorious action which did not distinguish a man from his peers, was not sufficient. An individual needed to stand out from others in a very marked way. Seeking to add some clarity to this situation, Lee offered a suggestion of the changing statistical ratio of those who should be included which seemed to increase century by century, so that up to the end of the seventeenth century, the ratio was 1 in 6,250, but in the nineteenth century it was 1 in 4,000.

Every aspect of Lee's definition underlines his **gendered assumptions** and belief that the typical subject of a national biography would be an educated and privileged man. It is scarcely surprising, under these circumstances, to find that less than 3 per cent of the entries in the original *DNB* dealt with women. Even at the time that Lee was editing this work and setting out his guidelines for it, the question of women's inclusion was being raised, and it was clearly a source of some discomfort to him. Taking his statistical break-down into the realms of gender, Lee suggested that while at the time there were 'about 600 adult persons qualifying for admission to a complete register of national biography' in the county of London, 'of these about twenty should be women'. It was possible, he conceded, that he had 'made inadequate allowance for the recently developed energy among women which seems likely to generate unlooked-for exploits of more or less distinction'. But no statistics were needed to show that 'women's opportunities of distinction were infinitesi-mal in the past' and are still small compared with men's so that women will not, 'I regret to reflect, have much claim on the attention of the national biographer for a very long time to come'. The awkwardness of his expression suggests some discomfort. But what is clear is his absolute refusal or inability to recognise that slightly different criteria might have allowed for the inclusion of more women.

In the years since Lee addressed this question, new approaches to history and a range of specialised collections of biographical studies, including dictionaries of labour biogra-phy and of women's biography, have included individuals never contemplated in the late nineteenth- and early twentieth-century dictionaries of national biography. Keith Thomas suggests that these works have produced a quite new biographical canon which constituted a frontal attack on the old *DNB*, making it look extremely limited and dated. It was this which lay behind the decision in the early 1990s to produce a new and updated *DNB* in which many existing entries were rewritten and some 16,000 new entries were added. His-toriographical change, a new recognition of the historical significance of popular culture and, above all, a new understanding of the nation and of the need to recognise its internal diversity and connection to other nations are all evident in some of the major changes to the Oxford *DNB*. The number of entries on women, for example, has been trebled so that they now make up some 10 per cent – still pitiful, but an improvement on the 3 per cent of the original – and it includes more foreign visitors and considerably more people of col-our. Rather than seeing itself as offering a view of national achievement, the new *DNB* works with an idea of the nation as 'fluid, practical and inclusive'.[15] While seeking to embody a new approach both to the nation and to the very idea of what producing such a dictionary involves, however, none of the people originally included have been dropped. Their lives have been rewritten in ways that offer both more critical comment and more information about private lives and familial and social relationships than was acceptable in the late nineteenth century. But the new *Oxford Dictionary of National Biography* still includes both the old approach and the new, with the lives deemed significant and the ideas about what constituted British national character in the late nineteenth and early twentieth centuries sitting alongside a new selection of lives created in a very different spirit.

The particular problems which arise when attempting to integrate an earlier dictionary of national biography with the current concerns so central in Britain are not ones faced directly by those countries for whom the establishment of a dictionary of national biography has happened relatively recently. Nonetheless, the continual shifts in focus that have occurred as a result of the growing concern about indigenous people, about women and about popular culture invariably place these works in a slightly difficult situation. Several of them articulate a more inclusive approach to history. They also establish a clear hierarchy in relation to the historical importance of those included, however, which is reflected in the size of their entries. Both the concern to be inclusive and this sense of hierarchy are made clear in the *Australian Dictionary of Biography*, for example. Its introduction explains that 'while the dictionary covers the orthodox fields of politics, business, religion, the land, the professions and the arts, it also attempts to reflect the rich variety of Australian life by including representatives of every social group and sphere of endeavour', the hierarchy of importance is emphatically indicated by length of entry: 'In the *ADB* the most eminent people in Australia's history are given articles of 2000 to 6000 words; other significant figures have entries that range in length from 500 to 2000 words. Articles on these representative people are usually 500 to 750 words in length.'[16] A similar distribution of words is evident in the Oxford *DNB* and in other national equivalents.

Although the overt nationalism evident in nineteenth- and early twentieth-century dictionaries of national biography is very muted in these later versions, the importance of dictionaries of national biography in the nation-building project continues. A *New Dictionary of South African Biography* was published in 1995, for example, just one year after the end of apartheid and the election of the government of Nelson Mandela. The earlier South African dictionaries of biography which gave pride of place to white male leaders, and most especially to those most significant in the history of Afrikaner nationalism, were no longer acceptable in the new South Africa, and many of those who were becoming prominent in government and in society were little known outside the African National Congress or the particular groups with whom they had been involved in underground resistance. In the foreword that he provided to this dictionary, Mandela made very clear his sense of the importance of this work appearing 'soon after the first democratically elected government of South Africa assumes power. Through this series it will be possible to both record and commemorate the role of the many hitherto unacclaimed people whose past work and struggle have contributed so much to the future of our nation.'[17]

▶ Women and collective biography

Although largely absent from the collective biography of classical times, at least from the late seventeenth century onwards some women had found their way into general biographical dictionaries. Bayle's *Dictionnaire Historique et Critique*, for example, included a small number of goddesses, women rulers, courtesans, religious women and even a few learned and literary women, although he paid as much attention to their appearance and personal charm as to their ideas and activities. But if women featured in very limited ways in general collections of biographical essays, from the eighteenth century onwards some collective biographies were devoted entirely to them.

One of the first of these was George Ballard's *Memoirs of Several Ladies of Great Britain Who Have Been Celebrated for Their Writings or Their Skill in the Learned Languages, Arts and Sciences* (1752).[18] Ballard was a self-educated man with strong antiquarian interests which he pursued energetically through an extensive array of correspondents. In his preface, Ballard pointed to the increasing interest in biography which was evident at that time, but he deplored the lack of attention to women's lives in Britain. Despite the fact 'that England hath produced more women famous for literary accomplishment than any other nation in Europe', less attention was paid to recording women's lives than was the case elsewhere in Europe. To remedy this situation, Ballard produced sketches and memoirs of some fifty women, choosing primarily those whose conservative political views and exemplary conduct he found acceptable. He paid particular attention to aristocratic and religious women and to devoted wives, omitting entirely well-known authors such as Aphra Behn, whose questionable life and exotic works he disliked.[19]

Ballard's work provided a basis for later writers such as Mary Hays, who expanded his work by including women who had been prominent in politics and religion as well as in literature, and by going beyond the confines of England to include Europe more generally. In her six-volume *Female Biography: Or Memoirs of Illustrious and Celebrated Women, of All Ages and Countries* (1803), Hays provided a compendium of the lives of some 288 women, many of whom had sought intellectual freedom and some form of political participation.[20] She included Catherine II of Russia, for example, amongst women rulers, as well as depicting the lives of French women whom she considered heroic, such as Madame Roland, who met her death during the course of the French Revolution. Hays addressed herself explicitly to women readers, seeking to offer them both education and moral instruction. Following a very traditional approach to celebratory lives, but directing it now towards women, Hays expressed her desire 'to excite a worthy emulation', by offering 'memories of those women whose endowments, or whose conduct, have reflected lustre upon the sex ... more especially to the rising generation, who have not grown old in folly'.[21]

In her interest in the domestic lives and virtues of women, and her emphasis on the ways in which admirable women combined all the appropriate feminine qualities with whatever public role they undertook, Hays anticipated developments which would become widespread in the nineteenth century. Her *Female Biography* was the first of what Rohan Maitzen argues became a distinctive genre of Victorian women's writing.[22] History was deemed a useful study for women, but it was not seen as one which their powers of mind would enable them to write. By contrast, 'the humbler walk of Biography' seemed well fitted 'to feminine power'.[23] Biography, and especially collective biography, also provided a much better way of exploring the activities of women in both the present and the past, and of establishing the conditions in which they lived, than was available in current models of history, which were concerned primarily with major public events.

The women who engaged in biographical writing accepted the strictures which excluded them from writing history, often stressing the personal and private nature of their work. Many women produced memoirs of historical figures, and particularly of women, which dealt with their private, domestic and daily lives in ways which reinforced their suitability as subjects for women. In the very process of doing so, however, they worked to expand the scope of history to include discussions of domestic and social life which were rarely encountered in other historical work. The lives of queens were particularly favoured, allowing as they did discussion of both private and of public matters. The advent of Queen Victoria to the throne in 1838 stimulated the production of these works. Agnes Strickland's very popular twelve-volume *Lives of the Queens of England from the Norman Conquest*, for example, which was published between 1840 and 1848, began appearing shortly after Queen Victoria's coronation.[24] Promising to 'portray equally the grandeur of the Queen, the attachments of the wife and the affections of the mother', Strickland offered a domestic version of British history which accorded well with nineteenth-century middle-class values. Her own close kinship with various members of the British aristocracy facilitated her access to documents and private papers which were not readily available, and added also to the authority of her work. Strickland followed her work on the queens of England with other collected works, including *Lives of the Queens of Scotland* (1850–59) and, finally, *Lives of the Last Four Princesses of the House of Stuart* (1872).[25]

Whereas Strickland remained largely within a female domestic environment, Julia Kavanagh offered a rather more feminist approach in her collective biographies, *Woman in France during the Eighteenth Century* and *Women of Christianity: Exemplary for Acts of Piety and Charity*.[26] In the latter of these works, she addressed directly the question of the share that women had 'in the history of men', and her answer pointed to the lack of any recognition of women or any recording of women's actions in the works of prominent nineteenth-century historians such as Carlyle and Macaulay. To emphasise her point, Kavanagh sought to demonstrate the agency and the importance of those women whose lives she wrote. Each of her detailed studies was framed by her general insistence on the importance of women in any form of royal household or government and her insistence on the power and influence that they exercised in both public and private realms. 'This power', she acknowledged, 'was not always pure and good; it was often corrupt in its source, evil and fatal in its results; but it was power.'[27]

▶ Prosopography

The question of whether or not all ways of addressing collective lives historically constitute forms of biography is one which is frequently raised, especially in relation to prosopography. Usefully defined by Lawrence Stone as 'the investigation of the common background characteristics of a group of actors in history by means of a collective study of their lives', prosopography played an important part in the development of both British and American history in the early and mid-twentieth century.[28] It was used very effectively by Charles Beard in the first decades of the twentieth century in his attempt to explain the establishment of the American Federal Constitution through a close analysis of the shared class backgrounds, economic interests and social outlooks of the Founding Fathers. In Britain, the emergence of prosopography occurred some two decades later with the publication of Namier's *Structure of Politics at the Accession of George III* in 1929, followed a decade later by Symes's *Roman Revolution*. Like Beard's earlier work, these later studies were concerned to explore the shared background, economic circumstances and sense of family and social and political connections amongst political elites in order to gain greater understanding of significant political events and more particularly of how particular political decisions were made.

Prosopography is heavily dependent on the huge quantities of biographical data contained within national dictionaries of biography, but in my view, and indeed in the view of many experts in prosopography, it is impossible to accept it as a biographical enterprise. This was certainly Namier's view. He included brief biographical sketches in his work, but as one with a deep interest in contemporary psychological theories and in the ways in which they assisted in the understanding of individual lives, Namier was very conscious of the differences between his work and biography. The information that he provided about individuals was intended to illustrate widely held and shared attitudes and sets of beliefs. 'Here is an ant heap', he wrote at the start of his best-known book, 'with the human ants hurrying in long files along their various paths; their joint achievement does not concern us, nor the changes which supervene in their community, only the pathetically intent, seemingly self-conscious running of individuals along beaten tracks.'[29] Long before there was any clear idea of political parties, he was particularly concerned to find a way to explain the nature of eighteenth-century political organisation and outlook and parliamentary behaviour. Focusing on the backgrounds, beliefs, expectations and conduct of those who went into parliament, and exploring the ways in which their shared outlook contributed to their political behaviour, offered a way to do this. He therefore combined members of parliament into a number of smaller groups which were differentiated by profession: soldiers, sailors, civil servants, lawyers, and so forth, seeking to find 'types' whose behaviours shared common characteristics. In doing this, he ignored all the personal and individual stories, the peculiarities and the relationships which essentially make any form of biography.

Although not as dominant within the study of history as Lawrence Stone anticipated, prosopography continues to play a very important part in the study of medieval history and also in some areas of ancient history. It is used particularly by those seeking to explore the social and cultural make-up of particular regions across Europe. But, though important in itself, it is not coming closer to biography and certainly not to group biography. On the contrary, while some of those engaged in it insist that there is an overlap between biography and prosopography, others reject entirely the idea that it is a form of group biography: 'it is not the study of life histories in groups (nor indeed the biography of groups)', Dion Smythe argues, 'but rather the study of biographical detail about individuals in aggregate.'[30] Katherine Keats-Rohan, agrees. 'Despite the use of unfortunate designations such as collective biography and group biography', she argues, 'prosopography does not privilege biography. It merely collects and exploits structured biographical data.'[31] It cannot exist without this data, of course, but its ultimate purpose is to produce something that targets the common aspects of people's lives and not their individual stories. Its aim is not in any way to create or establish a better understanding of individuals and their motives or their life experiences. Rather it is concerned with 'what the analysis of the sum of data about many individuals can tell us about the different types of connexion between them, and hence about how they operated within and upon the institutions – social, political, legal, economic, intellectual – of their time.'[32]

▶ Contemporary dictionaries of biography

Large-scale collective biographies appeared in a variety of different forms and fields across the twentieth century and continue to do so today. Some of these dictionaries follow earlier patterns in their framework and focus: dictionaries of biographies of poets, artists, writers, monarchs, military men, scholars and professionals of many kinds continue to appear now as they did in the eighteenth and nineteenth centuries, as do those dealing with religious figures and eminent and notable women. But there have been some notable late twentieth- and twenty-first-century additions to these works, including dictionaries of socialist and labour biography, of business biography and of political radicals and activists, environmentalists, feminist theorists and activists, and people connected in many different ways to popular culture.

Like their predecessors, these works are intended to provide biographical information about a number of individuals while also offering general information about particular groups of people. For the most part, these new dictionaries are concerned also to stake claims for the significance of their subjects and for their entitlement to both public and historical recognition. In many cases, they have also been closely connected to the emergence of new areas of historical research and inquiry. Just as the advent of labour history brought the sense of a need for dictionaries of labour biography, so too one can see a very close connection between the emergence of feminist history and dictionaries of women's biography during the course of the 1970s, and between environmental history and the emergence of dictionaries of 'naturalists' with an explicit environmental concern in the 1990s.

In most cases biographical dictionaries offered resources to a field which was already being developed; however, in some cases they played a major part in establishing new fields. Radcliffe College (a women's college in the United States), for example, decided in the 1950s to sponsor a comprehensive biographical dictionary of American women. It did this explicitly as an attempt to counteract the absence of women from existing American dictionaries of national biography as indeed from much American history. The work took nearly two decades to complete, appearing fortuitously in the early 1970s just as the demand for women's history and for feminist approaches to history were beginning to be articulated. The first volume, which provided 1,359 entries and covered women who had died between 1607 and 1950, appeared in 1971[33]; the second volume included 442 brief lives of women who had died between 1951 and 1975[34]; the third volume, which profiled 483 women who died between 1972 and 1999, has brought the project to an end.[35]

In Britain, which has never had a women's project of that scale, the many smaller dictionaries of biography dealing with prominent women in general, or more specifically with feminists, political activists, writers or philanthropists, were all products of the rise of women's history and began to appear during the course of the 1980s. In the foreword to the first edition of her *Dictionary of Women's Biography*, Jenny Uglow points quite explicitly to the need for more biographical information about women, which became clear to her when she was teaching women's studies, and to her desire to 'look at women's strength in action', which underlay her interest in compiling the dictionary.[36] The *Dictionary of Women's Biography* that she produced promised 'short biographies on notable women from Eva Braun to Marie Curie to Dorothy Parker' and sought to offer international coverage across time. Inevitably, as she recognised, the selection was more expansive when it came to European and American women than it was with regard to Asian, African and South American women. But the fact that an attempt could be made to include *all* notable women in a single volume in the 1980s testifies to how little information about women was generally known or included within either the historical or the national biographical frameworks at the time. Uglow's dictionary was followed two or three years later by Olive Banks's *The Biographical Dictionary of British Feminists*.[37] In the intervening period, there have been literally dozens of dictionaries or collections of women's biography, most now organised nationally and in terms of either their importance or their particular interests and activity but others having an international focus, like the *Biographical Dictionary of Women's Movements and Feminisms: Central, Eastern and South Eastern Europe, 19th and 20th Centuries*, edited by Francesca de Haan, Krassimira Daskalova and Anna Loutfi.[38]

▶ From collective to group biography

Although dictionaries of biography continue to focus on individual lives, one can see in the ways in which many of them are now presenting and publicising themselves a similar move towards the notion of group biography to that which is emerging in full-length biographical studies. This move has been facilitated – indeed, it has only been made possible – by the advent of new technologies that have transformed the ways in which dictionaries of biography can be accessed and used. Digitisation and the possibilities of digital searching are the key developments here, as they enable the dictionaries, while continuing to be set out alphabetically, to be searched through subjects and key words. This enables readers to find material on all members of particular groups or organisations, including the names and details of those who were fringe rather than full members or who were opposed to the group. Thus, for example, if one enters 'Bloomsbury Group' as a theme into the online *Oxford Dictionary of National Biography*, it not only brings up biographical information on the core of what Virginia Woolf called 'Old Bloomsbury' (Woolf herself and her sister Vanessa Bell and husband Leonard Woolf, alongside Lytton Strachey, Maynard Keynes, Clive Bell, Roger Fry, Duncan Grant, etc.) but also points to the importance of the group for some younger people and establishes some of their international connections. One can do the same with many other themes or keywords, locating, for example, all the material on suffragists or militant suffragettes or pacifists. The putting together of groups is of great importance to those editing the dictionary and updating information on how to use it, and new groupings appear on a regular basis. Recent groupings include Participants in the battle of Agincourt (*act.* 1415), Auden group (*act. c.* 1930–39), Benedictine reformers (*act. c.* 960–c. 1000) and Bluestocking circle (*act. c.* 1755–c. 1795).[39] In addition, under the heading of 'themes', the *Oxford Dictionary of National Biography* now includes essays on particular groups and on their activities and the lives of their members.

While this creation of groups and the pooling of biographical information are most developed in the *Oxford National Dictionary of Biography*, it is also evident in other dictionaries of biography. The *Dictionary of Canadian Biography Online*, for example, also has a very sophisticated search engine which enables people to be grouped on the basis of keywords or geographical location or 'identification', a very broad category which extends from religious, ethnic and tribal identification through to connections with particular political, literary and artistic groups and movements.[40] While the *Australian Dictionary of Biography* does not list groups or put them together in this way, it does allow people to search it in terms of particular categories, including gender, religious influences, cultural heritage and occupation. These keywords allow one to group together people of the same cultural heritage or religious beliefs living in a particular area at a particular time: for example, all the feminist activists working in Australia during a particular period.

This new emphasis on connecting people and on locating those who share either a background or a set of beliefs, or who are directly linked through membership of a political, social or cultural organisation, is clearly intended to increase the usefulness of these biographical dictionaries as a historical resource. In so doing, it points both to the growing interest in groups and group biography and to the changing ways in which biography and history are now seen to relate as historians are increasingly seeking illustrations of typical lives and of wider social patterns through the study of individual lives.

▶ Group biography

One of the most significant new developments in the writing of biography since the 1970s has been the emergence of group biography, focusing on families and siblings, on social and cultural groups and sometimes on intellectual networks. Group biography has been particularly attractive to those concerned to link life stories with wider historical processes and to use them to illustrate particular historical developments or patterns. But it has been of interest also to many seeking new approaches to intellectual biography, as it offers a way of showing not only social and personal connections but also political developments which have directed the attention of people in particular ways as well as how important personal interaction has been in the development of particular ideas.

The great advantage of group biography is that it avoids the artificial isolation which inevitably accompanies an intense focus on a single individual in which all others become secondary to the main figure under discussion. Few individuals live their lives in that way. But while it is possible to establish the meaning of intimate relationships and of family and friends in the life of an individual, they remain as a kind of background. Group biography, by contrast, takes as its primary subject the relationships between a group of people: their importance for each other, whether emotional or intellectual, becomes the primary issue for discussion. Family biography is particularly valuable here, as it allows for an ongoing analysis of the interaction between parents and children and amongst children, and of the ways in which these dynamics either remain the same or alter over time. But biographies of groups of friends and of networks also allow for the sustained analysis of how people are linked to each other and of the importance of the changing nature of those links over time.

As all feminist theorists of biography have pointed out, most women's lives are closely enmeshed in the lives of parents and siblings or of husbands and children. It is not surprising, therefore, that women were the first subjects for group biography. From the 1980s onwards, there has been a steady stream of group biographies of women which take sisters as their subject. My own book *Destined to be Wives: The Sisters of Beatrice Webb* was one of these, and it focused considerable attention on the nature of the sisterhood as well as on the similarities and differences in the ways in which the nine Potter sisters went from childhood to adulthood and then to old age. Beatrice Webb herself, as befits a woman who was a wonderful diarist as well as being a very significant social investigator and an important figure in the Fabian Society and the British Labour party and in the establishment of the London School of Economics, has been the subject of several biographies. Although several of her sisters led interesting and even dramatic lives, not one of them has been seen as a fitting subject for an individual biography. Taken together, however, they offer wonderful insights into the lives and life patterns of upper middle-class Victorian women. The fact that the oldest of these sisters was born more than twenty years before her youngest sister meant that within this family it was possible to chart changes over time in the ways in which childhood, adolescence and marriage were lived and understood within one family. The differences in personality and in the nature of their experiences made it possible also to show the extent to which different women could negotiate the oppressive structures and the legal and political discrimination faced by all women in the nineteenth and early twentieth centuries.

While the sisters of an important woman, or a family of prominent sisters, such as the Lennox sisters, the subject of Stella Tillyard's widely acclaimed *The Aristocrats*, have featured in some group biographies of sisters,[41] in other cases women who did not stand out in any particular way have become the subject of group biographies. These include the Paget women, who were studied by M. Jeanne Peterson, and the McDonald sisters, about whom Judith Flanders has written recently.[42] All of these works explore the intensity of the interpersonal sibling relationships which dominated many women's lives, while also pointing to the ways in which their lives illuminate broader social and historical patterns. In order to emphasise the link between the detailed biographical study and the wider social pattern, some authors have chosen to organise their group biographies thematically around childhood, education, coming out, marriage and motherhood, rather than to follow the life of each individual or to organise the study chronologically. This thematic arrangement allows the similarities and differences in the experience of members of the same family to be shown. Sometimes this is also a feature of wider historical change: in large Victorian families, for example, such as the Stracheys, there was an age gap of almost thirty years between the oldest and the youngest child. Not only did this lead to the children having very different relationships with their parents, it also meant that the youngest children (especially the girls) in some cases had access to educational institutions, including universities, which simply did not exist when their older siblings were growing up.[43] A thematic approach also helps to focus attention on the different ways in which members of one family respond to familial and social beliefs and pressures: a family's imperial heritage, for example, or prevailing concepts of femininity.

A different kind of thematic approach was chosen by Emma Rothschild in her book *The Inner Life of Empires: an Eighteenth-Century History*. Rothschild's study of the Johnstone family begins with a brief narrative of the lives of the eleven Johnstone siblings, each of whom is introduced in the kind of brief paragraph that one finds in dictionaries of biography. Rothschild then discusses the circumstances and experiences of the group before going on to the larger questions that interest her concerning how the Johnstones understand, reflect or illustrate wider questions about commercial empires and the eighteenth-century enlightenment, as well as the new economic theories of the time and the new understanding and emphasis on sentiment.[44]

Not all family biographies are thematically organised. In some there is a concern, rather, to place the lives of sisters or brothers side by side sequentially, so that the overall experience of each serves to illuminate the others. This is the case in James Fox's *The Langhorne Sisters*, for example, which explores the lives of Nancy Astor and her sisters, moving from the story of one sister to the next, although showing how the lives of the sisters were linked.[45] A similar approach has also been taken in Anne de Courcy's study of the daughters of Lord Curzon[46] and in Mary Lovell's recent book on the Mitford sisters.[47]

If not quite as popular a subject as sisters, brothers have certainly not been ignored. Indeed, biographies of Wilbur and Orville Wright and of the Rockefellers, for example, appeared some time before the current spate of group biographies.[48] The tendency to focus on men who have been prominent in the worlds of politics and business and of art and literature has continued in group biography. Unlike the biographies of sisters, therefore, those of brothers rarely suggest common patterns that these particular siblings might share with other men of their class. It is, rather, their rivalry or dependence and the roles that they have played in promoting, or hampering, their separate and collaborative ventures which have been of interest. The Kennedy brothers have probably been the subject of greatest interest to historians and biographers, but many other sets of brothers have also been the focus of interest. In the case of the United States, the Emerson brothers in the nineteenth century, the Dodge brothers and their successful involvement in the motor car industry and, of course, the Marx brothers have all been the subject of recent biographical study. In Britain, such subjects have included the Knox brothers and the Duke of Wellington and his brothers.[49]

As we shall see, marriage has also been a subject of great interest to biographers who trace both the early lives of the two people involved and the nature of their marital relationship. But many biographers have chosen to go beyond this and to encompass whole families, often over more than one generation. This approach offers the possibility of an even more extended look at change across time by showing generational differences in education, social attitudes and life experience. In studies such as my own two-generational work on the Strachey family, one can also explore in these works the changing meaning or resonance of a family name. In the case of the Stracheys, the change was from the idea of an imperial family with a major role in the government of India in the nineteenth century, to the close connection of the name with Bloomsbury and with its aesthetic interests and new ideas about sexuality. Prominent British political families, such as the Gladstones and the Stevensons, and literary and intellectual ones, such as the Godwins and the Shelleys, have appealed strongly to biographers.[50] Others, including major banking families with multi-national activities, such as the Rothschilds and the Warburgs, and families which include amongst their members industrialists, musicians and major intellectual figures, such as the Wittgensteins, have also been extremely attractive to biographers.[51]

Group biography began with families, but it soon extended beyond that. Friendship has provided a significant alternative focus. Norma Clarke's exploration of the themes of writing, friendship and love in relationship to Jane Carlyle and her friends, the Jewsbury sisters and Felicia Hemans, was a pioneering work of this kind.[52] But friendship circles amongst feminists and college women have also been the subject of biographical study, as have cross-racial friendships such as that of Mary Todd Lincoln and the seamstress and former slave who became for many years her most intimate friend.[53] Biographies of friendship have not been confined to women, and there have been many recent biographical studies of male friendships, including works on political friendships, such as those of John Adams or Abraham Lincoln; on friendships amongst major composers, such as Brahms; and on literary friendships, such as that between Coleridge and Wordsworth.[54]

Group biographies have also been written about social, political, intellectual and cultural networks, offering a way to link the ideas and activities of a particular set of people with their close personal relationships. Norman and Jeanne Mackenzie's *The First Fabians* and Leon Edel's *Bloomsbury House of Lions* were amongst the first works of this kind.[55] Both of these works deal with very well-known political and cultural groups who also shared close friendships and provided an excellent way of showing how important these personal links were in developing the ideas and the literary and artistic works of those involved. But other groups and networks have also been studied, and there are now group biographies of Enlightenment intellectuals in both France and Scotland; and of the group of men who were central to the development of American pragmatism and for whom the American Civil War was a defining experience, who are the subject of Louis Menand's *The Metaphysical Club*.[56]

Over the last decade, close attention has also been paid to the interlinked lives and stories of significant scientists and industrialists and to the shared values, beliefs and social networks which underlay their discoveries and new ideas. Jenny Uglow's *Lunar Men* traces the lives, interests and activities of a small group of scientists and industrialists, living around Birmingham, who formed a club to engage in scientific discussions and experiments.[57] Uglow's approach emphasises the importance of the friendships of these men and of the ways in which their shared scientific enthusiasm permeated not only their commercial and industrial ventures but also aspects of their personal lives and domestic relationships. More recently, Richard Holmes' *The Age of Wonder: How the Romantic Generation Discovered the Beauty and Terror of Science* provides a group biography focused on the shared desire to expand dramatically the understanding of the natural and physical world felt by scientists, the explorers Joseph Banks and Mungo Park and the Romantic poets Coleridge, Wordsworth, Byron, Keats and Shelley.[58] Ian McCalman offers a slightly different approach in *Darwin's Armada*, his recent study of the close-knit group of scientists that formed around Charles Darwin. All of them were employed as naturalists on long sea voyages, which was important in both providing their scientific training and in forging their friendships.[59]

In the view of Richard Holmes, this interest in group lives is not only one of the current strengths of biography but also a development which holds out some of the greatest promise for the future. While I agree with Holmes, I would like to stress here the importance of group .... significant ones. I would like to stress here the importance of group biographies of women in extending our knowledge of women's history at least from the eighteenth century to the present. But there are other areas where group biography is beginning to make inroads. Sheila Fitzpatrick has recently turned to group biography as offering a new a way to understand high politics in the Soviet Union. In her recently published work *On Stalin's Team: The Years of Living Dangerously in Soviet Politics*, Fizpatrick turns her attention to the members of the Politburo with whom Stalin not only worked but also socialized on a very regular basis from the early 1920s until his death. Membership of the team was not fixed: some early members, including Kirov and Ordzhonikidze, died in the 1930s, and new members, including Kruschev and Beria, joined in the late 1930s. Several members of the team held very important positions, running major sectors like the military, the economy or state security, often, Fitzpatrick notes, with great competence. Ordzhonikidze, for example, managed heavy industry with great flair. But in Fitzpatrick's analogy, Stalin was unquestionably the leader, the captain of the team, whose prerogatives included selecting and dismissing the other members – and indeed naming those who would become victims of the purges. Hence they all held their positions at Stalin's will and were required to spend their own time with him and to bring their families too. Nonetheless, as Fitzpatrick shows, their personalities and interactions allow one an extraordinary new insight into how the Politburo operated under Stalin and hence into the high politics of this period of Soviet history.[60]

4 Auto/Biography and Life Writing

▶ Introduction

The introduction of the term 'life writing' to describe and encompass a wide range of different forms of personal writing has been a very important development in the humanities and social sciences. The term emerged in the 1970s and clearly contained an explicit critique of the fairly rigid and restrictive nature of earlier approaches to biography in terms of both its subject matter and its form. The idea of life writing also allowed a new way of looking at a range of different kinds of writing, such as letters and diaries, which had little place in the established literary canons. The literature that was studied in university departments was confined to what were seen as the most significant genres, such as drama, poetry and fiction. It offered no place for informal or unpublished work. In the course of the 1970s, feminist scholars demanded recognition that these forms of writing that were so much more accessible to women be considered as literature. At the same time, others were demanding a further extension of the field of literature to include both autobiography and biography. 'Life writing' offered an umbrella term which could encompass all of these different forms of writing, connecting them to one another through their concerns with and revelations of individual lives.

The term 'life writing' appeared at much the same time as that of the hyphenated 'auto-biography'. This new term also served to question earlier definitions and ideas about biography by suggesting that autobiography and biography were closely linked in form and that the writing of a biography usually involved some form of autobiographical involvement on the part of the author. The idea that there is a close connection between these two forms of writing lives is not entirely new. It was generally accepted until the 1970s that writing a biography of someone else was something quite distinct from writing one's autobiography. Nonetheless, the involvement of close friends and of family members in the writing of biography in the eighteenth and nineteenth centuries and the insistence by Freud on the emotional involvement of biographers with their subjects certainly pointed to some kind of link between the two. This has been made particularly clear in a number of works which are simultaneously autobiographies and biographies. Many critics and literary theorists now argue that that there is some element of autobiography in all biography and that 'the same analytic apparatus is required for engaging in all forms of life writing'.[1]

The massive increase in interest in biography over the past four decades has been equalled or even surpassed by that evident in relation to autobiography. This can be seen not only in the number of autobiographies and memoirs currently being published but also in the vast amount of theoretical and critical attention which has been paid to autobiography. Particular interest has been taken in the ways in which autobiography reveals different forms of subjectivity, on the one hand, and in the ways in which members of marginal and subordinate groups have used autobiographies to make claims for social recognition, on the other. Although most published autobiographies and memoirs have been written by those who see their lives as both significant and unusual, this has not been universal. At least since the eighteenth century, many people with little access to wealth or political power have written autobiographies, although not all of them have been published. Felicity Nussbaum has explored in some detail the 'politics of subjectivity' in eighteenth-century autobiography, arguing that autobiographical writing allows previously illiterate and disenfranchised groups, including women and the poor, to construct particular identities for themselves and to challenge existing stereotypes and ideas of social hierarchy and significance, and Regenia Gagnier has made a similar case for the nineteenth century.[2] In a similar way, slave narratives and dictated autobiographies provided ways not only of showing in great detail the sufferings of slaves and conveying their feelings but also of underlining the need for them to be recognised as fellow human beings.

The concept of life writing draws quite clearly on this much more democratic tendency in autobiographical writing, allowing for and indeed encouraging acceptance of the notion that many, and indeed potentially all, lives are of interest and worth writing and reading about. Within this framework, it is not always the exceptional nature of a life which makes it worth understanding, but often the extent to which one individual shares experiences and problems with others. Thus while there continue to be stories which focus on very unusual life experiences, over the past few decades there has also been a tendency for many autobiographies and memoirs to explore or expose the difficulties and the pain and suffering which individuals have experienced or undergone in particularly harsh political and economic situations and military conflicts. Sometimes the emphasis in this writing is on the impact of public and political events on private and domestic life, as if to ensure the making of individual private records at a time when public record-keeping becomes more and more comprehensive and dense. These works serve as much as a way of bearing witness to the sufferings of many as they do of offering insight into a particular individual life and personality.

Some of these autobiographies and memoirs follow the tradition of slave narratives in their concern to provide an immediate account of one individual's experience of a major historical (and usually catastrophic) situation or episode or event, and in a way which will engage much wider sympathies for the victims. But many also make claims to recount the history of these episodes or events, suggesting that a direct and individual insight offers the possibility of a particularly deep understanding of significant events. These personal accounts of traumatic events have become the subject of immense interest over the past few decades, but the autobiographical impulse was very much in evidence in earlier periods of historical change and disruption, during the English Civil War, for example, or the French Revolution. Indeed, there are more than 1,500 known autobiographies and memoirs of the French Revolution, which have enabled historians to pinpoint some of the differences in the ways in which it was understood and experienced by men as compared with women, and with people across both the social hierarchy and the geographical spread of France.

The question of the relationship between autobiography and the writing of history has been taken up in a slightly different way since the 1970s, one which challenges some of the basic assumptions on which history has traditionally rested. As we have seen, the establishment of history as an academic discipline involved an insistence on the importance of a particular historical method and of objectivity, and on the role of special training to ensure that historians understood both of these things. The objectivity of established academic history was questioned in the course of the 1970s and the 1980s by feminist scholars who pointed to the narrow ways in which history engaged with the past and to its privileging of masculine voices and male experiences and its omission of women. This criticism was expanded and enlarged by others, concerned particularly with postcolonial and subaltern studies, who showed how the voices, experiences, activities and resistance of many different subordinate or colonised groups had been excluded from the study of history. These comments and criticisms led to a huge expansion in the field of history and to a range of new forms of historical investigation. They also led to a new sense of the importance of recognising the standpoint from which historians wrote.

Over the last two decades, this questioning of the complete impartiality of historians and a sense of the need to understand their backgrounds, beliefs and interests has been articulated in a new way with the emergence of a new field or approach termed 'ego-histoire' by the French historian, Pierre Nora, who has encouraged its development in France. Nora is a central figure in the study of memory and, for him, there is a close connection between the current interest in memory and its relationship to history, on the one hand, and the importance of the historian's own life and connection to his research, on the other. 'The historian's role used to be simple', he argues, as was his place in society:

> He was to make himself the voice of the past and to pass it along to the future. In his role, his personality mattered less than his function: he was to be no more than an erudite transparence [sic], a means of transmission ... In the final analysis, an absence obsessed with

objectivity. A new personage emerges from the upsurge of history conceived as memory, one ready, unlike his predecessors, to acknowledge the close, intimate, personal liaison he maintains with his subject.[3]

In the light of this recognition of the relationship between the historian and the object of his or her study, Nora encouraged a group of colleagues and friends to write about their own lives and to explore the connection between those lives and their historical investigation. His approach and this example have worked as a stimulus to others, including Luisa Passerini and Annie Kreigel, who have both written extensively about the close connection between their political experiences and beliefs and their historical writing.[4] This development has accompanied the proliferation of historians' autobiographies which have served to underline the close links between personal experience and scholarly approaches.[5]

This chapter explores the emergence of the new terms 'life writing' and 'auto/biography', and their importance for historians, before going on to look more closely at the changing ways in which historians have thought about autobiography.

▶ Life writing

The term 'life writing' is rarely defined in any very clear way – and indeed for many who use the term, a strict definition would be inappropriate as it is its very breadth which makes the term most attractive and useful.[6] Rather than constituting a particular literary form, life writing is a broad category encompassing many different kinds of writing which record or describe an individual life, including not only diaries, memoirs, letters, autobiography and biography but also travel writing and indeed any other form of writing which involves a construction of the self. Sometimes the term is even used in a way which extends its reach beyond written sources to include the ways in which lives can be recorded or represented through photographs and material objects.

It is scarcely surprising that the term 'life writing' came into use in the course of the 1970s, a decade in which much attention was focussed on critiquing the underlying assumptions and the concealed gender, ethnic and imperial hierarchies which underlay academic disciplines and authorised particular voices and stories while ignoring or silencing others. Scholars in many fields stressed the importance of exploring the lives, experiences, beliefs and assumptions of ordinary, marginalised and oppressed people, of recognising the value of popular and personal writing and of coming to terms with cultural forms which had not previously been accepted within dominant literary or cultural canons. The expression of this new interest was evident in history in the huge expansion of social history and in the study of plebeian life, often referred to as 'history from below'. These developments reinforced feminist attempts to challenge existing ideas about the nature of history by including the lives and experiences of women, and stressing the importance of the private realm and domestic life, in a discipline which had always privileged the public world of politics and paid work. There was a counterpart to these demands in literature, with a new emphasis on the significance of women's writing and on that of indigenous and oppressed groups – and on the need to encompass within the realm of literature not only works which fell within the accepted genre of novels, poetry and drama but also private writings such as letters and diaries, which had not previously been thought worthy of literary analysis. These forms of writing were often ones practised by women, and feminist literary scholars stressed the importance of studying them both because of the insights into women's lives that they offered and because they provided a way of incorporating more women's writing within the study of literature.

Although often associated with creative writing and with literary studies, the flexibility which the term 'life writing' allowed has proved attractive to many historians, and especially to those who work closely with literary colleagues. In his edited collection *Life Writing and Victorian Culture*, for example, David Amigoni explains his own reasons for choosing to use 'life writing' rather than 'biography' in the title. He contrasts the concern expressed by Nigel Nicolson in the 1920s to separate and establish the proper relation of biography to 'such cognate modes of expression as journals, diaries, memoirs, imaginary portraits or the mere jottings of conversation' with the insistence of later writers and critics on the instability, and complexity of biography as a form and its closeness to other forms of life narratives, including collective lives and obituaries.[7] The wide scope offered by the term 'life writing', Amigoni argues, allowed for the inclusion of many different kinds of life story and many different forms of writing – including sermons and eulogies, privately written sketches produced for members of a family, and fragmentary sketches of lives – in ways that expanded greatly the historical understanding of how lives in past societies had been written about, seen and understood and which enabled one to show how important those approaches to individual lives were for the broader culture of the period. Amigoni's collection of essays is an interdisciplinary one which includes literary scholars as well as historians, and it is worth noting the extent to which the term 'life writing' encourages this form of endeavour. By contrast, some of those historians interested in rethinking the place of individual lives within their own historical period have ignored the term and have retained the use of 'biography' in reference to their work.[8]

▶ Auto/biography

There is a difficulty similar to that evident in relation to 'life writing' in defining precisely what the composite term 'auto/biography' means. For this composite both problematises the relationship between autobiography and biography and seems to obliterate any distinction between them. Although the widespread use of the term 'auto/biography' has only emerged in the last couple of decades, the idea that writing someone else's life could not be kept completely separate from writing one's own had certainly been raised before then.

A number of writers have quite explicitly incorporated their own lives into their discussions of others, especially when writing biographies about members of their own families. Edmund Gosse's *Father and Son* (1909) is probably the earliest work of this kind, anticipating the new biography of Strachey and Woolf in its puncturing of Victorian religious and moral assumptions and its sharp insights into the blindness and the pain in this particular family and father–son relationship. Carolyn Steedman's widely read and much discussed *Landscape for a Good Woman* repeated this experiment in relation to a mother and daughter, as did Kim Chernin's *My Mother's House*. There have been other approaches to this too: Philip Roth's portrait of himself and his father in *Patrimony*, for example, and Mikal Gilmore's *Shot in the Heart*, which details the family life that he shared with his brother, the convicted murderer Gary Gilmore.[9]

The question of the relationship between biographer and subject has been of particular interest to those whose approach is informed by psychoanalysis. Freud himself had suggested early in the twentieth century that the emotional investment that biographers often had in their subjects limited their capacities to write critically about them:

> In many cases they have chosen their hero as the subject of studies because – for reasons of their personal emotional life – they have felt a special affection for him from the very first. They then devote their energies to a task of idealization, aimed at enrolling the great man among the class of their infantile models – at reviving in him, perhaps, the child's idea of his father.[10]

Following Freud, Leon Edel, the doyen of biography studies in the 1960s and 1970s, argued that **transference** is at the core of all biographical writing.[11] Sometimes it leads to an excessive idealisation of a subject – although it can sometimes do the reverse and produce an unbalanced form of vilification. In order to write a successful biography, Edel argues, it is necessary for biographers to disengage themselves from their subjects and to write about them in a dispassionate and detached way. Edel drew this general picture from his own experience as the biographer of Henry James, whom he felt he had lived with over many years and regarded as 'a father figure, and a mother figure, and also a brother figure'. But he had to overcome this sense of his relationship with James in order to write about him, and he advised others of the need 'to learn to fall out of love with' their own biographical subjects.[12]

Some would suggest that transference can be traced back to the very origins of modern biography. Stuart Feder, for example, points to its importance in the work of Samuel Johnson. Johnson's *Life of Savage*, sometimes considered the first modern biography, owes its sympathy and its power, Feder argues, to Johnson's strong identification with Richard Savage and to his sense of the similarities in some aspects of their lives, most notably their difficult relationships with their mothers.[13]

Although articulated in a rather different way, the issue of transference was an important one for some feminist historians and biographers in the 1970s and 1980s. As we have seen, several of them recognised that they were seeking an idealised maternal figure or a role model as they researched the life of an older feminist leader and that their biographical research offered new ways of understanding difficulties that they faced in their own lives.[14]

It is not only those with an interest in psychoanalysis who have pointed to the problems which arise from too close a tie or relationship between biographer and subject. Several literary theorists have also raised questions about the ethical issues which arise when the boundaries between biographer and subject are breached. These issues come to the fore particularly in those works which are simultaneously autobiographies and biographies, and in which questions arise concerning whether privacy is breached, or confidences betrayed, in the telling of a parent's story by a child. In some cases too, there are questions to ask about the ways in which the voice of the passive partner in this autobiographical relationship is permanently appropriated by the one who writes the joint autobiography – ways which can be deleterious for both.[15]

These ethical issues and questions about the voice and ownership of the narrative have been especially acute in the writing and recording of the lives of indigenous people. Over the last few decades, many scholars, particularly historians and anthropologists, have sought to record the life narratives of indigenous people, often as an attempt to see and understand their perspective and world view and to give them an independent and authentic voice in recording their own histories. But while much of this endeavour was motivated by a desire to enable indigenous people to speak for themselves rather than being spoken for or about by white scholars and officials, it has been hard to remove the imperialist framework entirely. As scholars in Australia, New Zealand and Canada have all pointed out, not only are many indigenous people illiterate, they also come from cultures which do not share any of the Western conventions concerning how a life story is understood or told. Many of them lack the basic data on which such stories depend – such as precise information about birth, education, and the significant points in a career unfolding or progress through life – and, moreover, they do not see these dates as particularly significant. Religious ideas or totems are often more important as markers of an identity – just as dance might be a more significant way of encapsulating a life than a verbal narrative. Basil Sanson explains extremely well the process whereby what is presented as an 'authentic autobiography' is actually a life story that has been taken over and made into something which is recognisable to white audiences, but bears little relationship to how life is understood within Australian Aboriginal culture. 'In the majority of instances', he writes,

> aboriginal life stories are works mediated by second parties in which personal narratives once orally given are rendered into prose. First order mediation is with translation or 'Englishing'; then there is arrangement and editing; but, most often, there is appropriation distinguished by the telltale authorial urge to have the reported life make sense as a whole

and this is inescapably part of the Western literary heritage ... In the balancing of the bio –
against the – graph in 'biography', it is usually the graph (with its transfer of authorship and
authority from original subject to latter-day reporter) that wins out.[16]

▶ History and autobiography

If the differences between history and biography were clearly articulated at least from
the time of Plutarch, those between history and autobiography, as Jeremy Popkin argues,
were rather less clear until a much later period. Autobiographical elements are included in
much historical writing up until the eighteenth century, as a number of those who wrote
histories had witnessed the events they described and often used their personal knowledge
and experience to support the validity of their accounts. Thucydides, for example, cites
his own involvement in the war, and the fact that he had heard many of the speeches
he reports, to reinforce his claims about the accuracy of his *History of the Peloponnesian
War*. And, indeed, the idea that a history or chronicle of events could be provided – and
could perhaps best be provided – by a person with direct knowledge and experience of the
events under consideration continued until the early nineteenth century. It was the establishment of history as an academic discipline requiring a particular form of training and
method which brought an end to this idea. Once that happened, eyewitness accounts of
any kind, like memoirs, came to be seen as the sources on which historians drew. From this
moment on, the roles of the historian, on the one hand, and of actors in historical events,
on the other, were clearly differentiated. As Pierre Nora notes, it now 'fell to historians to
collect sources and to provide a definitive judgement of past events, while it was the role of
the actors in history and the servants of the state to bear witness and to furnish a detailed
account of their responsibilities'.[17]

Once history was thought of as a discipline – even, for some, as a science – it became
imperative to differentiate it from autobiography, and for much of the nineteenth
and twentieth centuries, not only were autobiographies not seen as history, they were
regarded with great suspicion as historical sources. The basic questions that historians
were taught to ask about every document – who created it, where, under what circumstances and for what purpose – were designed above all to guard against the problems
of 'bias' and 'inaccuracy' in documentary sources. Autobiographies and memoirs, which
by definition gave accounts of events and developments from the point of view of one
particular individual, were seen as particularly likely to be biased – especially if the
author had been involved in the events described and sought to record and justify his
or her own actions. G. Kitson Clark, a leading British historian of the mid-twentieth
century, deemed 'the memoirs and autobiographies written by eminent persons' to be
'the least convincing of all personal records', and this view was widely shared by his
colleagues.[18]

Over the last few decades, however, historians have come to think about autobiographies and their historical value in rather different ways and to value them, rather, as unique and important sources. In part, this new approach reflects a recognition of the scope of auto-biography and of the access that it provides to the lives and experiences of many different kinds of humble or marginal people whose only records are what they have written about their own lives. This includes slaves, workingmen and women, even paupers, as well as many devoutly religious individuals concerned to chart their spiritual life. Both historians and literary scholars have become extremely interested in collecting and reading this work because it offers an insight into the voices, views, outlooks and experiences of people who have usually been excluded from the historical record – or at best included in statistical form and through the comments of others. The growth of social history and the interest in 'history from below' which emerged in the late 1960s and early 1970s made these works particularly interesting and important to many historians. But this new interest in autobi-ography and memoir has extended to literate and prominent people and even to political leaders.

These personal writings are now read in a variety of different ways, and not simply as Kitson Clark had read the memoirs of eminent people earlier in the twentieth century, in order to assess the accuracy of their recollections of particular events. Most historians now look to autobiographies for what they reveal about the beliefs, ideas and subjectivity of their authors and for the insight they offer into how people saw and understood them-selves and their worlds or how they constructed a persona or a public self. Rather than providing information about specific events, autobiographies are read for what they reveal about how religion, community, fate, gender, work, class, family life and the nature of the self were addressed and what the forms of address revealed about the mental and moral horizons of their authors. For many of those using or writing about autobiographies, the elements of fiction, the literary tropes, the moral comments, the calls on Providence that they contain are quite as important as any information that is offered about work, the family formation or the daily life of their authors. This is not to say that historians are no longer concerned about the accuracy or truth of an autobiography, but rather that they are equally interested in understanding how or why an individual might have seen an event in a particular way, or in exploring what their recollections or reconstruction reveal about their mindset or world view.

One of the first historians to use this approach was Natalie Zemon Davis, who discussed the autobiographical writings of three seventeenth-century women in her pioneering *Women on the Margins*. In this work, Davis sought to explore how these women had seen their own worlds and worked within the restrictions that they faced to shape their own lives. She chose to write about a Jew, a Catholic and a Protestant in order to explore the differences that religion made in women's lives, and to see both what it allowed and what it prevented. Davis accepts that there were many omissions in the autobiographical writ-ings of these women. Although all talked about their work and about some aspects of their lives, 'sensitive events were alluded to without details that would compromise the mother or embarrass the children, and some matters were skipped over entirely'.[19] But the reticence and the omissions are an important part of her story, along with the lamentations and exhortations and the fables and moral tales with which these autobiographies abound. For Davis is as concerned to explore the ways in which these women articulate and describe their spiritual and religious lives and seek to instruct or to explain things to their children as she is to follow their life course. Their recourse to storytelling as a way to explain and to deal with their lives is itself of great interest and importance and offers additional insights both into the women's religious faiths and into the ways in which they sought to make sense of their own worlds.[20] Davis spells out her approach very clearly in outlining what she will look for in her analysis of the autobiography of the Jewess, 'known in published works since the end of the nineteenth century as "Glückel von Hameln"':

> We will listen for her dialogues, for the inner contention around which her life swirled, and for her account of why things happened to her and others as they did ... How did Glikl locate herself and her people in a world where Christians thought Jews should be on margins or in ghettos or excluded altogether? And what cultural resources were available to a Jewish woman in seventeenth-century Europe – resources that she could bend to her own use, that would supply the notes with which she could find her own voice?

Far from criticising the use of traditional stories in Glikl's autobiography, Davis points to the contrasts between Jewish and Christian autobiography, which help us to understand the ways in which Glikl mixes genres and blends stories and memoirs in her autobiography.

James O'Donnell offers a slightly different example of this new kind of approach in his biography of Augustine, in which he both draws on and warns against too much reliance on Augustine's *Confessions*. 'This book', he writes, 'that remains the most widely read of Augustine's work, is a work of extraordinary artifice and power':

> If we use that book and his other books to imagine his life, we might then fall into the same trap his contemporaries did; of being overpowered by him, of being seduced by his art, of being driven to accept his words as he intended them, of taking his world his way. By writing these famous confessions, he wanted us to learn his story; wanted to make us think he was coming entirely clean. But no one ever comes entirely clean. No one tells the whole story. We cannot tell the whole of our own story, much less that of someone who lived and died sixteen hundred years ago. But we can tell more of the story than Augustine told us, more than he sometimes knew. If we read his words and those of his contemporaries with resistance and imagination they will reveal him to us in many ways.[21]

O'Donnell then goes on to explore not only the story that Augustine offers in the *Confessions* but also the one which he does not tell but which can be gleaned from other sources, using both to try to gain the greatest possible insight into the life, motivations, desires, sorrows and feelings of Augustine.

A similar approach was taken by Vincent Carretta in his biography of the eighteenth-century freed slave Olaudah Equiano.[22] Reading Equiano's celebrated autobiography alongside a range of other sources, Carretta came to the conclusion that the moving and terrible account that Equiano provided of his African childhood, his kidnapping and his voyage on a slave ship were all untrue. There was no evidence that he had ever been in Africa; on the contrary, he seems to have been born in America. But while pointing to the large gulf between Equiano's account and what can be gleaned from other sources, Carretta is not interested in suggesting that Equiano was a liar. What interests him is rather the question of why it was so important to Equiano to write this account. He explains this by pointing to the need evident in the abolitionist movement at the time for an 'authentic' account of the horrors of slavery, described by one who had experienced it. Such an account would help greatly to energise their movement and promote their cause. Equiano provided this account in a way which more than fulfilled the needs of the movement. For Carretta, this serves to show both his intelligence and how very much he was a man who had made himself in impressive ways. Carretta then includes Equiano's own account of his childhood in his biography, not as a way to undermine his credibility, but rather as a way of showing how closely connected Equiano was to the abolitionist cause and the dominant political currents of his time.

This interest in autobiographical writing in the past has its counterpart in the attention paid to contemporary memoirs and autobiographies. Over the past fifteen years, there has been an extraordinary boom in the writing and publishing of memoirs and autobiographies, not only in the West, as Kay Ferris and Sidonie Smith have pointed out, but globally: in English-speaking countries around the world, across Europe and in much of Asia and Africa.[23] As was the case in earlier times, autobiographical writing seems to be particularly prevalent in countries which have undergone massive suffering and considerable political and social change, such as China, Cambodia, Rwanda, Bosnia, South Africa and Iran. Suffering and survival are often the primary focus, and there are now hundreds, even thousands, of works describing the lives of those who have survived violent oppression, torture, dispossession, enslavement, forced displacement, genocide or some other form of historical or environmental catastrophe. This work reflects the extreme violence which was so pronounced in the twentieth century. The emphasis on suffering and on bearing witness to appalling events which is so central to many of these works has led several critics and literary theorists to suggest that what has emerged is a culture of confession and testimony amongst those seeking to tell their stories of oppression, suffering and trauma and, in so doing, to inform a less oppressed readership of what they have been through.[24]

Although much of this work reflects contemporary events, a great deal of it looks back to the 1930s and the 1940s and to the terrible suffering of Jews during the Nazi genocide which has come to be called the **Holocaust**. Indeed, the Holocaust and the life stories and descriptions of those who survived it make up the largest single group of twentieth-century autobiographies and memoirs and have been the subject of the most debate, discussion and theorising. In the eyes of many, the Holocaust has become the paradigm case for twentieth-century genocide and suffering and for the ways in which survivors write about their experiences. One of the notable features of Holocaust memoirs and autobiographies has been the way in which they proliferated only after the term 'Holocaust' came to be accepted as one which named and described the sufferings of Jews as a result of Nazi genocide. Although some of those who had survived concentration camps spoke about them and wrote their stories immediately after the end of the Second World War, few others wanted to hear or to read about them. It was not until the late 1960s and early 1970s, after some of the highly public trials of perpetrators of the genocide, most notably Adolf Eichmann, that people began to talk about what had happened to Jews in Germany and to label it 'the Holocaust'. The existence of the term and the discussion it provoked offered a framework which made it easier for people to tell their own stories and to bear witness to their sufferings and experiences, and to those of others in ghettoes and concentration camps who had not survived, by providing an interested audience for them. There have also been several major projects set up, especially in the United States, seeking to record the lives and the testimonies of Holocaust survivors who have not written or published memoirs, and to make these available in digital and video as well as written form. As the term 'Holocaust' became more widely used, so too the suffering of the Jews under Nazism came to be seen as an archetypal example of trauma which could be both comprehensible and significant for people other than the individuals directly involved.[25]

As this suggests, the concept of **trauma** has been central to much discussion of Holocaust memoirs and autobiography. First described by Freud as something which might involve a psychic rather than a physical wound, the concept of trauma was first applied to victims of childhood sexual abuse. When it was later applied to those who had experienced particularly extreme and shocking forms of oppression, violence or torture, it retained its earlier connection with questions about memory, particularly in terms of whether and how traumatic episodes could be remembered. As Freud had suggested with regard to his patients, trauma was not something which could be fully remembered. It tended, rather, to return constantly and partially in dreams. 'In its most general definition', writes Cathy Caruth, 'trauma describes an overwhelming experience of sudden or catastrophic events, in which the response to the event occurs in the often delayed, and uncontrolled repetitive occurrence of hallucinations and other intrusive phenomena. The experience of the soldier faced with sudden and massive death around him, for example, who suffers this sight in a numbed state, only to relive it later on in repeated nightmares, is a central and recurring image of trauma in our century.'[26] If traumatic events cannot be fully remembered, they cannot be accurately or completely described in memoirs and autobiographies. Many critics and commentators would argue, as Dominick LaCapra has, that one reads these autobiographies not for simple factual detail, but for a sense of how and in what form survivors of particularly traumatic events remember, describe and deal with that trauma.[27]

But although theorists of trauma have advanced reasons why individuals cannot recall some events with complete accuracy, this has not stopped vehement debate and discussion about the truth or lack of it in some celebrated autobiographical works. Literary theorists point constantly to the instability of autobiography and to the elements of fiction which are inevitably part of it, but this issue is not one that historians can readily accept.[28] As the immense international controversy occasioned by the autobiography of Rigoberta Menchú shows, great importance is still attached not only to factual accuracy but also to the ways in which autobiographies are written. In *I, Rigoberta Menchú*, Guatemalan human-rights activist and winner of the Nobel Peace prize Rigoberta Menchú detailed the terrible sufferings that she and her family, as indigenous people, had experienced at the hands of a repressive government and its army. The book was based on tape-recorded interviews and so was always complex as a result of the fact that two people were involved in the telling of the story. Later research suggested that there were marked inaccuracies in the way in which Menchú described the origins and financial status of her family and that she had claimed to witness events (such as the torture of her brother) at which she had not been present.

Many people insist that even though she makes false claims about her own presence as a witness, the events she describes are generally held to be true; however, some historians who had seen the work as offering important insights into the lives and sufferings of indigenous people in Latin America have ceased to set it for their students.[29]

A slightly different controversy arose in relation to another once-celebrated work, Binjamin Wilkomirski's *Fragments*. Purporting to describe the sad and horrifying childhood of a young Jewish boy hiding out in Poland before being sent to a concentration camp, *Fragments* was widely read and acclaimed when it was first published in 1995. However questions about its veracity arose almost immediately, and there are now at least five book-length studies and several shorter ones showing in detail the falsehoods involved in the story – beginning with the fact that Wilkomirski is not a Jew; he came from Switzerland, not Poland; and he was never interned.[30]

The controversy surrounding these works has raised a number of general issues about the relationship between autobiography, memory and history. The debate around Wilkomirski, in particular, has served to question the weight which has been given to the apparent authenticity of testimony and autobiography. It has made many prominent historians insist on the differences between history and memory and on the need for historians to maintain their traditional rigour and their careful analysis and interrogation of sources, rather than accepting the primacy of individual voices. Although the absolute lack of veracity in Wilkomirski's account has left it with few defenders, this has not been the case with Rigoberta Menchú. But here one can see differences in approach between historians and scholars in other disciplines. Thus while historians express unease about the book, some literary scholars have argued that *I, Rigoberta Menchú* needs to be read not simply as a single person's autobiography, but rather as a form of testimony in which the life of one person has served to illustrate the experiences of a whole group.

This approach to autobiography as a form which is important, not so much for the insights that it offers into individual subjectivity as for the ways in which it links one particular life to significant political and social developments and transformations, has become increasingly significant in thinking about postcolonial autobiography. The auto-biographies of leaders of anti-colonial and independence movements in both Asia and Africa are particularly notable here, and many of them have assumed a privileged status in providing the narrative of how colonial power ended and the new nation came into existence. As Philip Holden has argued, the autobiographies of Nehru, Nkrumah, Sukarno and Mandela, along with those of many other national leaders, are primarily concerned 'to mould the nation, incite colonial subjects to recognize themselves as citizens of the new nation and to spark recognition in an international audience by placing the nation's narrative within a larger one of human self-realization'.[31] Holden points to the ways in which particular tropes and motifs move backwards and forwards across these various anti-colonial autobiographies, and to the ways in which earlier stories from heroic auto-biographies are sometimes incorporated into them. The best-known autobiography to combine an individual story with that of the making of a new nation is unquestionably Nelson Mandela's *Long Walk to Freedom*, which has become effectively the founding narra-tive of the new post-1994 South Africa.[32] It is an epic story of apartheid and resistance to it, describing tremendous suffering under the harsh prison system of the South African apart-heid regime, detailing the life of Mandela and his fellow inmates on Robben Island and the turning of a prison into a university, and finally their release and the establishment of a new multiracial South Africa. It offers also a strong sense of the value of traditional tribal culture and of the positive ways in which this contributed to a sense of black iden-tity. Mandela's autobiography was carefully crafted both inside and outside prison, vetted by many senior members of the African National Congress to ensure that the story it told was one acceptable to the leaders of the party, and finally turned into a literary form with the help of an outside collaborating author, Richard Stengel. But any inaccuracies it might contain are of almost no importance beside its place as the founding story of the nation.

▶ Historian's autobiographies

Historians have not been immune to the autobiographical impulse. On the contrary, increasing numbers of them have written memoirs and autobiographies, especially over the last two decades. Rather than being seen as falling within the broader sweep of auto-biography, there has been a tendency to separate out the autobiographical writing of his-torians as something special or at least different from that of others. The reason for this centres on the training that historians receive: by virtue of this training, some would argue, historians have a much greater capacity than other writers to explore the historical period through which they have lived – and to comment on it in significant ways. The relationship between an individual life and the larger historical framework within which that person has lived is always important in autobiographical writing, although, as Paul John Eakin suggests, it is usually taken for granted. Autobiographers with a trained historical consciousness, in Eakin's view, 'may be uniquely capable of exploring and problematising that relationship and explaining what it means to be living in history'.[33] Some of the historians who have written autobiographies both endorse this approach and point to its significance for them. Eric Hobsbawm, for example, suggests that his autobiography, *Interesting Times: A Twentieth Century Life*, is in some ways 'the flip side' of his widely acclaimed history of the twentieth century, *The Age of Extremes*. That book benefited from his direct experience of and involvement in some of the events and issues which he discussed. This later book is 'not world history illustrated by the experiences of an individual, but world history shaping that experience, or rather offering a shifting, but always limited set of choices'.[34]

The specific characteristics of historians' autobiographies, and the similarities and differences between those written by British, American, Australian and French historians, have been discussed at some length by Jeremy Popkin.[35] In his view, the sheer volume of autobiographies published by historians makes it clear that their writing is not generated simply out of personal concerns, but rather that they write 'as members of a particular disciplinary community'. Following Eakin's suggestion, Popkin is concerned to explore the influence of their historical training and understanding on the ways in which they write about their lives, and to document how different historians show their own individual lives as ones lived within and affected by larger historical currents. At the same time, Popkin stresses the differences between the demands of autobiography and those of writing history, noting particularly the inevitable subjectivity and personal focus of autobiography and the priority that it accords memory rather than other forms of documentation. The demands of autobiography can, therefore, come into conflict with the methodology and approach required by historical writing. This conflict sometimes produces both tension and a sense of unease in the published autobiographies of historians.

Seeking to extend beyond Popkin, James Aurrell has argued that, writing autobiography extends historians' understanding of themselves and of the human experiences about which they write. Historians' autobiographies should also, in his view, be seen as privileged sources both of intellectual history and of historiographical inquiry. In writing their autobiographies, historians engage with broader contemporary critical and scholarly frameworks and so provide new insight into significant developments in intellectual history and into their impact on historical practice.[36] To substantiate this claim about the importance of historians' autobiographies as sources of intellectual history, Aurrell establishes a way of classifying contemporary historians' autobiographies that is both thematic and chronological. The most crucial point, he insists, is not the date of publication of the autobiography, but the dates of its author's training because it is this that determines the author's intellectual outlook. Those trained in the inter-war period are inflected with a humanistic perspective, whereas those who came of age after the Second World War tend rather to a structuralist approach, and the next generation was influenced by the postmodernism of the 1970s. But these intellectual approaches affected the form and genre that their autobiographies took: the first group articulated their autobiographies as biography, the second as monographs and the third as 'individually conceived or created narratives'. This last group is also more likely to be poetic and narrative in form and more performative than its predecessors.[37]

Although contemporary historians seem particularly inclined towards the writing of autobiography, they are not the first to have done so. Historians have been writing autobiographies at least since the eighteenth century, when the autobiographies of Hume and Gibbon appeared. In some cases, the better known of these early works served as models for their later counterparts. Popkin is interested particularly in pointing to the similarities and the contrasts evident between Edward Gibbon's *Memoirs* (1796) and Henry Adams's *The Education of Henry Adams* (1918). Gibbon places his own historical research at the centre of his life. Adams does not do this, but offers a rather more sophisticated way of connecting an individual life with wider historical developments. Gibbon's sense of the close connection between his historical writing and his *Memoirs* is evident from the very beginning of this work. One reason for undertaking it, he insists, is that he is better qualified than anyone else to provide a history of his own thoughts and learning, and he discusses at some length the development of his own interest in history and how he came to make it his central preoccupation. His sense of the demands of historical writing is followed in the *Memoirs*, in which he focuses on public life, offering very little in the way of intimate or emotional detail.[38]

Henry Adams did not share Gibbon's sense of achievement or enjoyment of his chosen profession and perhaps for this reason did not make it the centrepiece of his autobiography. In place of Gibbon's story of success and triumph in his education and in his later historical writing, *The Education of Henry Adams* (1918) offers rather a story of failure and decline. His sense of personal failure, made clear in his own relative insignificance when compared with his presidential forebears, is shown as a parallel to the broader decline of America from the great days of the early republic. The critical and even dire portrait of America and the idea of its decline from a heroic age to a corrupt and materialistic one that Adams offered were disputed by many at the time it was published. But the ways in which he depicted his own life as both affected by and illustrating the broader trends and patterns which were significant in the national history offered a new way of writing a life which has continued to be influential for many later historians – autobiographers.[39]

There has certainly been continuity in the ways in which some historians have generally written biographies from the eighteenth century to the present, most notably in the emphasis on external developments and public life and career rather than on private life.

Hobsbawm, for example, makes clear at the start of his autobiography that the book 'is more about the public than the private man', and the same is true in the autobiographical writing of many other historians. At the same time, however, the dramatic and violent nature of much twentieth-century history and the intense political involvement of a number of historians make their work very different in tenor from that of their nineteenth-century counterparts. Henry Adams may have been very critical of America, but his place within it was very secure. By contrast, the autobiographies of many prominent twentieth-century historians deal with their experiences as Jews, of the rise of Nazism and the Holocaust, or with being refugees and immigrants in a less than welcoming world. The Cold War and the McCarthy era loom large in the autobiographical writings of many American historians who share with many of their European Jewish counterparts their left-wing political commitments and their sense of engaging in passionate but minority political activism. In some cases, it is precisely the question of this political involvement and engagement that the autobiographies address. Thus Hobsbawm suggests, as many reviewers have since noted, that his autobiography contains the answers to the questions that he has 'been most often asked by journalists and others interested in the somewhat unusual case of a lifelong but anomalous communist'.[40]

A different version of this kind of impersonal autobiography that draws on particular intellectual or political experiences while eschewing the personal is evident in some historians' autobiographies, like that of Geoff Eley. Eley is concerned to chart and explain the developments in twentieth century historiography, and particularly the shifts from social history through cultural history and then to a new kind of history of society. But he does so by looking at his own education and ideas, drawing heavily on his own student life and subsequent intellectual development. Far from wanting to collapse the discussion of historiographical developments into the story of the historian, he sees his use of the first person in the text as a way of linking wider historiographical debates with the social practice and processes of the intellects that engage with them and as a way of stressing the collective nature of historical and political debate.[41]

The entry of significant numbers of women into the historical profession has brought some marked changes in the writing of historians' autobiographies. A number of women historians have written autobiographies that offer very different pictures from those of their male counterparts, beginning with their discussions of the ways in which their careers were chosen and taken up or in which they responded to the dominant ways in which history was understood and written about. The challenge to the prevailing idea that history ought properly to deal only with the public world and not the private is strongly evident here. Thus, for example, Gerda Lerner's *Fireweed: A Political Autobiography* deals in considerable detail with her early years in Vienna in the 1920s and 1930s, linking very closely her own dawning political involvement and commitment with her experiences within a bourgeois Jewish household – and with her growing disillusionment with her father's family and their refusal to recognise what was happening in the world around them. Her political struggles were waged as much within her family as they were against the Nazi regime which came to dominate Austria in the mid-1930s.[42] There are few women historians, moreover, who did not at some point have to deal with the prevailing assumptions about gender and about appropriate lives for women. This did not always take the form of open discrimination within universities and academic institutions. On the contrary, Jill Kerr Conway, for example, turned back to the university when, as a woman, she was refused entry into the diplomatic corps.[43] The separation of their public and private lives is also often harder for women, many of whom postponed their own careers in the early years of marriage or while they were responsible for young children. For many women seeking to become historians across much of the twentieth century, there was a battle to be fought or at least a struggle against social, institutional and often disciplinary assumptions which privileged men and rendered women outsiders.

This struggle has been chronicled and detailed in a series of autobiographical essays written by American women and published in a volume called *Voices of Women Historians: The Personal, the Political, the Professional*. The collecting of these essays was an explicitly feminist endeavour. All the participants were women who had been on the board of the Coordinating Council for Women in History and had thus been actively engaged in campaigning for women within the historical profession. In seeking to use personal narratives in a way which would weave together 'the past and present of women's history and women in the historical profession to leave a record for those who shape the future', this book was intended as a way both to commemorate three decades of feminist activism and scholarship and to explore the impact of these women on the discipline of history.[44] Many of the women involved had sought not only to gain entry into the historical profession but also to point to the ways in which history as a discipline had excluded women – and to offer new approaches and new kinds of history which dealt explicitly with gender and allowed for a more comprehensive analysis of women's experience.

But there have also been other and very different kinds of autobiography written by women historians, linking their personal life with their historical understanding. Sheila Fitzpatrick's *A Spy in the Archives* details her time as a student researching Soviet History in Moscow in the late 1960s, beginning with the incident in which she was named as a spy in a daily newspaper, an event with no ill consequences as the article used her married name which was not the one by which she was known to friends and colleagues.[45] Fitzpatrick offers an extraordinarily detailed account of the texture of daily life in Moscow in the time she lived there, with much commentary on what could and could not be discussed and on the complexities of relationships between foreigners and Soviet citizens. But it is a deeply personal account, including discussion of her parents and the ways in which they, particularly her beloved father, featured in her decision to become a historian of the Soviet Union. Her story also draws extensively on the letters that she wrote at the time to her mother, to whom she makes clear, she was not as close as she was to her father. It includes also details of friendships and love affairs and relationships with teachers and other students so that she and her feelings and experiences are integral to the depiction of Moscow in the Cold War.

A more personal note is also evident in some autobiographies by male historians reflecting on their own particular experiences in relation to their study or understanding of history, rather than wanting to use their own lives to illustrate wider or more general trends. David Walker's *Not Dark Yet* is a particularly interesting example, which focuses on Walker's sudden loss of sight through macular degeneration, a catastrophic event that prevented him from continuing to pursue his earlier historical research on the relationship between Australia and Asia. Instead, he turned his attention to the history of his own family, something which he could research in a variety of different ways and which was closely linked also to his memories.[46] But his discovery and his recreation of the story of his own family also offers a very interesting reading of Australian history that links small-scale experiences and values with wider social forces and patterns.

Another historian's memoir that links a personal experience of illness with a wider social and historical analysis is Barbara Taylor's brave and moving *The Last Asylum: A Memoir of Madness in our Times*.[47] Taylor's work deals with the years in the 1980s that she spent in the mental health system, some of them as a patient in Friern Barnett, a mental hospital which closed the year after she was finally discharged in 1992. Her book is, as she says, 'the story of my madness years, set inside the story of the death of the asylum system in the late twentieth century'. It combines a strong argument about the need for such asylums for those who are seriously mentally ill with a clear-sighted analysis of the lives and difficulties of many inmates and a history of the asylum and the politics surrounding its final end. Here, as with Fitzpatrick and Walker, it is the particularity and the intensity of the individual experience and the desire to link that with an historical understanding that is especially valuable. Right from the start of her time at Friern Barnett, Taylor's historian friends made sure she was aware of its important history, beginning with its founding as Colney Hatch, a showcase for enlightened psychiatry in 1851.[48] And in her memoir, she provides brief histories both of this institution and of psychoanalysis and psychiatry in Britain. But all of this is connected to and illuminated by her own life and experience.

These historians' autobiographies differ markedly from earlier ones and from those late twentieth-century ones like Hobsbawm's and Geoff Eley's that eschew the personal. But what is particularly interesting about them is that none of them deal with 'the personal' in the sense of domestic life and revelations about intimate relationships. Their focus on the personal is rather more one that deals with their own subjectivity and sense of self and the accommodations that they have to make as individuals to the various different worlds in which they live. Thus they offer a range of new and different ways of thinking about the importance of an individual life in the writing and understanding of history.

5 Interpreting and Constructing Lives

▶ Introduction

'My God, how does one write a biography?' Virginia Woolf asked one of her close friends in 1938 as she wrestled with the problem of writing the life of Roger Fry, another very close friend who had died some four years earlier.[1] Woolf commented frequently in her diaries and letters on the difficulties she faced in this task: on the tedium of being submerged in factual material for days on end; on the pain of reading some of the letters; on the prohibition she faced from Fry's sisters and friends on dealing with aspects of Fry's sexual and emotional life which were integral to her understanding of him; on the impossibility of rendering a person as complex as Fry and with as many different facets to his personality in a single work. The issues that Woolf faced in her own struggles with writing this biography and her sense of how different biography was, and how much more limited and constricted than the writing of fiction, reflect quite closely the ideas that she had earlier discussed in a number of essays throughout the 1920s and the early 1930s. 'Is biography an art?' she asked in one of these, arguing that as a relatively new literary form in England, biography had had little chance to become established as an art form. At the same time, the restrictions necessarily placed on biographers by the need to deal with letters, diaries and other documents and to produce a portrait or a life story which accorded with the facts limited its artistic possibilities. Unlike the novelist, the biographer could not invent a character, but had to produce one which reflected the available material. And yet, Woolf pointed out, the facts which a biographer needed to understand and incorporate were 'not like the facts of science – once discovered always the same'.[2] On the contrary, the biographer's facts were subject to changes of opinion and to the impact of new beliefs and ideas: 'What was thought a sin is now known, by the light of facts won for us by the psychologists, to be perhaps a misfortune ... [or] a trifling foible of no great importance.'[3]

With the 'new biography' of Strachey and others, moreover, the nature of biography itself had changed. As we have seen, the primary concern of the new biography, in Woolf's view, was with the 'inner life' of an individual rather than with his or her actions. This in turn meant that the biographer was involved in attempting to discern 'the thought and emotion which meanders darkly and obscurely through the hidden channels of the soul'. This required imagination and was also very much the province of the novelist.[4] Difficult as this was, it gave the biographer new freedoms and hence changed the nature of his work: 'He [sic] chooses; he synthesizes; in short he has ceased to be a chronicler; he has become an artist.'[5] But for Woolf, valuable as biography was, both the freedom and the kind of art practised by the biographer remained limited by their tie to the factual record.

Woolf continues to be a very influential figure for those engaged in writing biography.[6] In the decades since she wrote, however, many other biographers, literary theorists, psychoanalysts and historians have also published their reflections and ideas on the nature of biography and on how best to research, interpret and write a life. This chapter explores these reflections, beginning with a look at some literary discussions about biography before turning to the question of psychoanalysis and biography and then to the ways in which some contemporary biographers have incorporated theoretical approaches derived from literary and gender studies in their biographical writing.

▶ The biographer's craft

Although the satirical approach that Lytton Strachey developed in *Eminent Victorians* did not dominate biography in subsequent decades, other facets of the 'new biography', especially its concern with personality and the inner life, its insistence on the need for careful selection of material and for independent criticism and analysis from the biographer, continued to define the approach of most biographers across much of the twentieth century. Prominent mid-century biographer and theorist Leon Edel illustrates this in his use of the heading 'The new biography' to define his own approach even in the 1980s.[7]

While providing an extensive discussion of Strachey and Woolf, Edel felt a great need to go beyond their comments and suggestions in order to establish what he saw as the basic principles of the new biography, and he published a stream of lectures and essays from the 1950s to the 1980s which outlined these principles.[8] Working much more closely within the framework of established academic disciplines than did Strachey and Woolf, Edel stressed the importance of recognising biography as a form of literature, while pointing also to its important links with other disciplines. The research methods of the biographer were the same as those of the historian, he argued, and biographers needed to take the critical approach to their sources that all historians did.[9] But biography also shared much with both anthropology and the social sciences, which were concerned with the study of the individual psyche.

According to Edel, there are four basic principles involved in the writing of good biography. Three of them centre on the approach and attitude of the biographer and show very clearly Edel's interest in psychoanalysis. His first principle concerns the need for the biographer to 'learn to understand man's ways of dreaming, thinking and using his fancy'. Edel is not, he insists, suggesting that the biographer engage in any attempted form of psychoanalysis, but rather arguing that some **psychoanalytic** insights and approaches are essential to biography as biographers need to 'see through the rationalizations, the postures, the self-delusions and self-deceptions ... in a word the manifestations of the unconscious as they are projected in conscious forms of action'. The second principle takes up Freud's concern about the tendency of a biographer to identify with or hero-worship his or her subject and then to fail to maintain a critical distance from that subject. Biographers, Edel insisted, 'must struggle constantly not to be taken over by their subjects, or to fall in love with them'. His third principle – which is similar in some ways to the first – is 'that a biographer must analyse his materials to discover certain keys to the deeper truths of his subjects' and analyse his public activity or his literary work in order to understand his 'private mythology'. This can be found in 'the patterns and modes of a man's works' and the biographer needs also to explore the hidden private mythology which is concealed in the public endeavour. Finally, the fourth principle deals with form and structure: the biographer needs to find the ideal and unique literary form which is most suited to a particular life. This also involves careful selection of details and some form of literary style and elegance.[10]

The particular way in which Edel set about his task: the insistence on scepticism from the researcher as he read the documents and sought to find the untruths and evasions which would reveal the hidden truth about his subject, for example, points to the extent to which biography was for him a **modernist** project, with its underlying assumptions that the biographer needed to unmask and reveal his subject as he really was – and often in ways that the subject himself would not have recognised. Although it is clear that biographers seek and often find ways of interpreting the behaviour of their subjects which require knowledge and insights that their subjects do not have, many later or perhaps **postmodern** biographers question whether this is always possible. Biographers, they argue, are often unable to penetrate beneath the documents that they read or the representations of themselves that subjects create, and they need to accept the limits of their knowledge, focussing their attention rather on the ways in which a subject performs or creates a sense of self.[11]

But some of Edel's other assumptions have also been the subject of criticism. Although he discussed Virginia Woolf at some length, his own work and the examples he cites make clear the extent to which, for him, both the biographer and the biographical subject were emphatically male. His likening of biography to history, at a time when history was concerned primarily with public life and institutions and was secure in its belief in the objectivity and impersonal nature of historical research and writing, serves to underline the gendered nature of these assumptions. Edel also assumed that a biographical subject would exhibit a strong and unified sense of self which could be grasped through a careful reading of the documents and could then be written about in an appropriate literary form. While the inner life is important to him, he sees it as something which is revealed through the extensive collections of papers, letters and other documents that a significant or prominent public individual would be expected to leave. There is no place here for the gaps and silences which have caused such problems for so many later biographers, or for the conflicts that many individuals faced in attempting to deal with domestic responsibilities while trying also to establish a place in a world which was not normally open to members of their sex, class or ethnicity.

Edel's final and most magisterial work on biography, *Writing Lives: Principia Biographica*, appeared in 1984. Even before its publication, most of its assumptions were being questioned in practice by the many biographies of women which had begun to appear during the course of the 1970s, and they were soon also to be questioned in more general and theoretical terms. This period, as Carolyn Heilbrun argued in *Writing a Woman's Life*, was the start of a new one in the writing of women's biography as a result not only of the number of life stories of women which were being published but also of the new ways in which women's stories were now being told. In place of earlier biographies which either stressed the womanliness of writers and other women of achievement, such as Jane Austen and Charlotte Brontë, or pointed to the exceptional and even monstrous nature of women rulers, such as Queen Elizabeth I, these new biographies focussed rather on the struggles that many women faced as they sought independence or a voice of their own against prevailing stereotypes and assumptions which silenced women and took for granted their subordinate status and domestic concerns. What was important to the biographers writing about significant women was not so much to discern the rationalisations or the life myths that Edel had stressed, but rather how to structure and formulate the story of a woman's life in a way which allowed for an exploration of the particular desires, interests and struggles which were involved in overcoming obstacles and obtaining a particular goal, while still addressing adequately the ways in which women experienced their own lives as women and dealt with the expectations and constraints that they faced.[12] Linda Wagner-Martin carried this argument further in her discussion of the ways in which stereotypical views of women, which assumed that their entire lives could be explained and encompassed in the notion of them as wives or mothers, had to be relinquished in order for women's life stories to be told from their own perspectives.

Heilbrun's work differs from that of Edel as much in its approach and style as in its contents. Edel sought to speak for all biography and biography writers, insisting that the time in literary history had been reached 'when time and circumstances summon biography to declare itself and its principles'.[13] Heilbrun wrote in a much more personal and impressionistic way, drawing on the works of other women and on her own experiences and making clear how impressionistic and experiential her work was. To some extent she pointed in the direction of most of the later works on biography in her concern to reflect on the practices and approaches of other biographers and to see what general propositions one might draw from them, in contrast to Edel's enunciation of a single set of principles that everyone should follow.

This sense that the principles of biography could only be derived from looking at the actual practices of contemporary biographers underlies a number of contemporary general works. It is central to the approach of Linda Wagner-Martin's *Telling Women's Lives: The New Biography*,[14] as it is to Paula Backscheider's *Reflections on Biography* and David Ellis's *Literary Lives: Biography and the Search for Understanding*. Like Edel, both Backscheider and Ellis bemoan the lack of theoretical discussion about biography and of any clear aesthetic principles underlying it which can be recognised by both biographers and their readers.[15] However, both attempt to deal with this lack in an informal and nonprescriptive way by looking at what a large number of biographers do. Of course the questions which are being posed by each of these authors to the biographies that they read frames and even determines the way in which they depict biography. Ellis is much more concerned with the question of interpretation: with the importance of family of origin, of 'primal scenes' which determine psychic formations and of bodily health or illness in how a life is shaped. Backscheider, on the other hand, is rather more preoccupied with the choices that a biographer makes about voice and interpretation. However, neither is attempting to provide definitive works. Rather, in Backscheider's words, they are engaged in 'a tour of the decisions biographers make' showing 'some of the implications of those decisions'.[16]

As the one who offers the broader discussion of how biographers face their task, Backscheider is the more interesting here, and it is her views that I want to discuss. She begins her book not with four principles but rather with what she sees as the four basic questions that all biographers need to address and which readers too need to think about in reading biography. These centre on the voice of the biographer, the nature of the relationship between biographer and subject, the ways in which evidence is understood and dealt with and, finally, how the personality of the subject is understood, represented and used to give the life its shape. Rather than suggesting answers to these questions, she elaborates on how the questions are best understood and then looks at the range of different ways of answering them which can be seen in current biographical work. With regard to the question of the biographer's voice, for example, she makes it clear that it is the biographer's voice which establishes the writer's relationship with the readers and which determines whether readers will trust the biographer and accept that they are in the expert hands of someone who will enable them to understand and know the subject.[17] Establishing a voice is a complex matter, however, and it involves first answering several questions such as whether the biographer should appear in the work, whether the voice should be magisterial – like that of the omniscient author of a great nineteenth-century novel – and whether there is space for personal reflection which allows the author to come into view. Writing as she did with a strong feminist commitment and interest, Backscheider also raised the question about whether women's biographies sounded, or should sound, different from those of men, pointing out how much more likely women biographers were to include personal detail in the preface and introduction.

When it comes to the question of research and of dealing with the evidence from which to construct a biography, Backscheider rejects the idea that there is any definite formula. Research is a complex matter: people often approach it in different ways and have very different feelings about it. Indeed, Backscheider suggests that the attitudes of biographers towards the evidence they have to work with is as psychologically revealing about *them* as it is about their subjects. For Virginia Woolf, for example, the mass of factual data that she had to deal with became overwhelming and made the task of creating a portrait of Fry more difficult. For others, however, rich primary material provides one of the great pleasures in writing biography. And then, of course, there is the problem of inadequate material – years with no letters or diaries, for example, even amongst literate and literary people, and much scarcer resources for those who were illiterate, poor or itinerant and hence did not keep extensive record.[18] Biographers often have to work with limited material, Backscheider points out, either because material has been destroyed or because gaining access to what exists may be impossible if family members or trustees refuse it. Many people, therefore, have to work around a sense of incomplete knowledge and evidence, but even when all the material is there and it has been read, there is still the question of how to assemble it and to create a life. Turning to Woolf, as she often does to illustrate her points, Backscheider quotes the question that Woolf asked with regard to Roger Fry: 'How can one make a life out of six cardboard boxes full of tailor's bills, love letters and old picture postcards?' It was 'such a mass of odds and ends out of which to make a whole'.[19] Here again, Backscheider does not attempt to provide a definitive answer, preferring to emphasise how complex the issue is as biographers 'combine, assimilate, extract – arrange, draw inferences, and build chains'.[20] There are two crucial concepts which should, in her view, guide this process. The first is the need to find the 'fertile fact' which points beyond itself and leads to new inferences and suggestions which enrich the interpretation. The second is the need to explore the 'emotional centres' which offer insight into the personality and life shape of individuals and the organising structures of their lives.

The hardest issue to deal with, Backscheider suggests, is that concerning how best to understand and depict the personality of a subject and find the appropriate shape for depicting a life. On this question, as she makes clear, her own views changed as she read the work of others: while she began with the assumption that all biographers should have a theory of personality which included insights from developmental psychology, she ended up rejecting this position. The demands of a biography as a literary work, the dynamic nature of the relationship between biographer and subject and the many ways in which insights into a personality might be derived from that, and the numerous different ways in which a life could be read and written made her reject her earlier views as she came to feel that single developmental theory was adequate to meet all the demands that a biography required. Biographies might need to establish the identity of their subject, but there are so many social and historical issues concerning what their own world might allow a person to be as to make a single focus on personality inadequate.[21]

▶ Biography and psychoanalysis

If Backscheider ultimately gave up on the idea that any specific theory of personality was necessary for biography, psychoanalysts have certainly not given up their sense that there is a particularly close connection between their own disciplines and biography: 'Parallels between psychoanalysis and biography as our two most prominent ways of constituting life histories make close relations inevitable', wrote David Hoddeson in a special issue of the psychoanalytical journal *American Imago* which was devoted to biography: 'Psychoanalysts are always doing biography as they reconstruct and record their patients' case histories and contemporary biographers are virtually obligated to anatomize the psychic lives of their subjects.'[22] Elizabeth Young-Bruehl, who wrote highly acclaimed biographies of both Anna Freud and Hannah Arendt before becoming an analyst, has offered some new ways of looking at the relationship between psychoanalysis and biography.[23] Young-Bruehl sees the development of modern biography as intertwined with that of psychoanalysis, but in a sometimes uneven way. In her view, the biographical framing of case studies influenced the development of biography from early in the twentieth century, but it was only much later, in the 1950s, that analysts became interested in biography per se and, in many cases, began to write the history of psychoanalysis itself through biographical studies of its key figures. She is interested here in the ways in which many aspects of psychoanalytical theory, and particularly ones which originated with Freud but have since been seen as problematic – such as his ideas about femininity – are now being explored in biographical terms. Thus while biographers necessarily draw on theories of childhood and development which derive from psychoanalysis, those very theories are often approached through biographical studies of the people who first devised them.

Freud himself, as Adam Phillips has argued, 'had a lifelong aversion to biography and biographers'.[24] The intensity of this aversion, Phillips suggests, is partly because of his desire to differentiate psychoanalysis (which is a kind of conversation, without a definite beginning, middle and end and in which the patient can speak back) from a written biography which claims or seeks to tell the truth. Phillips quotes the rancorous reply that Freud sent to the writer Arnold Zweig when he offered to write Freud's biography. 'To be a biographer', he wrote, 'you must tie yourself up in lies, concealments, hypocrisies, false colourings, and even in hiding a lack of understanding, for biographical truth is not to be had, and if it were to be had, we could not use it.' But this in turn leads Phillips to question whether Freud is so defensive because he feels that there is a similarity between the biographer and the psychoanalyst who trades in biographical truth 'and that something immoral, something suspect about the analyst, is exposed by the art of biography'.[25]

But this aversion did not prevent Freud from engaging in his own speculative biographical accounts, or indeed from insisting that psychoanalysis was essential for the writing of biography, particularly when it involved the complex lives of artists. He had a lifelong fascination with Leonardo da Vinci and spent many years pondering what he saw as the 'riddle' of da Vinci's character, which suddenly became clear to him in 1901. His sense that he alone had been able to understand Leonardo da Vinci led him to the general belief that 'the domain of biography, too, must become ours.[26]

It is not only in terms of the interpretation of the subjects of biography that Freud saw psychoanalysis as having something to offer, but also in terms of the questions it might raise about the relationship between biographers and their subjects. As we have seen in Chapter 4, Freud pointed to the perils of excessive identification of a biographer with a subject and to the likelihood that, in the process of idealising a subject, biographers sacrifice truth to an illusion 'and for the sake of their infantile practices abandon the opportunity of penetrating the most fascinating secrets of human nature'.[27]

Seeing himself as able to overcome all of this, Freud proceeded to explore the paradoxes that da Vinci presented both in his life and in his art and which required some analysis. In his art, they could be seen in the difficulty he had in finishing any of his works, or indeed of committing himself to art at all – despite his artistic genius. Ultimately da Vinci relinquished his artistic work and turned rather to scientific endeavours. His personal life, and his apparent lack of any form of sexual interest, was equally hard to understand. Freud saw the enigmatic smile of the *Mona Lisa* as a kind of symbol of da Vinci's own enigmatic life, and he attempted to resolve the riddle by seeking the underlying causes in da Vinci's childhood. Accepting that there was little information about this part of da Vinci's life, he found the clue he was seeking in a childhood memory that da Vinci reported in one of his later writings. 'While I was in my cradle', wrote da Vinci, 'a vulture came down to me, and opened my mouth with its tail, and struck me many times with its tail against my lips.'[28] In the light of his sense that da Vinci was a homosexual, Freud interpreted this fantasy as one of being suckled by his mother but having the mother replaced by a vulture – a bird perceived as both male and female, hence suggesting the shift in da Vinci's desire from the maternal breast to the penis.

As many later commentators have pointed out, Freud's belief that he had solved the riddle of da Vinci's character proved unfounded.[29] His analysis was based on serious errors: in the original Italian version of this memory, da Vinci used the term *nibio*, which refers to a kite rather than a vulture. There is no symbolism attached to kites, however, which is similar to that upon which Freud insists in relation to vultures. This issue, therefore, raises questions about the whole sexual interpretation that Freud provided. There are also many false assumptions and inaccuracies in Freud's knowledge and depiction of da Vinci's relationships with his birth mother, his stepmother and his father, which serves further to undermine his analysis of da Vinci's childhood and its impact on his adult life. For his critics, Freud demonstrated both the reductiveness of psychoanalytical approaches to biography and the perils which await those who place more weight on their supposed theoretical insight than on careful empirical research. But for his supporters, Freud's essay on da Vinci, despite its errors, remains important, illustrating as it does the difficulties and problems that all biographers face. In working on da Vinci, Freud combined insights that he gained from his clinical practice, which provided his interpretive framework with what empirical material he could find. In doing this, he struggled constantly with the need to maintain da Vinci's individuality and unique personality while making his life coherent and comprehensible through a paradigm of infantile sexuality and adult neurosis which was not uncommon. In this very conflict, Malcolm Bowie suggests, Freud shows how psychoanalysis 'redramatizes one of the paradoxes that the modern biographer confronts from day to day: you need a simplifying model, a schematic life-pattern, in order to give your work an arresting plot and prevent it from becoming a mere chronicle of particulars'.[30] But if the model is too rigid, one loses all sense of the human life being lived and moving between inner and outer circumstances.

Several later analysts also made serious claims to particular expertise and insights in the writing of biography. Erik Erikson, a very influential figure, especially in the United States in the 1950s and 1960s, was the first of these. Erikson moved away from Freud's emphasis on both childhood and sexuality, insisting rather on the importance of psychic development beyond the childhood years and into adolescence and adulthood. His theory of personality development posited seven separate stages of life from infancy to late adulthood, each of which involved particular challenges and developments. In his view, adolescence was the most significant phase. It was then that issues of identity came to the fore, with the possibility of an identity crisis as young people sought to establish a sense of direction and purpose which also allowed for a sense of unity between their childhood and their anticipated adulthood.

Erikson's approach involved an analysis of society as well as of individuals. He argued that different social institutions, familial arrangements and customs would have an impact on the ways in which individuals experienced and dealt with the crucial stages of development. Erikson's concern to encompass individuals, groups and whole societies in his analysis was made very clear in his use of the term 'psychohistory' to describe his project, which was 'to understand the social conditions shaping the development of the individual (and group) psyche, and then the psychological factors forming the social conditions'.[31] Like Freud, Erikson sought to apply his own theoretical framework to a particular individual, and in 1958, he published *Young Man Luther*, his most widely read and controversial biographical work. Again like Freud, Erikson combined his own biographical work with critical comments on the blindness and unconscious emotional investments of non-psychoanalytical historians and biographers. Historians were often too immersed in the 'disguises, rationalizations and idealizations of the historical process' to be able to comment critically on it. Hence, in his view, it was imperative that trained clinicians become involved in historical and biographical research.[32] But Erikson sought to do more than simply investigate a historical individual and event; he wanted also to use history to expand and enhance his own discussion of the problem of the identity crisis as the central and formative issue for young men in all societies by showing how important it had been for leading figures in the past. In a final similarity with Freud, Erikson used a particular episode in Luther's life as the focal point of his analysis. He chose as his central event a very dramatic fit which Luther had in church one day in his mid-twenties, during the course of which he cried out aloud and then fainted. Erikson argued that this fit illustrated Luther's inner torment and his identity crisis, and he analysed it in relation to Luther's earlier familial experiences and to his later religious actions and beliefs.

Here too, Erikson faced a problem similar to that earlier with regard to Freud: there was no clear record of the crucial episode which illustrated Luther's identity crisis, and Erikson himself acknowledged that it was not absolutely clear that it had ever occurred. A couple of Luther's contemporaries reported the event, but Luther himself never mentioned it. For Erikson, the lack of evidence was of little importance.[33] What mattered rather was the way in which this episode seemed to encapsulate all the questions concerning the difficulties of Luther's relationship with his father, the nature of his monastic experience and the spiritual solution that he found as a way to resolve his inner conflict.

While Erikson's somewhat cavalier approach to empirical evidence was castigated by a number of reformation scholars, his general approach and his insistence on the need to bring psychoanalytical theory and insight to bear on the analysis of significant religious and political figures was applauded by many others and made Erikson a prominent figure in the writing of history and biography for a number of decades. In the 1950s and 1960s, courses on psychohistory were introduced into a number of leading universities, and several major biographical projects were undertaken following his method.[34] Erikson's influence waned rapidly, however, during the course of the 1970s.[35] His lack of detailed archival or primary research and his assumptions that his own clinical expertise offered insights which obviated the need for this kind of work were subject to ever more criticism and made his work appear extremely amateurish. At the same time, the complete lack of interest in questions about gender – or, indeed, the extent to which his ideas about life stages and identity might be applied to women – meant that he was subject to stringent feminist critiques and out of step with the burgeoning interest in women's history which was so important during this decade. In a similar way, his ready assumptions about the universal applicability of his theories across cultures were also queried in the light of their exclusive concern with particular Western societies and values.

Interest in the best ways to link psychoanalysis, biography and history has continued up to the present. In the United States, where Erikson continues to have a high standing among some historians and analysts, there is an ongoing interest in psychohistory, with societies and journals that continue to promulgate and develop it and to discuss what psychohistory might be or mean today. But there are also alternate approaches from some who, while clearly acknowledging their indebtedness to both Freud and Erikson, have recognised the need to modify their approach and to recognise the primary importance of extensive empirical research and of historical method in the writing of biography. This emphasis on the importance of historical research has gone along with a very different tone and set of assumptions about what psychoanalysis can offer. In his attempt to reformulate psychohistory in the mid-1980s, Thomas A. Kohut, who is both an analyst and a historian, began by accepting that there were acute difficulties in applying psychoanalytical approaches to history and that previous attempts to do so had been seriously flawed. In seeking to understand a historical figure through a single narrow interpretative formulation, psychoanalytical theory tended to be both 'psychologically simplistic and historically reductionistic'.[36] The preoccupation of psychoanalysis with the present posed problems for its approach to history, but he insisted that analysis provided useful insights for the historian and biographer. The concept of transference is, in his view, particularly important. It is the transference, which is established between the patient and the analyst during analytic treatment, that enables the analyst to understand the thwarted childhood needs and frustrated childhood wishes of the patient, as these are remobilised during the analysis and 'transferred' by the patient on to the analyst. The historian does not have the benefit of this form of transference, of course, but if he or she understands how it works, it can be used in writing a biography. The historical record and the empirical data often enable the researcher to see the transferences that the biographical subject experienced in relation to important figures in his or her life. But it is not only childhood which is important: 'the whole course of an individual's life expresses the psychological essence of the person – his [*sic*] needs and wishes, his aims and ideals, his loves and hates, his conflicts ... the basic pattern of his self'.[37] Psychoanalysis, he suggested, might help historians and biographers to think about the life course of their subject and what it revealed.

Despite their differences, history and psychoanalysis share a concern to understand human feelings, thoughts and actions, Kohut argued. They also 'share what the philosopher Wilhelm Dilthey defined as the methodology of the human sciences – that is, knowing by empathic understanding ... In both disciplines the investigator feels or, perhaps better, thinks his way inside the experience of the other when he understands him.' Empathy here does not mean sympathy or compassion, but rather 'the ability to transcend subjective responses and to experience, although to a necessarily attenuated degree, the experience of another'. Although the analyst seeks through his interpretations to help the patient achieve empathy with himself and to give him an understanding of why – given his past and present – he feels, thinks and acts as he does, the historian seeks through his interpretations to make the reader empathise with the historical subject, and to show the reader why – given the historical subject's experiences and circumstances – what happened did happen.[38]

In later work, Kohut takes a rather different approach, turning away from the study of individuals towards that of groups and stressing the importance of history in relation to the psyche rather than assuming that a psychoanalytic approach might provide superior insights. In *A German Generation*, Kohut points to his own shift away from an earlier concern that he shared with other psychohistorians about the impact of the individual psyche on history and towards a recognition of the importance of the influence of history on the psyche. Psychologically, he argues, we are all constituted to some extent through our environment, which is historically constituted. Therefore, history constitutes our psyche.[39] Kohut has moved so far away from his earlier preoccupation with individuals that in this study, which is based on interviews with sixty-four people born in Germany before the First World War and living through Weimar and then Nazi German and into the present, he reduces the sixty-four to six composite individuals, seeing them all as so similar in outlook and experience that no violence is done to them by reducing them to composites to provide a picture of a particular generation.[40]

In Britain, attempts directly to apply psychoanalytical theory to biography have not been met sympathetically. As Daniel Pick, who did precisely this in his work on Garibaldi, argues, in both its older and newer forms, psychohistory has provoked considerable scepticism in Britain.[41] But although psychoanalytic approaches remain suspect to many, there are also influential adherents to it, including not only Daniel Pick but also Lyndal Roper as well as Barbara Taylor and Sally Alexander. There are not many biographies that extol the virtues of a psychoanalytic approach, Taylor argues, and the new literary boldness that some exhibit has not been matched by any comparable change in its psychological dimension.[42] Both biographers and historians use psychology – 'it is impossible to write human history without it – but the psychology that most historians deploy is of the pick-and-mix variety, blending commonplace assumptions about human motivation with bits of pop psychology, often Freudian in flavour'.[43] But Taylor herself is one of a small number of prominent historians interested in using psychoanalytical approaches and concepts both historically and biographically, as she has done both in her work on Mary Wollstonecraft and, as we will see, in her own memoir.[44] To her work one needs to add the 2014 biography of Freud by Adam Phillips and Lyndal Roper's long awaited and widely acclaimed 2012 biography, *Martin Luther*.[45]

Roper's work is particularly significant here. While accepting that it 'may seem foolhardy to attempt a psychoanalytically influenced biography of the very man whose biography has become a byword for the worst kinds of reductionist history', Roper argues that the material on Luther offers extraordinary insights into his inner life that enable the historian both to understand him and the contradictions that are so evident, especially in his views about women and about marriage. They also allow a new understanding of how a sixteenth-century individual perceived the world around him.[46] In making use both of the insights into his personality and conflicts and into the social and intellectual context that formed him, Roper sees it as possible also to offer a new approach to his theology and a new vision of the Reformation. What is notable in Roper's work is the depth and complexity of her analysis of Luther's ongoing development, as well as a recognition of her almost life-long engagement with Luther who was a feature of her childhood because for a short time her own father was a Presbyterian minister.

▶ Texts and performances

While psychoanalysts and some biographers seek the inner core or psychological essence of their subjects, others have come to question not only whether it is possible to gain access to an inner core but even whether looking for one is the best way to approach biography. Drawing on some new theoretical developments which have emerged in literary and gender studies, they have sought rather to focus on the different ways in which individuals represent, construct or fashion their identities either in texts or in a range of different kinds of performance. These representations, they would argue, are all the biographer really has to work with and are extremely important. Not only do they show how individuals wish to appear but also how they negotiate the social structures and the assumptions about gender, class and ethnicity which are dominant in their societies and to which they often have to conform.

In some cases, this interest in the ways in which individuals construct or represent themselves is a response to one of the problems that all biographers face in working out how best to encompass the very different ways in which individuals are seen and understood by those who know them. An even more difficult problem centres on how to deal with the conflicting accounts of themselves, of their experiences and feelings, and of particular episodes in their own lives that some individuals offer. These differences can often be seen if one compares the accounts provided in letters to a range of recipients or if one looks at the difference between accounts provided in letters, diaries and, in the case of those who wrote them, in autobiographies and other literary texts. Clearly there are issues about memory which need to be taken into account. But there are many examples of individuals who write different versions of events or who describe themselves and their feelings in completely different terms – even in letters or other accounts written on the same day. The need to deal with contrasting and conflicting accounts is not something new to historians. They have always insisted on the need to interrogate sources and to treat them with care and indeed with scepticism, seeking to establish when and why they were written and how any given document might deviate from the truth or give only a partial truth. Older theorists of biography, such as Leon Edel for example, insisted that biographers should follow suit in interrogating their sources. For the most part, however, this scepticism and critical reading of sources by historians was based on a sense of the need to establish the truth beneath what each document might suggest. By contrast, many contemporary literary theorists and scholars reject the very idea that one can get 'behind' or 'beneath' the text to reveal the 'real' aims, intentions and ideas of the person who wrote it. All one has to work with *is* the text, they would argue, and what is important is to see how best the text might be read and what meanings it might reveal when close attention is paid to its structure, its language, its obvious omissions and the ways in which particular texts draw on or refer to other texts. When applied to various different forms of life writing, including letters, diaries and autobiographies, this new literary approach leads to a rejection of the idea of letters and diaries as authentic personal writings in which an individual reveals his or her inner self, and a recognition that even in these ostensibly personal documents individuals are engaged in a literary exercise, constructing and representing themselves and telling their own story in a range of different ways. Rather than seeking to reconcile apparent contradictions in their sources or to find the coherent inner core of a person, many biographers now see it as important to encompass the full range of those representations and to explore their variation. It is often helpful to look at the particular audiences that the individual was addressing or at the needs of a particular moment which made one kind of representation more appropriate than another.

Biographers are not, of course, the only writers or scholars interested in reading that images and representations of an individual and their new concern with this as an approach overlaps with the work of others interested in political analysis or in cultural studies. Garry Wills's *Cincinnatus: George Washington and the Enlightenment* offers an interesting example of such an overlap.[47] This work combines Washington's self-representation, in his speeches and letters, with depictions of him by others in both a written and a visual form. What is important, Wills suggests, is not to get below the images to find some kind of 'real' Washington, but rather to explore these images in order to see and understand how Washington appeared to his contemporaries. In order to do this, Wills chose three crucial moments in Washington's career: his resignation as commander-in-chief of the Continental Army, his presiding over the Constitutional Convention, and his farewell address at the end of his presidency. All of them were to some extent staged, and all worked to reinforce Washington's courage, sense of duty and lack of any personal ambition. In insisting on resigning his commission and leaving public life when he saw himself as no longer needed, Washington drew on the image of the Roman hero Cincinnatus, who agreed to leave his farm when called upon to protect Rome, but insisted on returning to his farm once the crisis he had been asked to resolve was over. Wills's study serves well to illustrate the nature of the eighteenth-century republican values and virtues that Washington embodied and for which he was revered. Although some critics and reviewers did see this work as a biography, and aspects of Washington's life and earlier biographical accounts of him are central to Wills's own work, he does not present his account as a biography. He is concerned rather to study Washington as a political leader and particularly to see the correspondence between his conduct and self-representation and the republican ideals and values of the Enlightenment. But he does suggest that this is the only Washington that we can really get to know and that this study of Washington's character supplants biographical ones which seek to focus more closely on his private life.

The question of whether a study of the different representations that an individual produces about herself constitutes a biography is raised in a particularly interesting way in Toril Moi's study of Simone de Beauvoir. In her book, *Simone de Beauvoir: The Making of an Intellectual Woman*, Moi was concerned to explore de Beauvoir's intellectual development and to see how she came to be both an intellectual woman and the figure who has been so important to so many late twentieth-century literary scholars and feminists. At the start, Moi argued that she was not writing a biography: 'When I say that I am interested in Simone de Beauvoir as an intellectual woman', she explained, 'it may sound as if I am mostly concerned with biography. Yet my work is based on the assumption that there can be no *methodological* distinction between life and text.' In his *Interpretation of Dreams*, she argued, Freud seemed unable to differentiate between psyche and text: he offered us a map of the mind as he gave us an interpretation. This approach was particularly relevant to de Beauvoir, who left hundreds of letters and diaries in addition to her books. In many cases her novels depict or reflect on episodes in her life in even more detail than do either her autobiography or her letters. What interests Moi is not how best to bring together these different accounts to establish what really happened in de Beauvoir's life, but rather to see how the different texts play off, contrast with and indeed sometimes destabilise one another. It is the writer, and not the person, who is of interest to her: 'The intertextual network of fictional, philosophical, autobiographical and epistolary texts she left us *is* our Simone de Beauvoir', she insists.[48]

Moi's insistence that she was not writing a biography derived both from her primary interest in literary and intellectual questions and from her sense that her study focussed on particular episodes in de Beauvoir's life rather than depicting it in its entirety. But of course many biographies now focus on parts of a life, rather than the whole. Paula Backscheider pointed this out, arguing that de Beauvoir's life was absolutely central to the book and that Moi's interest in combining the life with the writings was similar to that evident in a number of other 'neo-biographies that are ideological, consider a portion of a person's life or work, or are a blend of intellectual biography and cultural studies'. Moi reconsidered her own approach in the light of this comment, quoting Backscheider in the second edition of her book and agreeing that her work was really a biography, as she tried to bring out the 'meaning and resonance of different aspects of de Beauvoir's life or writing, by coming at them from different angles, often using different methods too'.[49]

This focus on particular texts and episodes as a way to explore a life is indeed evident in a number of biographies. While some authors, like Moi, are most interested in how to read different texts, others have turned rather to the idea of performance and to the ways in which some individuals perform different roles and different versions of themselves. Interest in performance and in theatrical forms of self-presentation has been considerably more noticeable in writing the lives of women than of men. This is not surprising in view of the widespread recognition of the ways in which women have been expected to modify their speech, dress and behaviour in order to conform to prevailing codes of femininity. The idea that many women perform femininity has thus become a familiar one in gender studies. The concept of 'performance' which is used here is derived in a general way from linguistic anthropology, but also in a more direct way from the ideas of Judith Butler concerning the importance of **performativity** in establishing gender identity. Gender, in Butler's view, centres on what one *does* rather than on what one *is*. It involves actions which have been learned or rehearsed, often ones derived from the gender scripts which women are expected to learn. These gender performances usually involve the enactment or restatement of dominant or hegemonic practices and hence serve to demonstrate the extent to which women accept and acknowledge the assumptions of their society. But they can also include deliberate acts which challenge dominant ideologies.

Both literary theory and ideas of performance have been used effectively in a number of biographies in the past few years. Angela John's biography of the Edwardian suffragette and actress Elizabeth Robbins offers one example. Pointing to the many different ways in which Robbins wrote her own life story in her diaries, notebooks and memoirs, John argued that it was impossible to impose a definitive shape on her and necessary rather to write about her using the various different versions of her life that she had created. Robbins was a professional actress who produced a number of versions of herself, enacting different roles in her life as well as on the stage. She adopted different names as she moved from the United States to Britain and from one social world and set of activities to another. What John focuses on is precisely the different ways in which Elizabeth Robbins both created and staged her life. Rather than attempting to 'unveil her quintessential self', John looks at 'how multiple, shifting identities were constructed by and for her at particular times and in different places'.[50] Of course actors and actresses lend themselves particularly well to this approach, as Lisa Merrill showed in her biography of the nineteenth-century American actress Charlotte Cushman. Like Robbins, Cushman's performances worked across both her private and her public life as she sought to create a particular image of her life and an acceptance of her lesbian relationships which both drew on her theatrical representations of male characters and on her extensive public reputation.[51]

These concepts of 'staging' and 'performance' have also been used in biographies of women who never set foot on the stage, but who performed their femininity as a highly deliberate and self-aware form of social display. The importance of performing femininity was explored in the 1970s in Hartmann's *Victorian Murderesses* and was shown to be a key issue in determining whether a woman accused of murder was found to be guilty or innocent. In 2000, in an edited collection of essays entitled *The New Biography: Performing Femininity in Nineteenth-Century France*, Jo Burr Margadant argued that many women from elite backgrounds who sought to move outside a circumscribed feminine sphere in nineteenth-century France 'had to craft a feminine self legible to the public and credible to herself that might also win approval in at least some influential circles'.[52] This self could be constructed through writing as well as through actions undertaken in private or in public life, and it often enabled women to engage in activities which would otherwise have been impossible.

The importance of performance as a way for a woman to gain acceptance and legitimacy when seeking to engage in activities generally regarded as unacceptable for women is demonstrated clearly by Susan Grogan with regard to the nineteenth-century French socialist and activist Flora Tristan.[53] Tristan played her various roles quite self-consciously, describing herself in her diary on one occasion as 'playing the princess', as she watched an altercation between soldiers and a group of working men and women whom she had been encouraging to join a union which would engage in political activism with a view to establishing a socialist society. But while seeing herself as acting in this way on occasion, Grogan suggests that the idea of performance can be seen as embracing almost all of Tristan's life. Her desire for a public role and for some influence over the society in which she lived meant that she had to overcome her own society's assumption that virtuous women confined themselves to the domestic realm. Tristan needed to find a way not only to challenge prevailing assumptions about the link between domesticity and femininity but also to establish an alternative female model which would give her the authority that she needed in order to engage effectively in political debate and activity. She needed to find and to enact other models of femininity which would legitimate and authorise her claim to public notice, and she found these sometimes by suggesting alternative forms of motherhood, but at other times by basing her performance of herself on upper-class women whose appearance in public was acceptable.

While the approach to looking at a life and writing a biography in terms of the self-representation and performances of its subject comes from other disciplines, it is a way of writing lives which is of particular value to historians. For while the choice of roles and representations that a person makes clearly reflects something of her personality, both the need for particular forms of self-representation and the range of available possibilities is determined by a particular society and period of time. In all the biographies of women that have looked at these representations, considerable emphasis has been placed on the way that particular assumptions about femininity made it necessary or at least advantageous for a number of women to adopt the roles they did and to perform their lives in the ways in which they did. The focus on performance, therefore, serves to illustrate in both detailed and subtle ways the gendered expectations that women face and some of the ways in which they negotiate them in order to live their lives.

Finally it is worth emphasising the range of different ways of approaching, understanding and constructing lives which is currently evident amongst those engaged in the writing of biographies and life stories, and especially in historical biography. For some, it is gaining access to the inner life of an individual, to his or her hidden and unconscious motives and feelings, that is most important in understanding and making sense of that person's life. But to others, it is the very ways in which individuals created and performed not only specific roles, but themselves. In this latter case, it is important to historians and biographers not to decode these performances to get to an ultimate truth, but rather to explore and understand the various stories and the ways in which individuals represented or performed their lives because it is those performances that stand as their public record.

6 Changing Biographical Practices

▶ Introduction

Although there is clearly some new and experimental work being done in contemporary biography, there is a marked difference of opinion about how extensive it is. In the view of some writers, the continuities in the form of most biography, and especially in political biography, point to a lack of change. Some biographies now follow a thematic rather than a chronological structure, and even new political biographies sometimes begin with a significant episode or one that illustrates a character rather than with an account that follows a trajectory from birth to death. Nonetheless, for the most part biography has not abandoned the chronological structure and the unified narrative so prevalent in its nineteenth-century predecessor in the way that the contemporary novel has. Even the demands of the 'new biographers' for selection of details and economy of size have been rejected, so the 'nineteenth- and twentieth-century biographies look increasingly alike. Stuffed with corroborating materials, more-recent volumes have bulked up to resemble their Victorian ancestors.'[1] But there is also, as Richard Holmes notes, some development. 'It is true that the traditional form of major Life and Times biographies, often in two volumes, are still being written,' he concedes, 'but at the cutting edge, clearly, something is happening.' Holmes notes particularly 'a fascination with briefer and more experimental work. There is renewed interest in marginal and subversive subject matter. The "monolithic" single Life is giving way to biographies of groups, of friendships, of love affairs, of "spots of time" (micro biographies), or of collective movements in art, literature or science.' It is new subjects, Holmes rightly suggests, and the interest now taken in previously neglected lives, or in writing about groups of people, held together for an historic moment by a common endeavour, place or ideal, that has driven the change. Their stories often do not fit into a traditional 'womb-to-tomb story' and hence have led to the development of unusual narrative forms.[2]

There is a much stronger sense of the extent and the importance of change in biographical practice at least since the 1970s amongst those who have focussed on women's lives. Carolyn Heilbrun, Paula Backscheider and Linda Wagner-Martin are amongst the scholars who have discussed this question at some length.[3] None of them suggest that writing women's lives involves a radically different form of narrative or of structuring and organising the story. On the contrary, as Wagner-Martin argues, it is not form that matters so much as conceptualisation and the understanding and depiction of a life in all its complexity. It is here, she suggests, that one can see the changes evident in women's biography: in the need to explore more fully the personal and emotional conflicts in an individual life, to focus more attention on domestic and family life, and to assume a different biographical perspective which leads to the questioning of earlier assumptions and interpretations which tended to rely heavily on feminine stereotypes.[4] Many of these biographies of women have also served to show the gendered assumptions evident in traditional biography and to question the accepted accounts of a number prominent men.

Those who stress the conservatism of biography as a form and the continuities in the ways in which it has been written are surely correct when it comes to the vast mass of biography. For all the interest in women's lives that has been evident over the past three or four decades, there is no question that the dominant subject in biographical writing continues to be significant and important men. The proportions evident in the new Dictionary of National Biography – in which some 10 per cent of entries are now women while the remaining 90 per cent are men – is probably a fairly accurate indicator of the overall picture of biographical writing and publishing. Political and military leaders make up a very large percentage of this number, followed closely by literary figures, but there has also been a great deal of interest in scientists and explorers. The majority of these biographies are traditional in form, conceptualisation and content, focussing primarily on the public lives and achievements of their subjects, with perhaps a little more discussion of their intimate private life, and a greater sense of the need to explore their personalities and to point to weaknesses as well as strengths than was evident in the nineteenth and early twentieth centuries. But they still have a basic concern to tell the life story of an outstanding individual in a way that demonstrates that person's exceptional abilities and historical significance. Even amongst these works, however, there have been some quite marked changes at the 'cutting edge', in the ways in which the life stories of prominent and important individual lives have been understood and told. In some cases, this has been a result of bringing the women with whom they were involved into the biographer's focus more centrally; in others, it is a result rather of a re-evaluation of the importance of context, or an interrogation of how a particular individual gained not only his power and position, but also created the image that sustained him. All of this has tended to emphasise the need to explore more closely the connection of significant individuals with the world in which they lived.

Although powerful men continue to dominate biography, there has nonetheless been a significant expansion in the range of other people as biographical subjects over the past four decades. The spate of books on little-known individuals who had interesting lives or relationships, or on the mothers, wives, daughters and sisters of prominent men, are examples of this current interest in the lives of many people who would not have been deemed sufficiently important to warrant a biography in earlier decades. The idea that 'ordinary people' are appropriate subjects for biography is not entirely new. In the 1920s, Virginia Woolf had asked 'whether the lives of great men only should be recorded. Is not anyone who has lived a life, and left a record of that life, worthy of biography – the failures as well as the successes, the humble as well as the illustrious? And what is greatness? And what smallness?'[5] But although she turned her hand to a very amusing life of a dog, Woolf herself did not attempt to answer these questions by writing an actual or even a fictional biography of an 'ordinary' individual.[6] It was not until the final decades of the twentieth century that historians and biographers began seriously to explore this possibility. This new interest in obscure lives is closely connected to the democratising impulses of the new social histories of the 1970s, with their concern not only to explore the lives and experiences of ordinary people but also to see the world from their viewpoint and to allow them to speak for themselves. It can be seen most clearly in the increasing interest in women's biography that was linked to the emergence of women's history in Britain and the United States and in the development of microhistory. As we will see, interest in new biographical subjects also required the development of some new approaches to biography. Some of these were a result of having to work with fewer sources and to find ways to tell life stories without the full documentation that traditional biography assumes. But others came from the ways in which those dealing with obscure lives sought to connect their subjects to the wider world in which they lived and to use their stories to illustrate wider historical patterns.

This chapter begins by looking at the gendering of biography and at the significant ways in which the introduction of women has challenged traditional assumptions and ideas. It then moves on to explore some of the changing biographical practices that have been introduced by the introduction of new biographical subjects whose lives had long been hidden or forgotten. It concludes with a discussion of the new ways of seeing and understanding the relationship of individuals to the wider world in some biographical work.

▶ The gender of biography

The new approach to biography that was driven by the feminism of the late 1960s and 1970s began with a critique of the gendered assumptions and stereotypes that were evident in earlier biographical practices. Those who wanted to know about the lives of past women in the 1970s were immediately struck by how hard it was to do this. Women's lives in past time had been of little interest either to historians or to biographers. Queens and women rulers had certainly been written about, as had important women writers, alongside some particularly prominent intellectuals, activists, women engaged in politics, society and political wives, and even some notorious courtesans. But there were few biographies that explored the lives of the many women engaged in local politics, trade unions, education, philanthropy or social activism or feminism who had not attained the standing of a national leader, and almost none that dealt with ordinary women who had not sought a public life. Little of the existing work offered insights into the private and familial lives of women, moreover, or into the ways in which those engaged in public life combined their feminine responsibilities with their other interests and activities.

The point made by many feminists concerning the ways in which the exclusion of women from much historical work reflected its preoccupation with a public world from which women were usually excluded was relevant also to biography. The heavy emphasis in biography on those who had made significant political or military contributions, or who had a place in the dominant literary and artistic canon, made it almost impossible for women to 'qualify' as suitable subjects for biography. Even when they did, the standard biographical pattern fitted them badly. The flow of a life through childhood, education at school and then often university, sometimes followed by or substituted with military training, leading into a career or a life of public activity involved constant interaction with institutions from which, until recently, women were excluded. Within this pattern, moreover, marriage, family responsibilities and domestic life usually played a very small part. But this was rarely the case for women, for whom domestic life and family relationships were generally far more important than for men. Even those nineteenth- and early twentieth-century women who were celebrated for their intense public involvement, like Josephine Butler or Elizabeth Cady Stanton in the nineteenth century, or Eleanor Roosevelt in the twentieth, for example, were closely enmeshed in domestic and familial responsibilities which took precedence over their public activities for a large portion of their lives. Even if a woman did not marry, she was likely to have close ties to and responsibilities for parents, siblings and relatives and possibly also to live with a close friend.

Although most biographies deal in some way with the marriage, family life and extra-marital relationships of male subjects, the treatment has often been reasonably cursory. It is rare for a biography written before the 1970s to take too much account of the behaviour of a man in relation to his wife and female relatives, or to attempt to see him from their perspective rather than his – and especially if there was any difficulty or tension within these domestic relationships. We have already seen the furore created in the nineteenth century when Froude included discussion of Carlyle's cruel treatment of Jane Welsh Carlyle, and her comments on this, in his biography of Carlyle. This silencing of women, along with the assumption that they were of relatively little account in the telling of man's life story, continued for several more decades. Hence the views and judgements given most weight by the biographer were taken from those who were involved in the same literary or political or scientific circles as their primary subject and often from their male friends.

Looking back at the question of how a new awareness of gender has affected the more traditional framework of biographical writing, one can see two very significant changes since the 1970s. The first is the growing interest in the lives of the mothers, wives and daughters of significant men and the inclusion of more discussion of their familial relationships and treatment of women in the biographies of some prominent men. In part this also reflects a new range of biographical subjects which has come to include the wives and sometimes also the daughters of prominent men. One of the first of these was *Zelda*, looking at the wife of Scott Fitzgerald – and offering a very different picture of Scott Fitzgerald himself in the process. This spate of new biographies of women includes works on Jennie Churchill, Emma Darwin, Jenny Marx, Frieda Lawrence and Martha Freud. In all of these works, what is significant is the recognition of the need to see married women as people in their own right, with their own interests, desires and conflicts, rather than to evaluate them simply in terms of their capacity to fulfil the duties of a wife. Many of these women did not seek a public life for themselves and were content to devote themselves to husbands and families, but even here, the point for their biographers is to show what this actually involved and to demonstrate the intelligence, skill and physical and emotional effort often required to deal with the expectations and demands of their famous husbands and the weight of domestic and familial responsibilities that they were required to shoulder.

Biographies of wives and daughters have taken a collective as well as an individual form. In the United States, there are now several new collective biographies of presidents' wives, for example, as well as studies of particular family groups, like the Roosevelt women.[7] In Britain too, there a number of collective biographies looking at a number of the women who were connected to a particular significant man, for example *The Viceroy's Daughters*, looking at the lives of the three daughters of Lord Curzon; or *Freud's Women*, offering biographical essays of several of the women closely connected to Freud as disciples and translators; or *Dr Johnson's Women*, looking at the close women friends of Samuel Johnson.[8] Like some of these other biographies, this last one was intended both to add a previously ignored element to Johnson's life and to use the correspondence of these women with Johnson to elucidate other aspects of the lives of eighteenth-century women. Women authors hardly feature in Boswell's biography, Norma Clarke pointed out in her Introduction, despite the amount of time that Johnson spent with a number of literary women or his obvious interest in them and enjoyment of their company. In writing about these relationships, Clarke wanted to add this story to a knowledge of his life, but also to show how much insight his correspondence with these women offered into what it meant to be a woman author in the eighteenth century.[9]

There has also been a new interest in exploring in great detail the intimate relationships of public figures, particularly marriage, leading to the publication of a number of works titled 'the biography of a marriage'. Some of these works were intended as much to explore particularly unusual marriages as to throw new light on the individuals involved.

Nigel Nicolson's *Portrait of a Marriage* (1973), for example, explored the extraordinary relationship of his parents, the diplomat Harold Nicolson and the writer Vita Sackville-West, who maintained a close and affectionate marriage in full knowledge of the same-sex relationships in which they were both simultaneously engaged.[10] Others have sought rather to examine the nature of creative and collaborative partnerships, like that of Leonard and Virginia Woolf, or the collaboration between a very different kind of couple, the Victorian bishop Mandel Creichton and his intelligent and very active wife, Louisa.[11] But there are others concerned to stress the importance of marriage and of the contribution of a wife to the life and work of significant men, as one can see in the biographical studies of the marriages of Abraham and Mary Lincoln and of Franklin and Eleanor Roosevelt.[12] And there are also a growing number of studies of the marriages of composers and of literary men: of the German composer Richard Wagner and his English wife, Cosima, or of D. H. and Frieda Lawrence or, once again, Thomas and Jane Welsh Carlyle.[13]

A second result of this concern with gender has been the re-evaluation of some notable men as their relationships with the women closest to them have come to be seen as aspects of their lives that cannot be ignored. The question of how biographers evaluate subjects in terms of their intimate lives and relationships is of course a very complicated one. The changing moral and sexual standards of our own time have tended to produce both a greater interest in the emotional lives and sexual proclivities of others and a much greater tolerance for them, and there is no suggestion here of a new moral turn becoming a feature of biography. Nonetheless, in some cases, familial and sexual relationships have served to question the picture of an individual that can be gained from concentrating on his or her public and social life.

Ironically, in view of his opposition to any discussion of marital or domestic discord in regard to Carlyle, Leslie Stephen was one of the first people whose life was re-evaluated in terms of his behaviour to the women in his family. Shortly after Stephen's death in 1904, his biography was written by the distinguished medieval historian Frederick Maitland, who was also a very close friend of Stephen's and a relative by marriage. Maitland provided a very sympathetic portrait of Stephen, showing him as an intelligent and very sensitive man, sometimes assailed by depression and doubt, but always a congenial companion and much loved by all who knew him.[14] Stephen's daughter, Virginia Woolf, however, knew a very different side of her father, as she made clear in fictional form, in the portrait of Mr Ramsay in *To the Lighthouse* (1927) and then in several autobiographical essays. While genial to his friends, Woolf insisted, to his family Stephen was insensitive, self-obsessed and unbearably demanding. His need for constant emotional support placed a heavy burden on his wife, which was increased after her death as he demanded an inordinate amount of care and support from his daughters and stepdaughter. He required not only that he be given total love, sympathy and devotion but that all his womenfolk share and feel all his emotions. 'When he was sad, he explained to Vanessa, she should be sad; when he was angry, as he was periodically when she asked him for a cheque, she should weep'.[15]

He made it hard for his stepdaughter, Stella Duckworth, to marry and then poisoned her very short married life. After Stella's death, Stephen attempted to follow the same pattern with his older daughter, Vanessa.

Woolf's literary prominence and the fact that critical views of her father were published meant that, however reluctantly, later biographers of Leslie Stephen had to address them. Noel Annan, Stephen's major biographer illustrates this well. In his first book on Stephen, written in the 1950s and before the publication of Woolf's *Reminiscences*, Annan followed Maitland in his depiction of Stephen, sympathising with his suffering after his wife died and taking pleasure in the ways in which first Stella and then Vanessa seemed to offer Stephen all the domestic care and comfort that he needed. They were clearly behaving as dutiful Victorian daughters should! A very different picture is evident in Annan's later biography, *Leslie Stephen: The Godless Victorian* (1984). In this work, Annan tried to put together the different views of Stephen in a chapter entitled 'What Was He Really Like?', in which he discusses Woolf's critical portraits of her father. Quoting Woolf's comment that living with her father was 'like being shut up in the same cage with a wild beast', Annan acknowledges that her views are supported by a great deal of other evidence, all of which illustrates how destructive Stephen's behaviour was to his stepdaughter and how hard he made the lives of his daughters. Seeking an explanation for Stephen's behaviour in his anxieties and emotional vulnerability, Annan stresses the ways in which Stephen sought to break out of the hypersensitivity and weakness that threatened to immobilise him.[16] There is no question of Annan's continuing affection and admiration for Stephen, but in this biography Stephen is depicted as both more complex and more flawed, and as a man whose outrageous domestic behaviour has to be seen as integral to any understanding or assessment of him.

Integrating the questionable domestic or sexual behaviour of greatly admired public figures into their lives has not always been easy for biographers, as one can see in the controversy concerning the relationship between Thomas Jefferson and Sally Hemings, the slave who apparently bore him several children. Sally Hemings, who was the daughter of Jefferson's father-in-law, John Wayles, and his slave, Elizabeth Hemings, was the half-sister of Jefferson's wife, Martha Wayles, and became a member of Jefferson's household shortly after his marriage. She looked after his daughters after the death of their mother in France and subsequently lived at Jefferson's home, Monticello, where her children were born. The suggestion that Jefferson was the father of Hemings's children was first raised by his Republican opponents in 1802 and resurfaced intermittently across the nineteenth and twentieth centuries. But few historians or biographers were prepared to accept it. The question of slavery was, of course, a major issue here. Merrill Peterson in his magisterial study *Jefferson and the New Nation* (1970) saw it as 'a tale that titillated Jefferson's enemies in the neighbourhood of Monticello for years', but was based on inconclusive and highly circumstantial evidence. 'Unless Jefferson was capable of slipping badly out of character in hidden moments', he wrote, 'it is difficult to imagine him caught up in a miscegenous relationship. Such a mixture of the races, such a ruthless exploitation of the master-slave relationship, revolted his whole being.'[17]

Drawing heavily on the reminiscences of Sally Hemings's son, Madison Hemings, and on a psychoanalytic reading of Jefferson's papers, Fawn Brodie attempted to reconstruct the relationship between Jefferson and Sally Hemings.[18] But Brodie's reliance on a psycho-analytic approach, her occasional factual errors, and her attempt to reconstruct the inner dynamic of a relationship for which there was so little direct evidence led both to fierce criticism of her book and to a rejection of her argument.[19] In the last decade, however, through the painstaking work of Annette Gordon-Reed, followed by an investigation of the Jefferson and Hemings DNA, and a recognition of the fact that Jefferson had been at Monticello nine months before the birth of each of Hemings's children made the case irrefutable. Gordon-Reed has since written the story of the extended Hemings family, incorporating Jefferson within it.[20]

Accepting this story as true has been hard for Jefferson biographers.[21] Indeed, even in the last few years, biographies have appeared in which Jefferson's relationship with Sally Hemings is denied.[22] But this new view of Jefferson is now being incorporated into biographical studies of him. It is given a very significant place in Joyce Appleby's *Thomas Jefferson* (2003), for example. This is not just because it raises the question of whether Jefferson was behaving like so many other slave owners in demanding sexual service from a slave but also because of the way in which it highlights his ambivalence about slavery and questions the nature of his commitment to natural rights.[23]

▶ New biographical subjects

One of the reasons that so many feminist scholars and others interested in plebeian or subaltern lives were attracted to the idea of replacing biography as a category with life writing in the 1970s was because it enabled detailed attention to be paid both to the lives of people who would not have been deemed as 'deserving' of a full-scale biography, or indeed have left sufficient records to write one. In the decades since then, the lives of many little-known individuals have been written, drawing on a range of different kinds of evidence and traces that have come to serve in place of a full archive. Women of many kinds have featured prominently in this work as once quite unknown or forgotten figures, like Elizabeth Marsh or Madame de Couvray, have become the subjects of imaginative and fascinating biographies. Seth Kovan's *The Match Girl and the Heiress*, the story of the lives and, as he says, the improbable but close and loving relationship between 'the cherished daughter of a wealthy Baptist ship builder' and the semi-orphaned Cockney who became a match girl at the age of twelve is another important example of this new interest in exploring in detail the lives of people who would once not even have been a footnote in other works.[24]

However, it is not only women who have captured the attention of biographers in the last few decades but also a large range of marginal and obscure men, including political and social dissidents, petty criminals, humble workers, slaves – or occasionally millionaires. Shane White's *Prince of Darkness: The Untold Story of Jeremiah Hamilton, Wall Street's First Black Millionaire*, for example, tells the story of a ruthless, aggressive and intermittently very successful black businessman who was extremely prominent in New York in the 1830s and 1840s, but who has been ignored by historians ever since. To a large extent, White suggests, this is precisely because, as a millionaire and a successful businessman, his 'very existence flies in the face of our understanding of how things were in nineteenth-century New York'.[25]

In most cases, these people have left very few documents behind, and their lives can only be put together using traces and fragments. Beginning with Nellie's death certificate and a few other details, Kovan traced her through census data and records from London School Boards, Poor Law institutions, public asylums, voluntary hospitals and ships logs to and from New Zealand.[26] White too faced a complete lack of the usual sources for a biography as 'there are no letters to or from Hamilton, no diaries or ledgers concerning him in any of the repositories historians usually haunt.' He has never discovered what the 'G' in his name stands for. Hence he too worked with the sources better known to social historians than biographers: newspapers, court cases and government files.

Linda Colley faced a similar problem in researching *The Ordeal of Elizabeth Marsh: A Woman in World History.* Marsh's story was unquestionably a compelling one, which Colley came across while working on her earlier book *Captives: Britain, Empire and the World.* Born in the West Indies in 1735, possibly of mixed-race parents, Marsh went to Morocco but was seized by Moroccan corsairs in 1756 while returning to England. She escaped unscathed – and subsequently wrote about her ordeal in an endeavour to raise money for herself and her children. But Marsh wrote nothing about her subsequent marriage and travel to or around India, or about her return to England to re-join her children. Lacking any letters or documents that offer any direct insight into her sense of her self or her feelings, Colley explores the complex societies in which Marsh lived, including not only Jamaica, Portsmouth, Menorca, Gibraltar at the time of the Seven Years' War, and Morocco, but also the inner life of the Navy Office and the nature of shipboard life. Details are offered about the smuggling trade, the processes of salt production in India and cotton trading.

In all of this, Colley, like Kovan and White, was concerned both to recreate one life – or in Kovan's case, two – and to show the ways in which individuals were caught up in or served to illustrate wider social patterns. Her work, Colley argues, is an account of an individual, a family and a global history. Marsh's life

> co-incided with a distinctive and markedly violent phase of world history in which connections between continents and oceans broadened and altered in multiple ways. These changes in the global landscape repeatedly shaped and distorted Elizabeth Marsh's personal

progress. So this book charts a world in a life and a life in the world. It is also an argument for re-casting and re-evaluating biography as a way of deepening our understanding of the global past.[27]

It is here, and especially in dealing with obscure lives that are linked with or serve to illustrate larger historical patterns, that the overlap between biography and microhistory becomes most noticeable and the difficulty in separating them most pronounced. For microhistorians too have taken a particular interest in exploring the lives of little-known and obscure people and have done some pioneering work in showing how such lives can be both researched and written. Neither White nor Kovan nor Colley describe their work as microhistory, framing it clearly within the methodological approach of biography. But one is hard-pressed to find an absolute way to differentiate between their work and that of Natalie Zemon Davis or Laurel Ulrich or Martha Hodes. The interest of microhistorians in individual lives derives from their concern to gain access to the inner lives, the patterns of thought and belief, the emotions and the voices of ordinary people, especially peasants and workers in past societies who are usually silent. Here too, an episode dealt with at length in court records, or occasionally in memoirs or other public reports or the unexpected discovery of a particular diary or set of letters, has directed the attention of historians towards the study of particular lives and life stories. In many cases, these microhistories focus on particular years rather than whole lives, as records do not permit a comprehensive coverage – but this is equally true for the work of Kovan, White and Colley.

Natalie Zemon Davis's *Return of Martin Guerre* was one of the first and most celebrated of the microhistories focussing on an individual life, taking as its subject the trial of a man accused of assuming the identity of another in the sixteenth century. Using the report of this episode by the prosecutor, the details of the trial and a range of other fragments, Zemon Davis sought to recreate the lives of all of those involved: the imposter, Martin Guerre and his wife. For Davis herself, the key point here was the way in which the report on this incident by one of the presiding judges 'leads us into the hidden world of peasant sentiment and aspiration'.[28] Unusual as the case was, she suggested, the adventures of the three young peasants involved might also offer insights into the emotions and expectations of their neighbours. There were many facets of their lives that remained unknown, but the existing sources on the village from which they came, alongside other sources on sixteenth-century peasant life and customs, provided the basis for recreating something of the lives of those involved.

Davis's very influential work has been followed by a number of others seeking to recreate the lives of obscure individuals from a particular source. Laurel Ulrich's *A Midwife's Tale: The Life of Martha Ballard Based on Her Diary, 1785–1812*, is another such work, using the diary of an ordinary American woman in the late eighteenth and early nineteenth centuries to explore her daily life and to throw light on many aspects of contemporary social life, including the role of women in the household and local market economy, the nature of marriage and sexual relations, and some aspects of medical practice. Martha Hanna's *Your Death Would Be Mine. Paul and Marie Pireaud in the Great War* (2006), looks at the relationship of a young soldier and his wife through the letters that they wrote to each other while separated during the First World War. Like Davis, Hanna provides some discussion of the earlier and later lives and the personalities of her subjects, Paul and Marie Pireaud. But she concentrates on the time period covered by their correspondence and seeks to use their story 'to understand in new ways aspects of the First World War that have previously been viewed only through a wide-angle lens' and to stress the intimacy of their correspondence in order to argue that soldiers were not alienated from family or home concerns during the war, but rather maintained a close interest in those at home while sharing with their loved ones a great deal about their own experiences.[29]

Davis's influence is also cited in works dealing with larger family groups such as Emma Rothschild's *The Inner Life of Empires: An Eighteenth-Century History*. Rothschild's work focuses on the Johnstone family, their households, friends, servants and slaves. This was not a prominent or celebrated family, although some members of it were quite successful and had notable connections. But, as Rothschild explains, 'They lived amidst new empires, and they were confronted throughout their lives with large and abstract questions about commerce and the state, laws and regulations, slavery and servitude.'[30] Rothschild sees her work as a new kind of microhistory because it explores 'new ways of connecting the microhistories of individuals and families to the larger scenes of which they were a part'. She sees different ways of connecting the microhistory to the macrohistory of the time: through the significance of some individuals and their explicit connection with the wider financial or political world, through their capacity to serve as a case study and through raising the question of their representativeness – or their absence of representativeness. Her focus throughout is on their inner life, their minds and sentiments and the ways they are affected by or influence their wider social and financial activity.

While dealing with particular lives, all of these works are seen by their authors as microhistories rather than biographies. The concern of their authors is to use these lives to show wider social patterns or to provide a mirror onto the society in which they live. Nonetheless, their works share many features with biography and are often read as biography by others. Their focus on only one particular episode or period in the lives of their subjects in not a problem here. Indeed, as Richard Holmes's comment on new directions in biography suggests, concentrating on one particularly crucial episode or period in the life of an individual or family has served to provide new ways of thinking about the possibility that biography might not cover the entire life of its subject, but rather deal only with one particularly significant part of that life, using it sometimes to illuminate the whole. This need to confine attention to that part or those parts of a life for which there is adequate source material is but one of the new approaches that has become necessary in addressing the lives of new biographical subjects who rarely left the extensive private and public papers on which earlier biographers had depended.

Jill Lepore has suggested that the emphasis within microhistory on using a life to illustrate a particular historical pattern or development differs from the biographer's belief in the uniqueness of his or her subject.[31] This sense of addressing wider historical concerns within microhistory, she suggests, also tends to distance the historian from the subject and to lessen the intense involvement of author and subject which is integral to so much biography. But while these differences, like those concerning the treatment of only some years rather than a whole life, may be possible to sustain if one is contrasting a biography of a prominent individual who left a full archive of personal and public papers to the study of a barely literate individual or of a rural couple with limited education who left only very limited material behind, they become less cogent when one is dealing with the current range of biographical subjects.

Ultimately, it seems to me more helpful to accept the similarities between biography and microhistory than to seek any rigid form of differentiation. The ways in which some books are given both terms seems to me helpful here in pointing out the overlap between the two and emphasising the ways in which microhistory and current historical biography share research methods, interpretive structures and also a sense that individual lives can tell the story of a particular – even a unique – individual while illustrating wider historical patterns. This overlap can be seen in many works that are presented as biographies. Martha Hodes's *The Sea Captain's Wife* provides a useful illustration. Based on a chance discovery of the letters of a previously unknown American woman, Eunice Merrill, the biography explores how Merrill found a way out of extreme poverty in the mid-nineteenth century by marrying an African Caribbean sea captain. Hodes is able to depict much of Merrill's earlier life and to follow her through her marriage. But there are years when there are no letters and no information about what she did, and there are major gaps in the information about the family to whom her letters were written, few of whose answers are available. Hence it is a biography with notably significant gaps. It is also a biography designed to tell a wider story. One of Hodes' key interests is to explore Merrill's cross-racial marriage in order to use it to illustrate the complexities of racism in the nineteenth century. She is particularly interested in analysing the different responses to this cross-racial marriage from Merrill's white American family, on the one hand, and from the local community in Cayman where they settled, on the other. Indeed, although Hodes was unapologetic about writing biography, for her, as for microhistorians, the illustrative capacity of this life is more important than the study of the life for its own sake.

In these works, as in many microhistories, writers struggle with limited materials, necessitating a hunt for clues and traces of evidence that have to be read in particular ways. In many of these works, the story of the search, the ways in which an understanding of the subject has been obtained and the issues involved in attempting to construct the life are incorporated into the text so that the biographer or the microhistorian is present throughout, explaining his or her approach and methods. The gaps in the record call for the exercise of imagination, and both microhistorians and some biographers have stressed the need to draw on their imaginations in order to produce their work. There is no suggestion here that the use of imagination makes the work into a fiction. On the contrary, Zemon Davis and others stress that their use of imagination is contained within the documents and sources available, and depends on their detailed knowledge of the period and place under discussion.

All of these issues are raised and discussed in Nina Gelbart's biography *The King's Midwife: A History and Mystery of Madame du Coudray*, the study of an eighteenth-century French midwife. This work, although similar in many ways to microhistory is emphatically presented as a biography. Gelbart came across du Coudray while doing other research on eighteenth-century France. As the title of Gelbart's work suggests, as the midwife charged with the task of improving maternity services and decreasing infant mortality throughout France in the second half of the eighteenth century, du Coudray was very prominent in her own lifetime. But the material available for a biography was very limited. Although du Coudray published manuals on midwifery and left many letters connected to her work, there are no private papers of any kind. Indeed, in the hundreds of letters of Mme du Coudray, there was not a single mention of her parents, childhood, siblings, education, young adulthood, training, marriage, children or friends. Gelbart sought to fill in some of the details by following Coudray's footsteps, and tried in this way to get a sense of the pattern of her life.

> I learned where she had lived during her stay, I wandered her neighbourhood, I smelled the waxy interior of churches where she baptized babies, I strolled along the rivers where water carriages sometimes carried her baggage, I ate regional specialities that she must have enjoyed, I explored numerous *hotels de ville* (town halls) where she gave her lessons in the main hall ... These are the things I could see today that make hers what Henry James calls a 'visitable past'. The rest I had to imagine.[32]

Gelbart came to feel that the obliteration of all private records was intentional on du Coudray's part, 'as if she chose to mute the feminine core of her being in exchange for appropriating the prerogatives of male behaviour'. But Gelbart herself *wanted* to tell the private as well as the public story and felt that she and du Coudray were locked into a struggle which led her to reflect on 'the nature of the historian's craft in general, the relationship between biographer and biographee, and on my particular subject, a woman who left behind a record at once so full and so spare'. Here too, the scarcity of material led to new approaches to the writing of the life. Gelbart abandoned any attempt at a chronological structure, using a thematic approach and inserting herself into the narrative by discussing the questions that arose for her as she sought to fill in the background to du Coudray's life and tried to establish the precise identities of all the people that du Coudray mentioned and to establish their importance in her life and story.

A similar determination to write the biography of a woman who was once very prominent, but for whom there are now few sources is evident in Nell Irving Painter's work on Sojourner Truth, the nineteenth-century African American feminist and anti-slavery agitator. After her death, Truth was quite well known as a very a significant figure in nineteenth-century feminist and abolitionist history. But though she appears at some dramatic moments in the histories of those movements, little was known of the details of her life. There was no possibility of letters in this case, as Truth was illiterate. She had dictated the story of her life to a sympathetic white auditor, and it had been published as *The Narrative of Sojourner Truth* in 1850. But although this narrative offers some information, it poses as many questions as it supplies answers, and needs to be used with very great care.[33]

It is imperative that biographers not be put off by the absence of conventional written sources, Painter argues, and that they find alternative material to work with. The Sojourner Truth biographical problem, she insists, 'becomes a larger question of how to deal with people who are in History but who have not left the kinds of sources to which historians and biographers ordinarily turn. In order not to cede biography to subjects who had the resources to secure the educations that would allow them the leave the usual sources for the usual kind of biographies, we need to construct a new biographical approach'.[34]

Painter herself made extensive use of the photographs and other visual images that have served to make a symbol of Sojourner Truth and of the many descriptions and stories of her provided by the religious communities with which she was involved. Using a variety of psychological and psychoanalytic insights, she has also sought to delve into the story presented in the dictated narrative and to get a sense of the inner life beneath. She was concerned particularly to try to understand the ways in which Truth dealt with the many losses, the physical and sexual abuse and the hardships which she had experienced. In doing this, she insisted on the need to see and understand Sojourner Truth as an individual living a particular life rather than merely as the symbol of a number of important causes. Like Davis and Gelbart, she makes clear that this approach has required some imaginative latitude in dealing with possible occurrences and with feelings for which there is no absolutely clear evidence.

▶ The individual and the wider world

Unlike most other biographers, for whom the particular personality and experiences of an individual subject is the primary concern, many historians insist that they are interested in events that extend beyond the individual, in examining lives 'in dialectical relationship to the multiple social, political, and cultural worlds they inhabit and give meaning to', and in exploring the ways in which, or the points at which, an individual and a society intersect. The larger objective of the historian who writes biography, David Nasaw suggests, 'is not simply to tell a life story, though often they do that well, but to deploy the individual in the study of the world outside that individual and to explore how the private informs the public and vice versa'.[35]

In Nasaw's view, this focus on the wider historical picture occurs at the expense of the individual personality and character. Historians, he insists, 'are neither equipped for, nor capable of, nor for the most part interested in constructing individual portraits with the density and depth of characterization that are available to and prized by writers who are differently bound by their evidence'.[36] This claim seems to me entirely incorrect. I do not accept it in my own work, nor would many others. Blanche Wiesen Cook, for example, while obviously working as an historian, and both knowledgeable and concerned about the world in which Eleanor Roosevelt lived, offers an incomparable and intimate portrait of her. As Cook saw it, her challenge was to answer the questions: 'Who in fact was Eleanor Roosevelt? What were the sources of her strength? What did she really think? What of the great range of her writings? How did she spend her days?' Her study is, of course, 'a life and times', offering a reconsideration of the events that served to define a life, and a life that served to define events. But it offers as detailed a discussion of Roosevelt's emotional life and development, of her personality and character, of her marriage, her familial difficulties and relationships and of her friendships as can be found in any biography preoccupied with an individual life. The picture is given added depth by Cook's historical knowledge, of course, as it is by her feminist interests and commitments. But it combines its interest in the world around with a very close focus on its actual subject.

This question of how best to relate the individual to the wider world is one that has been taken up by a number of historical biographers. What is new here is the move beyond the recognition that one needs to understand the world in which individuals lived, if one is depict their lives fully and to make sense of their ideas and activities, emotions and beliefs, and the insistence on the importance of this wider world in terms of how a particular life was enabled, how the exercise of power was possible or even how a set of ideas developed. This new attention to context has served to transform some biographical studies in recent years.

I am not suggesting here that context is not dealt with by other biographers. On the contrary, its importance been stressed in serious biographical writing for well over a century. Leslie Stephen deplored the hazy understanding of the time and place in which an individual lived and worked in much nineteenth-century biography. He insisted that all contributors to the *DNB* place the actions and ideas of their subjects within the appropriate social, intellectual or political context and that they also indicate the current state of historical scholarship in any area of their life or thought. Leon Edel was equally insistent about the need to understand context and locate a subject within it in his *Principia Biographica*. And there can be no question of the extent or depth of the understanding of the appropriate context in the work of many major contemporary biographers. Richard Holmes, Victoria Glendenning, Michael Holroyd and Clare Tomalin, for example, all place their biographical subjects within their social and literary worlds with extreme skill, offering insights also into the ways in which added depth can be brought to their inner lives and emotional registers by an understanding of the wider world in which people lived.

This approach to context is nonetheless very different from that of historians like Ian Kershaw or Richard Bosworth or Janet Browne, for whom context has a deeper meaning and importance. Their use of context is similar to much of the writing on women's lives as it is in microhistory. But in the work of these historians, it assumes a new importance in the lives of prominent and powerful individuals as well. Rather than depicting major political figures or leading scientists as exceptional individuals who dominate their worlds and are exceptional in every way, these historians point in their biographies to the extent to which their subjects shared and embodied values, beliefs and attitudes that were widely held within their own societies, and stress the importance of that society in making or allowing the exceptional individual to engage in his or her most significant endeavours.

One can see both the importance and the novelty of this new approach to context in comparing the two most widely read British biographies of Hitler: Alan Bullock's *Hitler: A Study in Tyranny* (1952) and Ian Kershaw's *Hitler: A Biography* (2008).[37] In the preface to his book, Bullock explains the two questions the book is seeking to answer, both of which came from issues raised at the Nuremburg Trials.

> The first ... was to discover how great a part Hitler played in the History of the Third Reich and whether Göring and the other defendants were exaggerating when they claimed that under the Nazi regime the will of one man, and of one man alone, was decisive. This led to the second and larger question: if the picture of Hitler given at Nuremberg was substantially accurate, what were the gifts Hitler possessed which enabled him first to secure and then to maintain such power.[38]

In order to do this, Bullock proposed to reconstruct Hitler's life from birth to death in the hopes that this reconstruction would enable him to account for his puzzling career. He begins immediately to explore Hitler's birth and early life in an attempt to provide the clues to his career. Underlying the whole study is a sense of Hitler's power, capacity and will, the things that made him such a great and evil ruler.

Kershaw rejects this approach completely. He rejects entirely the idea of 'historical greatness' implicit in the writing of conventional biography, arguing that 'it is a red-herring: misconstrued, pointless, irrelevant, and potentially apologetic'. It is an idea that emphasises the actions of an individual and minimises the importance of those who promoted, sustained and gave backing to his rule. His central concern, as he explains in a lengthy preface, is to explore the nature of Hitler's power, using Weber's concept of 'charismatic authority' and hence emphasising his belief in the importance of the hold Hitler exercised over his followers. To understand Hitler's power, it is necessary to come to terms with the political and social world of Germany which allowed Hitler to exercise that power. The important question, he insists, is to explain how someone with so few intellectual gifts and social attributes, someone no more than an empty vessel outside his political life, unapproachable and impenetrable even for those in his close company ... Without the background that bred high office, without even any experience of government before becoming Reich Chancellor, could nevertheless have such an immense historical impact.

Hitler is not for him the kind of person about whom a conventional biography can really be written. He was an 'unperson' with almost no personal life or history outside political events. His entire being was subsumed within the role of Fuhrer. Hence it is only the character of his power that can really be studied, and this was a 'social product ... a creation of social expectations and motivations invested in Hitler by his followers'. His personality and his actions were of course significant in his gaining and maintaining power, but they were no more significant than the expectations and motivations of German society. Hence Kershaw's study, while certainly discussing the childhood that so many have seen as the key to Hitler's personality and his rule, places much greater emphasis on the state of Germany and on those who made his way and gave him opportunities and support.[39]

Richard Bosworth modified Kershaw's approach in his 2002 biography *Mussolini*. Although intrigued by Kershaw's approach, he could not see that it fitted Mussolini. Mussolini did have a private life and a successful career before 1914, and once in office, he was a careful and conscientious executive. Once he became prime minister in 1922, even though some parallels with Hitler emerge, it is impossible to see Mussolini as charismatic in the same way or to accept that Italy had a Fascist 'revolution' that Mussolini led without restraint. Nor was Italy like Germany. There were too many 'Italies', and too many people still immersed in family and region to accept the dominance of nation and ideology that were so important in Germany. But while rejecting the idea of Mussolini as a charismatic leader, Bosworth does so in order to point to a different kind of relationship between Mussolini and his followers from that evident in Germany. It was not the case that Italians tried to do Mussolini's will, he argues, but rather that he worked towards them, trying to be popular and accommodating, but not always succeeding. Ultimately, Mussolini did not even dictate, Bosworth argues, but was swept along by a destiny which took him from the provinces to a blinding but brittle glory, and which ended in a squalid and deserved death. 'As a man and a fascist "thinker", Mussolini was adamant that he possessed absolute free will. But in this contention, as in so many matters, he was wrong.'[40]

A slightly different emphasis on the importance of context is evident in Judith Brown's *Nehru: A Political Life* (2003). Rather than stressing the specific family background, education, and personal abilities and characteristics that brought Nehru to power and determined his political life and activities, as other biographers do, she points rather to the generation to which he belonged and whose aspirations he served to illustrate. He 'was a man who belonged to a crucial generation in the history of Asia, and whose life thus illuminates the lives of many of his contemporaries. It shows the diversity and complexity of the major issues which confronted them in a time of profound and unusually rapid transition.'[41] In keeping with this approach, Brown begins her biography with a chapter on 'India and the British Raj: Opportunity and Challenge', in which she explores the complex nature of imperial rule and of Indian society at the turn of the twentieth century in order to show the situation and the problems and opportunities that Nehru and his contemporaries faced. This prelude provides the background to a close analysis of Nehru's personal and familial life, his education and intellectual make-up, his vision of India and the political battles and compromises in which he was engaged, and the personal struggles that left him often at odds with himself and with those around. Nehru's life, she insists, was emphatically a political one, dominated by political questions and concerns – and it was one in which, as Nehru himself recognised, deep and intimate family relations were often sacrificed to politics. But throughout, the concern is simultaneously to explore Nehru's life and through it to offer an insight into the inner world of the men and women of his generation.

This question of linking the lives of political leaders and the worlds in which they live has also been done in other ways. Some of these draw rather more clearly on the approaches developed through those interested in the biographies of little-known women and men. In *Garibaldi: Invention of a Hero*, Lucy Riall explicitly drew on the idea of 'self-fashioning' developed by Natalie Zemon Davis, Carolyn Steedman and Nell Painter in their studies of women and men who were excluded from the public sphere but who fashioned different versions of themselves in ways that gave them some kind of agency or power. Garibaldi was not excluded from the public sphere. But what interested Riall was how he had come to have the very high position that he occupied there and what he had done to promote it. Looking at all his own speeches, statements and writing and at the different ways in which he was represented by others and in the press, she argued that Garibaldi played a very significant role in his own image and standing. He fashioned himself as a popular hero, moulding his achievements to meet the wishes and expectations of his audience. Biography and his telling of his own life story were an integral part of this self-fashioning, and Riall pays particular attention to 'his prodigious talent for political mobilization and communication'.[42]

A very different approach can be seen in John Bew's award-winning *Citizen Clem: A Biography of Attlee*. Bew is interested here in trying to get a clearer insight into 'Attlee's brain and heart, before the age of Attlee fades from view entirely'.[43] He is also concerned to explore more deeply the seeming paradox whereby this most unremarkable of British prime ministers led a government that transformed Britain in the period from 1945 to 1951 – and to look at how one writes and engages an audience in writing about someone as unassuming as Attlee. The contrast with Churchill, with whom Attlee worked so closely and cooperatively throughout the Second World War and about whom so much has been written, is constantly pointed to by Bew, who argues that the insatiable appetite for books on Churchill 'have created something of an imbalance in our understanding of twentieth-century history'.[44] Attlee's resolute refusal to make dramatic speeches or to engage in dramatic gestures and his lack of any sense of self-importance make him an unusual political leader and one in many ways hard to write about. But he was, Bew argues, a man of strong views and values, with impressive negotiating and parliamentary skills. His life is also far more emblematic and representative of Britain in his time than was that of Churchill. Indeed, Bew argues

> it is difficult to think of another individual through whom one can better tell Britain's story from the high imperialism of Queen Victoria's Golden Jubilee of 1887, through two world wars, the Great Depression, the nuclear age and the cold war, and the transition from empire into commonwealth.

Thus Attlee serves in an incomparable way to reflect the values and beliefs of the society in which he lived, even while dramatically transforming it.

It is not just in biographies of political leaders that context is coming to have a new importance, but also in those dealing with leading scientists. One can see it particularly clearly in biographies of the dominating scientific figure of the nineteenth century, Charles Darwin. Here too, a comparison between earlier approaches and those current now is helpful. For most of the 20th century, biographies of Darwin concentrated on the magnitude and importance of his major scientific work, his development of the theory of evolution. Despite its quaint phrasing, Leonard Huxley's short biography of Darwin, published in 1921, offers a good illustration of earlier approaches. Huxley begins with a brief discussion of 1809, the year of Darwin's birth and one which also saw the birth of many others 'who profoundly modified the world into which they were born'.[45] His biography, Huxley explains, will explore 'What manner of man was he who put this new and fruitful life into the ancient evolutionary idea? How was he equipped for the task by his natural birthright and his early education?'

Huxley's approach contrasts markedly to that taken by Janet Browne in her celebrated biography of Darwin. At the start of her work, Browne rephrases Huxley's question in ways that point to a radically different answer. How, she asks, did 'the most unspectacular person of all time', produce one of the most radical books of the nineteenth century and indeed become in many ways its dominating figure? Darwin himself was quite unable to explain this. One answer, Browne suggests, 'surely lies in the intricate relations between a man, his ideas and the public. Darwinism was made by Darwin *and* Victorian society.' Darwin himself, Browne insists, was quite unable to see this connection. As a believer in the Victorian ethos of character, 'in the inbuilt advantages of mind', he unconsciously endorsed the cult of great men and public heroes that was so much part of nineteenth-century life.

> He did not – could not see – that figures like himself were the product of a complex interweaving of personality and opportunity with the movements of the times. Scientific ideas

and scientific fame did not come automatically to people who worked hard and collected insects, as Darwin seems to have half hoped they would. A love of natural history could not, on its own, take a governess or a mill-worker to the top of the nineteenth-century intellectual tree.[46]

The point here for Browne is the need not simply to take Darwin's family connections, wealth and social privilege for granted, but to stress their importance in enabling him to take up natural science and to pursue his own interests. More than this, she insists that his work itself was 'a social process'. He did not sit in the middle of Victorian society soaking up the overriding themes of the age.

> On the contrary, Victorian society made him. He built his theories out of information phys-
> ically extracted from others. He knew how to charm, how to make people help him. And
> the collaboration was always hierarchical, with Darwin acting as a greedy spider, throwing
> out a thread here, pulling in a fly there ... By no means can the *origin* be seen as an indi-
> vidual triumph.

Whereas Browne's key concern here is to insist on the importance to Darwin of the supportive world without which he could not have done his great work, and hence to move away from the idea of an individual genius living and working in isolation, the way in which she discusses her own biographical approach points to another change in biographical practice. For the most part, standard biographies of prominent individuals have been concerned primarily with telling their story, beginning with a discussion of the family of origin. Reflecting on the nature of their endeavour, on their approach and sources and on what they want their biography to do has been the preserve of those dealing with new subjects, many of whom have felt it incumbent upon themselves to explain their choice and to indicate why they see their subject as important. At the present time, however, even amongst those writing about dominant men, and especially those rejecting traditional approaches to biography, there is a tendency to begin with a reflective introduction or chapter in which the author sets out his or her own approach to biography in general and to that of this subject in particular. It is in these reflections that one can see most clearly the importance now accorded to biography and the new sense of its close ties to history.

Conclusion

▶ History and the individual life

As the previous chapters have shown, the question of the relationship of biography to history has been extensively debated over many centuries. This question has become the subject of renewed interest, in part because the breaking down of once accepted models of biography and the emergence of new approaches to history have suggested a range of new ways of formulating and interpreting the link between them. In the nineteenth and much of the twentieth century, discussion of the relationship of biography to history focused primarily on the biographies of significant political or religious figures and on their importance in national or institutional histories. The general issue here centred on how to assess the role and importance of individuals in history at a time when social and economic structures were assuming ever greater importance. But the breaking down of the singular model of biography along with the emergence of new categories like auto/biography and life writing, on the one hand, and new kinds of history, including women's history, social history, the history of sexuality and the new imperial history, on the other, have greatly expanded the ways in which individual life stories can be seen in relation to wider historical patterns. All of these newer forms of history are concerned to a greater or lesser extent with the lives and experiences of relatively little-known 'ordinary' or obscure individuals rather than with men (and occasionally women) of power and influence. Hence, rather than focusing attention in the importance of an individual life in affecting historical change, they raise questions about the illustrative or representative capacities of individual lives and about the insights that particular lives may offer into aspects of the past which otherwise remain hidden.

For some historians, this use of individual lives in order to explore or illustrate wider historical themes makes biography more important for history. Others, however, choose rather to see it as a way of approaching lives that differentiates historical endeavour from biography. Even some of those who write about famous individuals, exploring their lives from birth to death, reject the description of biography for their own work, preferring to see it as using 'the medium of "life histories" of individuals to probe a key historical issue', or as using an individual life to 'help us to see not only into particular events but into the larger cultural and social and even political processes of a moment in time'.[1] In a similar vein, some of those who work on the lives of obscure and humble folk, micro-history is often a preferred designation. Sometimes this label seems particularly justified when fragmentary documentation doesn't allow for a full-scale biography – or because the interest of the author was focussed on a particular aspect of a life or a particular episode within it. It is worth noting with the prominent biographers, like Richard Holmes, see no difficulty in encompassing obscure lives, partial lives or group lives within the framework of biography, welcoming the way that these newer approaches make biography a more capacious and inclusive category. Some historians take a different approach, continuing to insist that their work on an individual is not biography and seeking ways to underline the differences between their own approach and some fairly fixed notion of what a biog-raphy is.[2]

What seems curious here is the way in which moving away from the term 'biography' seems to solve the problem for these historians – rather than pointing to what seems to me to be the larger underlying issue of what precisely the use of any individual life can do in explaining or exploring a wider historical pattern. The absence of any discussion of this issue is a remarkable feature of much microhistory. The term 'microhistory' clearly signals a connection with a wider macrohistory, and those who have been engaged with it have often stressed their concern not simply to elucidate particular lives but also to give voice to humble or plebeian folk rather than seeing them either in statistical terms or only through the words of others. Carlo Ginzburg's *The Cheese and the Worms* is a case in point.[3] In bringing forward the beliefs and ideas, the cosmogony and the heretical world view of the miller Menocchio in his own words, Ginzburg sought to show in a detailed and quali-tative way the mental life and map of a particular humble individual. He noted his desire to take issue with an essay by Furet in the Annales, in which he asserted that the history of the subaltern classes in preindustrial societies can only be studied from a statistical point of view. Ginzburg's path-breaking work brought Menocchio – and not only his views but his very words – in to view.

But for Ginzburg, as for many other historians, the idea that one is accessing an authen-tic voice is of such great importance as to render other questions irrelevant: whether that voice is typical or exceptional and therefore what exactly it tells us about the world from which it came.

Ginzburg's work was of great importance to other historians of early modern Europe concerned to explore not only the beliefs but also the nature of the emotional life and sub-jectivity of the pre-industrial peasantry, including Natalie Zemon Davis and Lyndal Roper. But what is interesting in all of this discussion is the very limited reflection, either while the work in question was being written or after, that these authors offer about the insights that the particular life stories or the mental maps that were being presented provide into the broader historical period in which they were located and the methodological issues that this reliance on an individual life raised.

Critics of microhistory have certainly raised questions about whether the figures whom Carlo Ginzburg, Giovanni Levi or Natalie Zemon Davis have made so memorable were typical or exceptional and therefore precisely how their stories illuminate the wider social and cultural world, but for the most part these historians themselves have had little to say about it. This is not, of course, to suggest that these works lack methodological reflection. On the contrary, Ginzburg, Levi and Davis have all discussed at some length the theoretical underpinnings of their work. Anthropology was often formative in their approach to and understanding of the plebeian cultures that they sought to explore, and so too were different ways of approaching literature and literary criticism. But their concern has been far more to demonstrate the ways in which their theoretical approach and their reading of sources ensures the accuracy of their stories and interpretations than to argue for the overall significance of these individual cases in terms of the wider historical world. All of them clearly see the reconstruction of particular episodes in the lives of individuals and an understanding of those individuals as offering important historical insights into 'the hidden world of peasant sentiment and aspiration'.[4]

But the unusual nature of the cases that they sometimes choose has raised questions for critics about how much the cases actually reveal about the wider historical period. Davis has commented on her interest in 'decentring', or telling the story of the past from outside the world of powerful elites, often through marginal figures or ones who cross cultural and geographical barriers and in ways that 'introduce plural voices into the account'.[5] In the Introduction to *Trickster Travels: A Sixteenth-Century Muslim between Two Worlds*, Davis makes clear her disinclination to engage in a lengthy discussion of this issue. As a Muslim, captured by pirates and imprisoned by Pope Leo X until he converted to Christianity, her subject, known generally as *Leo Africanus*, but increasingly to her as al-Hasan al-Wazan as she came to know more about him, allowed her to explore how a man moved between and understood different cultural, political and religious worlds. He was, she accepts, an extreme case as few other Muslims were captured by Christian pirates or handed over to the pope, but she adds enigmatically, 'an extreme case can often reveal patterns available for more everyday experience and writing'.[6]

This problem was recognised by Emma Rothschild in *The Inner life of Empires: An Eighteenth-Century History*, but not in any way resolved. Rothschild describes her work on the Johnstone family as 'a microhistory, or a prosopography, a history of persons (of the face or the person in front of one's eye.).'[7] But she insists that it is also a new kind of microhiostory. Partly this is because it is a history of diverse individuals (including landowners, servants and slaves) living across vast spaces. But it is also new, she insists, 'because it is an exploration of new ways of connecting the microhistories of individuals and families to the larger histories of which they were a part'. Some of the individuals are important in their own right. There are other connections too that focus on the capacity of the Johnstones to offer a case study of a larger phenomenon. But this in turn depends on how one sees the Johnstones' representativeness – or their absence of representativeness. Rothschild does not really make clear precisely how she sees the Johnstones in relation to these general questions, pointing rather to the importance of the ways in which her study leads readers into the minds and sentiments of the Johnstones and their world. But by raising the issue, she does at least make clear the need to address explicitly this connection between individual lives and wider historical patterns. She also raises the possibility that this may be done differently in different works, depending on the nature of the subject and of the sources.

The use of individual lives to explore or illustrate wider themes is not confined to biographers or microhistorians. On the contrary, contemporary historians working in very diverse fields also focus attention on individual lives as a way to illustrate broader social trends and patterns. Catherine Hall and Leonore Davidoff's *Family Fortunes: Men and Women of the English Middle Class, 1780–1950* was one of the earliest works to use it. Davidoff and Hall insisted that 'the only way to trace the shifts in middle-class society and gender relations was to look in detail at local communities and particular individuals'. Their book begins with a portrait of James Luckcock a radical Birmingham jeweller, whose poems, autobiography and didactic writing, they argue, 'provide clues to the deep connections between religious belief, political practice, commercial activity and family life', the connections that have to be unravelled if one is to understand the inner dynamic of middle-class culture.[8] It is made clear throughout the work that, though Luckcock is not typical in any simple way, his beliefs and ideas as expressed in his extant writing serve to illustrate beliefs and values that were widely held in the middle-class society from which he came. The detailed portrayal of him provides a way both to concretise these views and to show how they work in a particular set of circumstances.

A similar approach is evident in many later analyses of women and middle-class family life, such as Eleanor Gordon and Gwyneth Nair's *Public Lives: Women, Family and Society in Victorian Britain*.[9] But of course it is evident elsewhere too, notably in some important histories of imperialism, including Linda Colley's *Captives* or Antoinette Burton's *At the Heart of the Empire: Indians and the Colonial Encounter in Late-Victorian Britain* or Catherine Hall's *Civilising Subjects*. Bill Schwarz's *The White Man's World* quite explicitly embraces a biographical approach in his concern to explore the notion of the white man and of the white man's country within British imperial culture. For Schwarz, then, stories of individual life and the concept of 'men's bodies' are essential if one is to understand not just the outlook, but the very construction of the idea of the white man in the later nineteenth century.

> The white man of the late nineteenth century, I suggest, was the product of an entire discursive apparatus. Both the state and powerful institutions were active in his making. His body, his sexual practices, his family arrangements, his contacts with others: all were regulated.[10]

In all of these works, the individual story works to explain and embody particular views or experiences and thus to expand understanding of their complexity.

A similar approach is evident in several works of social and sexual history. Seth Kovan's *Slumming: Sexual and Social Politics in Victorian London*, for example, on the radical priest James Adderley. There is no suggestion here that Adderley is typical. On the contrary, as Koven makes very clear, James Granville Adderley, with whom he begins his book, was 'far too iconoclastic to be representative of anything, but his life provides one point of entry into the lives of the men and women whose philanthropic labours are the subject of this book'.[11] As one who gave up the privileges of birth and wealth to live an impoverished celibate life amongst the poor, Adderley, Koven suggests, points to the need to explore the complex psychological and personal reasons why so many privileged young men and women devoted their lives to living in urban slums and serving their inhabitants in the later part of the nineteenth century. He is important not as an exemplar, but rather as one who shows the need to encompass the psychological and the sexual in any attempt to explain the pervasiveness of a social phenomenon once rather easily dismissed as a middle-class fad.

What I want to emphasise here is the similarity in approach between many of those who are writing works that they describe as historical biography with others who describe their work as microhistory – or who eschew such descriptions altogether and simply rely on individual voices and particular lives to illustrate their historical analysis or story, seeking to encompass actual voices and lives in their work or to embody the patterns or issues with which they are dealing in particular individuals or lives. These similarities can easily be seen in the emphasis within much historical biography on the need to link individual lives, beliefs, activities and even achievements more closely to the world in which they were produced in order to both understand and evaluate them and also because of what the particular case contributes to an understanding of a specific historical period or issue or set of beliefs and practices. A wider recognition of the similarities between the ways in which different kinds of history now focus on individual lives might make it possible to move beyond the somewhat limited terms in which current debates about the place of biography in history occur.

What seems noticeable here is that rather than there being a complete contrast between biography and history, there is a continuum that goes from the use of particular anecdotes about individuals, through different kinds of individual case studies, to works that seeks to explore historical issues and developments primarily through a detailed focus on an individual life – or a group of such lives.

Linking these different kinds of historical writings also seems to me to allow more recognition of the ongoing methodological questions that are rarely discussed and that sometimes slip through the net in debates about biography and history; these questions concern both the value and the problems that come from focussing heavily on individual lives in historical writing. What would be valuable here in both work called biography and that designated rather as history or microhistory is more analysis and reflection on what is being offered or suggested in each particular case in which an individual life forms the core of an historical interpretation. In some of the works dealt with in this book, it is clear that the individual is seen as illustrative of something that is typical or at least widespread, or that it becomes influential and even dominant. But in others, the case of Menocchio in *The Cheese and the Worms*, or equally in Martha Hodes's *The Sea Captain's Wife*,[12] what we are being offered is a life or a world view that is extraordinary and that changes our understanding of a period by bringing into view characters or situations that were previously not only unknown but almost unimaginable. Hodes leaves us in no doubt about her recognition of how unusual are the experiences of Eunice Connolly who, as a white woman who had known extreme hardship and poverty in her first marriage, found both emotional and financial security in marrying a black Jamaican sea captain, much to the horror of her family. As she makes clear, both the story and the fact that sufficient traces of it in the form of letters remain to be able to tell it are unusual.[13] The story, in her view, illustrates both how complex and, in some circumstances, how permeable racial boundaries were in North America in the nineteenth century. Ultimately what needs to be discussed and thought about in greater detail and more generally is the great importance currently accorded the study of individual lives in the writing of history and the many different ways in which such lives can be written.

Glossary

Annales A school of French social historians initially grouped around the journal *Annales*, including such historians as Lucien Febvre, Marc Bloch and Fernand Braudel, who sought to observe the long- and medium-term evolution of economy, society and civilisation.

Annaliste A member of the *Annales* school.

charismatic This term comes from Max Weber, who applied it to a certain quality of an individual personality by virtue of which this person is set apart from ordinary men and treated as endowed with supernatural, superhuman or at least specifically exceptional powers or qualities.

ethnographic A methodological strategy used to provide descriptions of human societies, founded on the idea that humans are best understood in the fullest possible context.

feminism A variety of beliefs, theories, philosophies and movements, all of which are concerned with issues of gender difference and advocate equality for women or campaign for women's rights and interests.

gender The socially constructed notions of femininity and masculinity, in contrast to sex, which is defined as biological difference.

gendered assumptions The ways in which ideas that incorporate particular beliefs about gender are used without any recognition that this is occurring.

Holocaust The mass murder of the Jews by the Nazis in the Second World War of 1939–45.

interiority Inner states of mind, and deep and often unexpressed feelings and desires.

materialist   Originally, the term applied to those who believed that nothing exists except matter and its movements and modifications. In history, it refers more often to the Marxist conception of historical development, which conceives historical change as proceeding through a dialectic between human needs and capacities and the material conditions and productive apparatus available to societies at particular times.

mentalités   The beliefs, outlook, values and attitudes of a person or group of people, including their understanding of the world and their conception of their place within it.

microhistory   First developed in the 1970s, microhistory is the study of the past on a very small scale. Most commonly this involves the study of a small town or village, but it includes the study of little-known individuals.

modernist   Literally, the usages, modes of thought and expressions or peculiarities of style which are characteristic of modern times, but it has come to include also particular theories, such as structuralism.

panegyric   A public speech or published text in praise of a person or thing; a laudatory discourse; a eulogy; an encomium.

performativity   Relating to performance, the term suggests that speech and actions can be seen and understood as a kind of performance.

postmodern   The phase of history in the arts, and so forth, beyond modernism, usually regarded also as having some specific qualities including irony, detachment, and a scepticism about universal theories or 'grand narratives'.

poststructuralism   An intellectual movement which originated in France in the 1960s and which rejected the structuralist view that society can be understood in terms of particular structures and patterns of behaviour, attitudes and rules.

psychoanalysis/psychoanalytic   A body of ideas developed by Sigmund Freud and continued by others, concerned with the study of human psychological functioning.

subjectivity/subjective   The quality or condition of viewing things exclusively through the medium of one's own mind or individuality; the condition of being dominated by or absorbed in one's personal feelings, thoughts, concerns, and so on; hence, individuality, personality.

transference A term used within psychoanalysis to refer to the transfer to the analyst by the patient of reawakened and powerful emotions previously directed (in childhood) at some other person or thing and since repressed or forgotten. It also refers more loosely to the transfer of such emotions to others.

trauma A psychic injury, usually one caused by an emotional shock, the memory of which is repressed and remains unhealed.

Notes

► Introduction

1 Prue Chamberlayne, Joanna Bornat and Tom Wengraf (eds), *The Turn to Biographical Methods in Social Science* (London: Verso, 2000). See particularly Chapter 1, Michael Rustin, 'Reflections on the Biographical Turn in Social Science', pp. 33–52.

2 Arthur M. Schlesinger, Jr, 'Editor's Note', in Joyce Appleby (ed.), *Thomas Jefferson* (New York: Henry Holt & Co., 2003), p. xvi.

3 Ibid.

4 Barbara Merrill and Linden West, *Using Biographical Methods in Social Research* (London: Sage, 2009), p. 2.

5 Ian Kershaw, 'Power and Personality', *The Historian*, 83, Autumn 2004, pp. 8–20.

6 See, for example, James O'Donnell, *Augustine: A New Biography* (New York: Ecco, 2005); Janet L. Nelson, 'Writing Early Medieval Biography', *History Workshop Journal*, 50, 2000, pp. 129–36; Ian Kershaw, *Hitler, 1889–1936: Hubris* (London: Allen Lane, 1998); and *Hitler, 1936–1945: Nemesis* (London: Allen Lane, 2000); R. J. B. Bosworth, *Mussolini* (London: Arnold, 2002).

7 Barbara Caine, *Destined to be Wives: The Sisters of Beatrice Webb* (Oxford: Oxford University Press, 1986).

► 1 Historians and the Question of Biography

1 Judith M. Brown. "Life Histories" and the History of Modern South Asia', *AHR* Roundtable: Historians and Biography, *The American Historical Review*, 114(3), June 2009, p. 598.

2 Alice Kessler Harris, 'Why Biography?' *AHR* Roundtable: Historians and Biography, *The American Historical Review*, 114(3), June 2009, p. 625.

3 Plutarch, *The Age of Alexander: Nine Greek Lives*, translated [from the Latin] and annotated by Ian Scott-Kilvert; introduction by G. T. Griffith (Harmondsworth: Penguin, 1973), p. 252.

4 Francis Bacon, *The Advancement of Learning and New Atlantis*, with a Preface by Thomas Case (London: Oxford University Press, 1960), p. 87.

5 Cited in Mark Salber Phillips, *Society and Sentiment: Genres of Historical Writing in Britain, 1740–1820* (Princeton, NJ: Princeton University Press, 2000), p. 134.

6 Edmund Bohan, *The Method and Order of Reading Both Civil and Ecclesiastical Histories* (1685), cited in Phillips, p. 105.

7 Phillips, Society and Sentiment, pp.103–40.

8 Phillips, *Society and Sentiment*, pp. 103–4.

9 David Wootton, 'Hume, "the Historian"', in David Fate Norton (ed.), *The Cambridge Companion to Hume* (Cambridge: Cambridge University Press), pp. 281–85.

10 Cited in Phillips, p. 264.

11 Cited in Phillips, p. 263.

12 Thomas Carlyle, *Critical and Miscellaneous Essays* (Philadelphia, PA: A. Hart, late Carey & Hart, 1852), pp. 219–22.

13 Blair Worden, 'Thomas Carlyle and Oliver Cromwell' [1999 Raleigh Lecture on History], *Proceedings of the British Academy*, Vol. 105 (Oxford: Oxford University Press, 2000).

14 Ralph Waldo Emerson, 'History', in his *Essays: Series One* (1841), https://www.gutenberg.org/files/2944/2944-h/2944-h.htm (accessed 12 March 2018).

15 Cited in Phillips, p. 345.

16 Worden, p. 140.

17 Fred Kaplan, *Thomas Cromwell: A Biography* (New York: Open Road Media, 2013).

18 Ralph Waldo Emerson, p. 3.

19 See Scott E. Casper, *Constructing American Lives: Biography & Culture in Nineteenth-Century America* (Chapel Hill, NC: University of North Carolina Press, 1999), p. 21.

20 James Parton, *Life of Andrew Jackson* (New York: Mason Brothers, 1860); *Life and Times of Benjamin Franklin* (New York: Mason Brothers, 1864); see also Casper, *Constructing American Lives*, pp. 220–45.

21 For a discussion of this process, see Bonnie G. Smith, *The Gender of History: Men, Women and Historical Practice* (Cambridge , MA: Harvard University Press, 1998), pp. 103–30.

22 Leopold von Ranke, *History of the Latin and Teutonic Nations (1494 to 1514)*, revised translation by G. R. Dennis and Introduction by Edward Armstrong (London: G. Bell & Sons, 1909), p. iv.

23 Andreas Boldt, 'Ranke: Objectivity and History', *Rethinking History* 18(4), 2014, pp. 457–74.

24 Leopold von Ranke, *The Theory and Practice of History*, edited by George G. Iggers and Konrad von Moltke (New York: Irvington Publishers Inc., 1983), pp. iv–vii.

25 *Cambridge University Commission Report* (1852), cited in Christopher J. W. Parker, 'Academic History: Paradigms and Dialectic', *Literature and History*, 5(2), 1979, p. 170.

26 David Amigoni, *Victorian Biography: Intellectuals and the Ordering of Discourse* (Hemel Hempstead: Harvester Wheatsheaf, 1993), p. 103.

27 Ibid., pp. 97–106.

28 Lord Acton, *A Lecture on the Study of History* (London: Macmillan & Co., 1896), p. 13.

29 Reba N. Soffer, 'Nation, Duty, Character and Confidence: History at Oxford, 1850–1914', *The Historical Journal*, 30(1), March 1987, p. 80; see also Reba N. Soffer, *Discipline and Power: The University, History, and the Making of an English Elite, 1870–1930* (Stanford, CA: Stanford University Press, 1994).

30 *English Historical Review*, 1(1), January 1886, prefatory note.

31 Matt Perry, *Marxism and History* (Houndmills, Basingstoke, Hampshire; New York: Palgrave, 2002), p. 9. Kershaw himself uses this quote, from Marx's introduction to his *Eighteenth Brumaire of Louis Bonaparte*, to explain his own approach to biography. Ian Kershaw, 'Personality and Power: The Individual's Role in the History of Twentieth-century Europe,' *Historian*, Autumn 2004, p. 28.

32 G. V. Plekhanov, *The Role of the Individual in History*, translated from the Russian by J. Fineberg (Moscow: Foreign Languages Publishing House, 1946), pp. 59–60.

33 Plekhanov, *The Role of the Individual in History*, p. 60.

34 Tamara Deutscher, 'Work in Progress', in David Horowitz (ed.), *Isaac Deutscher: The Man and His Work* (London: Macdonald, 1971), p. 57.

35 Ibid., pp. 72–73.

36 Pierre Nora, *Essais d'ego-histoire*, réunis et présentés par Pierre Nora (Paris: Gallimard, 1987).

37 Peter Burke comments on the nature of the commission that he undertook with it, involving the writing of a biography for a wider audience, in 'Historians Revisited. Lucien Febvre, Ecclesiastical Historian?', *Journal of Ecclesiastical History*, 50(4), October 1999, p. 3.

38 See, for example, Derek Beales, *History and Biography: An Inaugural Lecture* (Cambridge: Cambridge University Press, 1981).

39 Herbert Butterfield, 'The Role of the Individual in History', *History*, 40(138–139), p. 1.

40 See, for example, Peter Burke (ed.), *New Perspectives on Historical Writing* (Cambridge: Polity Press, 1991); or Peter Lambert and Philip Schofield (eds), *Making History: An Introduction to the History and Practices of a Discipline* (London: Routledge, 2004).

41 E. H. Carr, *What Is History?* (Harmondsworth: Penguin Books, 1964).

42 G. R. Elton, *The Practice of History* (London: Fontana Press, 1967).

43 Roland Barthes, 'The Death of the Author', in his *Image Music Text*, essays selected and translated by Stephen Heath (New York: Hill and Wang, 1977).

44 Roland Barthes, *Michelet*, translated by Richard Howard (New York: Hill and Wang, 1987).

45 B. Finkelstein, 'Revealing Human Agency: The Uses of Biography in the Study of Educational History', in C. Kridel (ed.), *Writing Educational Biography: Explorations in Quantitative Research* (New York: Garland Publishing, 1985), p. 45.

46 Kathryn Kish Sklar, *Catharine Beecher: A Study in American Domesticity* (New Haven, CT: Yale University Press, 1973), p. xv.

47 Mary S. Hartman, *Victorian Murderesses: A True History of Thirteen Respectable French and English Women Accused of Unspeakable Crimes* (New York: Schocken Books, 1977), p. ix.

48 Carlo Ginzburg and Carlo Poni, 'The Name and the Game,' in Edward Muir (ed.), *Microhistory and the Lost Peoples of Europe* (Baltimore, 1991), p. 3; see also Carlo Ginzburg, 'Microhistory: Two or Three Things That I Know about It,' *Critical Inquiry*, 20(1), 1993, pp. 10–35.

49 See, for example, Jill Lepore, 'Historians Who Love Too Much: Reflections on Microhistory and Biography', *The Journal of American History*, 88(1), June 2001, pp. 129–44.

50 Natalie Zemon Davies, *Women on the Margins: Three Seventeenth-Century Lives* (Cambridge, MA: Harvard University Press, 1995); Martha Hodes, The *Sea Captain's Wife: A True Story of Love, Race and War in the Nineteenth Century* (New York: W. W. Norton, 1996).

51 Brown, '"Life Histories" and the History of Modern South Asia', *Loc. cit.*

52 Kessler Harris, 'Why Biography?' *Loc. cit.*

53 See two Special Issues of the *Journal of Women's History*, edited by Marilyn Booth and Antoinette Burton, entitled 'Critical Feminist Biography', 21(3, 4), Autumn and Winter 2009.

54 Cited in James L. Conyers, Jr (ed.), *Black Lives: Essays in American Biography* (Armonk, NY: M.E. Sharpe, 1999), p. 3.

55 Achim von Oppen and Silke Strickrodt, 'Introduction: Biographies Between Spheres of Empire', *The Journal of Imperial and Commonwealth History*, 44(5), 2016, pp. 717–29.

56 Ludmilla Jordanova, *History in Practice* (London: Arnold, 2000), p. 41.

57 Shirley A. Leckie, 'Biography Matters: Why Historians Need Well Crafted Biographies More Than Ever', in Lloyd Ambrosius (ed.), *Writing Biography: Historians & Their Craft* (Lincoln, NE: University of Nebraska Press, 2004), p. 20.

58 Robert I. Rotberg, 'Biography and Historiography: Mutual Evidentiary and Interdisciplinary Considerations' *Journal of Interdisciplinary History*, 40(3), Winter 2010, pp. 305–24.

59 Lucy Riall, 'The Shallow End of History?: The Substance and Future of Political Biography', *Journal of Interdisciplinary History*, 40(3), Winter 2010, pp. 375–97.

60 Ian Kershaw, *Hitler* (London: Routledge, 2014), p. vii.

61 Kershaw, 'Personality and Power: The Individual's Role in the History of Twentieth-Century Europe', *Historian*, 83, 2004, pp. 8–20.

▶ 2 A History of Biography

1 John Dryden, 'Life of Plutarch' in *Plutarch's Lives Translated from the Greek by Several Hands to Which Is Prefixt the Life of Plutarch* (London: Jacob Tonson, 1683), pp. 60–61.

2 Donald A Stauffer, *English Biography before 1700* (Cambridge, MA: Harvard University Press, 1930), pp. 215–20.

3 Dryden, 'Life of Plutarch', p. 45.

4 Plutarch, Plutarch's Lives, ed. A. H. Clough, Project Guttenburg, 1996 http://www.gutenberg.org/files/674/674-h/674-h.htm

5 See Mark Longaker, *English Biography in the Eighteenth Century* (Philadelphia, PA: University of Pennsylvania Press, 1931).

6 Samuel Johnson, *The Rambler*, 60, 13 October 1750, in *Selected Essays*, edited and with an introduction and notes by David Womersley (London: Penguin, 2003), p. 131.

7 Johnson, *Selected Essays*, pp. 129–30.

8 *Boswell's Life of Johnson, Together with Boswell's Journal of a Tour to the Hebrides and Johnson's Diary of a Journey into North Wales*, edited by George Birkbeck Hill, revised and enlarged edition by L. F. Powell, in six volumes (Oxford: Clarendon Press, 1934), *Volume III: The Life*, p. 155.

9 Mark Salber Phillips, *Society and Sentiment: Genres of Historical Writing in Britain, 1740–1820* (Princeton, NJ: Princeton University Press, 2000), pp. 104–5.

10 Samuel Johnson, *Selected Essays*, pp. 131–32.

11 Richard Holmes, *Dr Johnson and Mr Savage* (London: Hodder & Stoughton, 1989), pp. 53–61.

12 Samuel Johnson, *The Life of Richard Savage, 1748* (Menston: The Scholar Press, 1971), pp. 2, 181–82.

13 *Boswell's Life of Johnson, Volume 1: The Life*, pp. 25–26, 29.

14 Adam Sisman, *Boswell's Presumptuous Task: The Making of the Life of Dr Johnson* (New York: Penguin, 2000).

15 This comment from Carlyle is quoted in J. A. Froude, *Thomas Carlyle*, vol. 1 (London: Longman's Green, 1884), p. v.

16 Barbara Caine, 'Victorian Feminism and the Ghost of Mary Wollstonecraft', *Women's Writing*, 4(2), 1997, pp. 261–75.

17 Barbara Taylor, *Mary Wollstonecraft and the Feminist Imagination* (Cambridge: Cambridge University Press, 2003), p. 9.

18 This letter, dated 20 December 1836, is included in the Preface of John G. Lockhart's *The Life of Sir Walter Scott* (London: Dent, 1906), p. xxxvii.

19 See Richard Altick, *Lives and Letters: A History of Literary Biography in England and America* (Westport, CT: Greenwood Press, 1979), pp. 146–80.

20 Cited in Altick, *Lives and Letters*, p. 155.

21 Elizabeth Gaskell, *The Life of Charlotte Brontë* (London: Smith, Elder and Co., 1857).

22 Arthur Pollard, *Mrs. Gaskell: Novelist and Biographer* (Manchester: Manchester University Press, 1965), pp. 139–71; Amy K. Levin, *The Suppressed Sister: A Relationship in Novels by Nineteenth- and Twentieth-Century British Women* (Lewisburg, PA: Bucknell University Press; London: Associated University Presses, 1992), pp. 70–73.

23 For the fullest discussion of this issue, see Trev Broughton, *Men of Letters, Writing Lives: Masculinity and Literary Auto/biography in the Late-Victorian Period* (New York: Routledge, 1999).

24 Thomas Carlyle, *Reminiscences*, edited by J. A. Froude (London: Longman's, Green and Co., 1881); *Letters and Memorials of Jane Welsh Carlyle*, edited by J. A. Froude (London: Longman's, Green and Co., 1883).

25 Cited in Altick, *Lives and Letters*, p. 235.

26 Broughton, *Men of Letters*.

27 Edmund Gosse, *Father and Son: A Study of Two Temperaments* (New York: C. Scribner's Sons; London: W. Heinemann, 1907).

28 Lytton Strachey, *Eminent Victorians* (London: Chatto and Windus, 1948), Preface.

29 See Laura Marcus, *Auto/biographical Discourses: Theory, Criticism, Practice* (Manchester: Manchester University Press, 1994).

30 Virginia Woolf, 'The New Biography', in *Granite and Rainbow: Essays by Virginia Woolf* (New York: Harcourt Brace Jovanovich, 1975), pp. 149–55.

31 Paula R. Backscheider, *Reflections on Biography* (Oxford: Oxford University Press, 2001), p. xii.

32 Ibid., p. 104.

33 Altick, *Lives and Letters*, p. 334.

34 Leon Edel, *Henry James: The Untried Years 1843–1870* (London: Hart-Davis, 1953).

35 Michael Holroyd, *Lytton Strachey: A Critical Biography*, 2 volumes (London: Heinemann, 1967–8).

36 Phyllis Grosskurth, *John Addington Symonds: A Biography* (New York: Arno Press, 1975).

37 Michael Holroyd, *Lytton Strachey: The New Biography* (New York: Farrar, Straus and Giroux, 1996), p. xv.

38 Derek Hudson, *Munby, Man of Two Worlds: The Life and Diaries of Arthur J. Munby, 1828–1910* (London: J. Murray, 1972).

39 Susan Chitty, *The Beast and the Monk* (London: Hodder and Stoughton, 1974).

40 Gerder Lerner, *The Grimke Sisters from South Carolina: Pioneers for Women's Rights and Abolition*, 2nd edn (Chapel Hill, NC: University of North Carolina Press, 1998), p. xiv.

41 Bell Gale Chevigny, 'Daughters Writing: Towards a Theory of Women's Biography', *Feminist Studies*, 9(1), 1983, pp. 79–102.

42 Elizabeth Kamarck Minnich, 'Friendship between Women: The Act of Feminist Biography', *Feminist Studies*, 11(2), Summer 1985, pp. 287–305.

► 3 Collective Biography

1 Bronwyn Davies and Susan Gannon, *Doing Collective Biography: Investigating the Production of Subjectivity* (London, McGraw-Hill Education, 2006); Roberta Hawkins et al., 'Practicing Collective Biography', *Geography Compass*, 10(4), 2016, pp. 165–78.

2 Keith Thomas, *Changing Conceptions of National Biography: The Oxford DNB in Historical Perspective* (Cambridge: Cambridge University Press, 2005), p. 3d.

3 Bede, the Venerable, Saint 673=345, Lives of the Abbots of Wearmouth and Jarrow, (Cambridge: Penguin Classics, 2011)

4 See G. Vasari, 'Prefaces to the Lives', from E. Fernie (ed.), *Art History and Its Methods: A Critical Anthology* (London: Phaidon Press, 1995), p. 33.

5 Thomas, *Changing Conceptions of National Biography*, p. 3.

6 Pierre Bayle (1647–1706), *The Dictionary Historical and Critical of Mr Peter Bayle ... to which is prefixed, The life of the author, revised, corrected, and enlarged, by Mr. Des Maizeaux, The second edition, carefully collated with several editions of the original; in which many passages are restored, and the whole greatly augmented, particularly with a translation of the quotations from eminent writers in various languages* (London: Printed for J. J. and P. Knapton, D. Midwinter [and others], 1734–38).

7 See A *General Dictionary, Historical and Critical: in which a new and accurate translation of that of ... Mr. Bayle, with the corrections and observations printed in the late edition at Paris, is included; and interspersed with several thousand lives never before published. ... With reflections on such passages of Mr. Bayle, as seem to favour scepticism and the Manichee System. By the Reverend Mr. John Peter Bernard; the Reverend Mr. Thomas Birch; Mr. John Lockman; and other hands. And the articles relating to Oriental history by George Sale ...* (London: printed by James Bettenham, for G. Strahan et al. and sold at their shop in Scarborough, 1734–41).

8 David Bell, *The Cult of the Nation in France: Inventing Nationalism 1680–1800* (Cambridge: Harvard University Press, 2001), pp. 108–09.

9 Donald A. Stauffer, *The Art of Biography in Eighteenth Century England* (Princeton, NJ: Princeton University Press, 1941), pp. 250–51.

10 Ernest Renan, *'Qu'est-ce qu'une nation?'* (1882), translated in Geoffrey Eley and Ronald Grigor Suny (eds), *Becoming National: A Reader* (New York: Oxford University Press, 1996), p. 52.

11 Thomas, *Changing Conceptions of National Biography*, p. 14.

12 Ibid., p. 15.

13 Leslie Stephen, 'National Biography', in his *Studies of a Biographer*, vol. I (London: Duckworth, 1898–1902), p. 12.

14 Sidney Lee, 'National Biography', *Cornhill Magazine*, 26, March 1896, pp. 258–79.

15 Thomas, *Changing Conceptions of National Biography*, p. 38.

16 Australian Dictionary of Biography, www.adb.online.anu.edu.au/about.htm, accessed 29 June 2018.

17 Nelson Mandela, 'Foreword', in E. J. Verwey (ed.), *New Dictionary of South African Biography* (Pretoria: HSRC Publishers, 1995), p. v.

18 George Ballard, *Memoirs of Several Ladies of Great Britain Who Have Been Celebrated for Their Writings or Their Skill in the Learned Languages, Arts and Sciences*, edited by Ruth Perry (Detroit, MI: Wayne State University Press, 1985), p. ii.

19 Ballard, *Memoirs of Several Ladies*, see Ruth Perry's 'Introduction'.

20 Mary Hays, *Female Biography: Or Memoirs of Illustrious and Celebrated Women, of All Ages and Countries* (London: R. Phillips, 1803).

21 Hays, *Female Biography*, vol. 1, Preface.

22 Rohan Maitzen, '"This Feminine Preserve": Historical Biographies by Victorian Women', Victorian Studies, 38(3), Spring 1995, pp. 371–94.

23 Maitzen, '"This Feminine Preserve"', p. 388.

24 Agnes Strickland, *Lives of the Queens of England, from the Norman Conquest*, 12 volumes (London: Henry Colburn, 1840–48).

25 Agnes Strickland, *Lives of the Queens of Scotland and English Princesses Connected with the Regal Succession of Great Britain*, 8 volumes (London: William Blackwood and Sons, 1850–59); *Lives of the Last Four Princesses of the House of Stuart* (London: Bell and Daldy, 1872).

26 Julia Kavanagh, *Woman in France during the Eighteenth Century*, 2 volumes (London: Smith, Elder and Co., 1850); and *Women of Christianity: Exemplary for Acts of Piety and Charity* (London: Smith, Elder and Co., 1852).

27 Julia Kavanagh, *Women in France in the Eighteenth Century* (London: Smith Elder & Co., 1864), p. 4.

28 Lawrence Stone, 'Prosopography', *Daedalus*, 100(1), 1971, pp. 46–71.

29 Lewis Namier, *The Structure of Politics at the Accession of George III*, 2nd edn (London: Macmillan and Co., 1957), p. xi.

30 Dion Smythe, 'Putting Technology to Work: The CD-ROM Version of the *Prosopography of the Byzantine Empire I (641–867)*', History and Computing, 12(1), 2000, p. 85.

31 K.S.B. Keats-Rohan, 'Introduction Chameleon or Chimera? Understanding Prosopography' in Idem. (ed.), *Prosopography Approaches and Applications: A Handbook* (Oxford: Occasional Publications of the Unit for Prosopographical Research, 2007), pp. 5–7.

32 K.S.B. Keats-Rohan, 'Progress or Perversion: Current Issues in Prosopography, an Introduction', 28 June 2003, http://users.ox.ac.uk/~prosop/progress-or-perversion.pdf accessed 12 March 2018.

33 Edward T. James, Janet Wilson James and Paul S. Boyer (eds), *Notable American Women, a Biographical Dictionary*, 3 volumes (Cambridge, MA: Belknap Press of Harvard University, 1971).

34 Barbara Sicherman, Carol Hurd Green, Ilene Kantrov, Harriet Walker (eds), *Notable American Women: The Modern Period* (Cambridge, MA: Belknap Press of Harvard University Press, 1980).

35 Susan Ware (ed.), *Notable American Women: A Biographical Dictionary Completing the Twentieth Century* (Cambridge, MA: Belknap Press of Harvard University Press, 2005).

36 Jenny Uglow, 'Foreword to First Edition', in Maggy Hendry and Jenny Uglow, *The Palgrave Macmillan Dictionary of Women's Biography* (Basingstoke: Palgrave Macmillan, 2005), p. vii.

37 Olive Banks, *The Biographical Dictionary of British Feminists, Volume 1: 1800–1930* (New York: New York University Press, 1985).

38 Francesca de Haan, Krassimira Daskalova and Anna Loutfi (eds), *Biographical Dictionary of Women's Movements and Feminisms: Central, Eastern and South Eastern Europe, 19th and 20th Centuries*, Central European University Press, 2007.

39 See Updates, October 2009, *Oxford Dictionary of National Biography*, www.oxforddnb.com.

40 Dictionnaire biographique du Canada, www.biographi.ca. Accessed 12 March 2018.

41 James Fox, *Five Sisters: The Langhorne Sisters of Virginia* (London: Granta, 1998); Stella Tillyard, *Aristocrats* (London: Weidenfeld and Nicolson, 1999).

42 M. Jeanne Peterson, *Family, Love, and Work in the Lives of Victorian Gentlewomen* (Bloomington: Indiana University Press, 1989); Judith Flanders, *A Circle of Sisters: Alice Kipling, Georgiana Burne-Jones, Agnes Poynter and Louisa Baldwin* (Harmondsworth: Penguin, 2001).

43 Barbara Caine, *Bombay to Bloomsbury: A Biography of the Stracheys* (Oxford: Oxford University Press, 2005).

44 Emma Rothschild, *The Inner Life of Empires, an Eighteenth-Century History* (Princeton NJ: Princeton University Press, 2011).

45 James Fox, *The Langhorne Sisters* (London: Granta, 1998).

46 Anne de Courcy, *The Viceroy's Daughters: The Lives of the Curzon Sisters* (London: Harper Collins, 2003).

47 Mary S. Lovell, *The Sisters: The Saga of the Mitford Family* (New York: Norton, 2003).

48 Joe Alex Morris, *Those Rockefeller Brothers: An Informal Biography of Five Extraordinary Young Men* (New York: Harper, 1953); Fred C. Kelly, *The Wright Brothers* (New York: Dover, 1989).

49 John Kenneth Severn, *Architects of Empire: The Duke of Wellington and His Brothers* (Norman, OK: University of Oklahoma Press, 2007); Penelope Fitzgerald, *The Knox Brothers* (London: Macmillan, 1977).

50 William St Clair, *The Godwins and the Shelleys: A Biography of a Family* (London: Faber, 1989).

51 Ron Chernow, *The Warburgs: The Twentieth-Century Odyssey of a Remarkable Jewish Family* (New York: Random House, 1993); Alexander Waugh, *The House of Wittgenstein: A Family at War* (London: Bloomsbury, 2008).

52 Norma Clarke, *Ambitious Heights – Writing, Friendship, Love: Jewsbury Sisters, Felicia Hemans and Jane Carlyle* (London: Routledge, 1990).

53 Jennifer Fleischner, *Mrs. Lincoln and Mrs. Keckly: The Remarkable Story of the Friendship Between a First Lady and a Former Slave* (New York: Broadway Books, 2004).

54 Jeffrey O'Connell and Thomas E. O'Connell *Friendships across Ages: Johnson and Boswell; Holmes and Laski* (New York: Lexington Books, 2008).

55 Norman and Jeanne Mackenzie, *The First Fabians* (London: Weidenfeld and Nicolson, 1979); Leon Edel, *Bloomsbury: A House of Lions* (London: Penguin, 1988).

56 Frank A. Kafker, *The Encyclopedists as a Group: A Collective Biography of the Authors of the Encyclopédie* (Paris: Voltaire Foundation, 1996), Louis Menand, *The Metaphysical Club* (New York: Farrar, 2001).

57 Jenny Uglow, *The Lunar Men: The Friends Who Made the Future, 1730–1810* (London: Faber and Faber, 2002).

58 Richard Holmes, *The Age of Wonder: How the Romantic Generation Discovered the Beauty and Terror of Science* (London: Harper Press, 2008).

59 Iain McCalman, *Darwin's Armada: How Four Voyages to Australia Won the Battle for Evolution and Changed the World* (Melbourne: Penguin, 2008).

60 Sheila Fitzpatrick, *On Stalin's Team: The Years of Living Dangerously in Soviet History* (Melbourne: Melbourne University Press, 2015).

▶ 4 Auto/Biography and Life Writing

1 Liz Stanley, *The Auto/Biographical I. The Theory and Practice of Feminist Auto/Biography* (Manchester: University of Manchester Press, 1992), p. 3.

2 Felicity A. Nussbaum, *The Autobiographical Subject: Gender and Ideology in Eighteenth-Century England* (Baltimore, MD: Johns Hopkins University Press, 1989); Regenia Gagnier, *Subjectivities: A History of Self-Representation in Britain, 1832–1920* (New York: Oxford University Press, 1991).

3 *Essais d'ego-histoire*, réunis et présentés par Pierre Nora (Paris: Gallimard, 1987), p. 5.

4 Luisa Passerini, *Autobiography of a Generation*, translated by Lisa Erdberg (Hanover: Wesleyan University Press, 1996); Annie Kreigel, *Ce que j'ai cru comprendre* (Paris: Robert Laffont, 1991); see also *Historein*, 3, 2001.

5 For an extended discussion of this connection, see the issue of *Rethinking History* on 'Academic Autobiography and/in the Discourse of History', 13(1), 2009.

6 It is worth noting here that there is no attempt at defining 'life writing' in the *Encyclopaedia of Life-writing*, edited by Margaretta Jolly (London: Fitzroy Dearborn, 2001).

7 David Amigoni, 'Introduction: Victorian Life Writing: Genres, Print, Constituencies', in Amigoni (ed.), *Life Writing and Victorian Culture* (London: Ashgate, 2006), pp. 2–21.

8 See, for example, Jo Burr Margadant, 'Introduction: The New Biography in Historical Practice', *French Historical Studies*, 19(4), 1996, pp. 1057–58; David Bates, Julia Crick and Sarah Hamilton (eds), *Writing Medieval Biography 750–1250* (Woodbridge, NJ: Boydell Press, 2006).

9 Leigh Gilmore, 'Last Words: Transference and the Autobiographical Demand in Mikal Gilmore's *Shot in the Heart*', *American Imago*, 55(2), 1998, pp. 277–98.

10 Sigmund Freud, *Leonardo da Vinci and a Memory of His Childhood*, translated by Alan Tyson, with an introduction by Brian Farrell (Harmondsworth: Penguin, 1963), p. 177.

11 Eva Schepeler, 'The Biographer's Transferences: A Chapter in Psychobiographical Epistemology', *Biography: An Interdisciplinary Quarterly*, 13(2), Spring 1990, pp. 111–27.

12 Leon Edel, *Writing Lives: Principia Biographica* (New York and London: Norton, 1984), p. 67; see also Leon Edel, 'Confessions of a Biographer', in George Moraitis and George Pollack (eds), *Psychoanalytic Studies of Biography* (Madison, WI: International Universities Press, 1987), pp. 3–29.

13 Stuart Feder, 'Transference Attended the Birth of Modern Biography', *American Imago*, 54(4), 1997, pp. 399–416.

14 Bell Gale Chevigny, 'Daughters Writing: Towards a Theory of Women's Biography', *Feminist Studies*, 9(1), 1983, pp. 79–102; Elizabeth Kamarck Minnich, 'Friendship between Women: The Act of Feminist Biography', *Feminist Studies*, 11(2), Summer 1985, pp. 287–305.

15 Paul John Eakin, '"The Unseemly Profession": Privacy, Inviolate Personality and the Ethics of Life Writing', in Jane Adamson, Richard Freadman, David Parker (eds), *Renegotiating Ethics in Literature, Philosophy, and Theory* (Cambridge: Cambridge University Press, 1998), pp. 161–81.

16 Basil Sanson, 'In the Absence of Vita as Genre. The Making of the Roy Kelly Story', in Bain Attwood and Fiona Magowan (eds), *Telling Stories: Indigenous History and Memory in Australia* (Sydney, NSW: Allen & Unwin, 2001), p. 102.

17 Pierre Nora, 'Memoirs of Men of State: From Commynes to De Gaulle', in *Rethinking France: Les lieux de mémoire* (Chicago, IL: University of Chicago Press, 2001), p. 411.

18 G. Kitson Clark, *The Critical Historian* (London: Heinemann, 1967), p. 67.

19 Natalie Zemon Davis, *Women on the Margins: Three Seventeenth-Century Lives* (Cambridge, MA: Harvard University Press, 1995), p. 207.

20 Davis, *Women on the Margins*, pp. 2–3.

21 James J. O'Donnell, *Augustine, Saint & Sinner: A New Biography* (London: Profile Books, 2005), pp. 5–8.

22 Vincent Carretta, *Equiano the African: Biography of a Self-Made Man* (Athens, GA: University of Georgia Press, 2005).

23 Kay Schaffer and Sidonie Smith, 'Conjunctions: Life Narratives in the Field of Human Rights', *Biography*, 21(1), Winter 2004, p. 1.

24 Annette Wieviorka. *The Era of the Witness*, translated by Jared Stark (Ithaca, NY: Cornell University Press, 2006).

25 For a discussion of this process, see Dominick LaCapra, *Writing History, Writing Trauma* (Baltimore, MD: Johns Hopkins University Press, 2001).

26 Cathy Caruth, 'Unexplained Experience: Trauma and the Possibility of History', *Yale French Studies*, 79, 1991.

27 Dominick LaCapra, *Writing History, Writing Trauma* (Baltimore, MD: Johns Hopkins University Press, 2000).

28 Laura Marcus, *Auto/Biographical Discourses: Theory, Criticism, Practice* (Manchester: Manchester University Press, 1994); James Olney, *Metaphors of the Self: The Meaning of Autobiography* (Princeton, NJ: Princeton University Press, 1980).

29 *I, Rigoberta Menchú: An Indian Woman in Guatemala*, edited and introduced by Elisabeth Burgos-Debray; translated by Ann Wright (London: Verso, 1984). For the controversy generated by Menchú, see Arturo Arias (ed.), *The Rigoberta Menchú Controversy; with a Response by David Stoll* (Minneapolis, MN: University of Minnesota Press, 2001).

30 Binjamin Wilkomirski, *Fragments: Memories of a Wartime Childhood*, transl. by Carol Brown Janeway (New York: Schocken Books, 1996). For the controversy, see Stefan Maechler, *The Wilkomirski Affair: A Study in Biographical Truth*, translated from the German by John E. Woods (New York: Schocken Books, 2001).

31 Philip Holden, *Autobiography and Decolonization: Modernity, Masculinity, and the Nation-State* (Madison, WI: University of Wisconsin Press, 2008).

32 Nelson Mandela, *Long Walk to Freedom: The Autobiography of Nelson Mandela* (Boston: Little Brown, 1994).

33 Paul John Eakin, *Touching the World: Reference in Autobiography* (Princeton, NJ: Princeton University Press, 1992), pp. 145–51.

34 Eric Hobsbawm, *Interesting Times: A Twentieth Century Life* (New York: Pantheon Books, 2002), p. xiii.

35 Jeremy D. Popkin, *History, Historians and Autobiography* (Chicago, IL: University of Chicago Press, 2005).

36 James Aurrell, *Theoretical Perspectives on Historians' Autobiography* (London: Routledge, 2016), pp. 4–10.

37 Aurrell, *Theoretical Perspectives on Historians' Autobiography*, p. 21.

38 Edward Gibbon, *Memoirs of My Life*, edited with an introduction by Betty Radice (London: Penguin, 1984); see also Popkin, *History, Historians and Autobiography*, pp. 89–105.

39 Henry Adams, *The Education of Henry Adams* (Boston: Houghton Mifflin, 1971).

40 Hobsbawm, *Interesting Times*, p. xii.

41 Geoff Eley, *A Crooked Line: From Cultural History to the History of Society* (Berkeley, CA: University of California Press, 1998) p. x.

42 Gerda Lerner, *Fireweed: A Political Autobiography* (Philadelphia, PA: Temple University Press, 2002).

43 Jill Kerr Conway, *The Road from Coorain* (London: Heinemann, 1989).

44 Eileen Boris and Nupur Chaudhuri (eds), *Voices of Women Historians: The Personal, the Political, the Professional* (Bloomington, IN: Indiana University Press, 1999), p. xii.

45 Sheila Fitzpatrick, *A Spy in the Archives* (Melbourne: Melbourne University Press, 2013), p. 1.

46 David Walker, *Not Dark Yet: A Personal History* (Sydney: Giramondo, 2011).

47 Barbara Taylor, *The Last Asylum: A Memoir of Madness in Our Times* (Harmondsworth: Penguin Books, 2013).

48 Taylor, *The Last Asylum*, p. 5.

▶ 5 Interpreting and Constructing Lives

1 Virginia Woolf to Vita Sackville-West, cited in Hermione Lee, *Virginia Woolf* (London: Chatto & Windus, 1996), p. 1.

2 Virginia Woolf, 'The Art of Biography', in Virginia Woolf (ed.), *Collected Essays*, edited by Leonard Woolf (London: Chatto & Windus, 1967), vol. IV, p. 226.

3 Ibid.

4 Virginia Woolf, 'The New Biography', p. 230

5 Ibid., p. 231.

6 Not everyone sees this as a good thing: see Ray Monk, 'This Fictitious Life: Virginia Woolf on Biography and Reality', *Philosophy and Literature*, 31(1), 2007, pp. 1–40.

7 This is the title of the first chapter of Leon Edel, *Writing Lives: Principia Biographica* (New York: W. W. Norton & Co., 1984; first pub. 1959). Edel is best known for his Pulitzer Prize–winning biography of Henry James.

8 His prominence within the field was made very clear as a result of his role in the prominent interdisciplinary journal *Biography*, which first appeared in 1978. Edel was not on the editorial board, but he was clearly the patron of this whole enterprise, and the first number carried a short Manifesto written by him.

9 Edel, *Writing Lives*, p. 25, pp. 93–108.

10 Ibid., pp. 28–31.

11 Jo Burr Margadant (ed.), *The New Biography: Performing Femininity in Nineteenth-Century France* (Berkeley, CA: University of California Press, 2000).

12 Carolyn G. Heilbrun, *Writing a Woman's Life* (London: The Women's Press, 1989), pp. 34–46.

13 Edel, *Writing Lives*, p. 23.

14 Linda Wagner-Martin, *Telling Women's Lives: The New Biography* (Brunswick, NJ: Rutgers University Press, 1994).

15 David Ellis, *Literary Lives: Biography and the Search for Understanding* (New York: Routledge, 2000).

16 Paula Backscheider, *Reflections on Biography* (New York: Oxford University Press, 2001), p. xiv. Backscheider issued a new edition of this work in 2013. But she did not in any way change her original text, choosing rather to write a new Introduction commenting on the choices she made when she first wrote the book and reflecting on some new biographies and more general literature on life writing. She also augmented her conclusion. See Paula R. Backscheider, *Reflections on Biography* (New York: Createspace Independent Publishing, 2013). As a result, I have kept the references which are to the original and more widely available Oxford edition of her book.

17 Backscheider, *Reflections*, pp. 10–13.

18 Ibid., pp. 70–90.

19 Ibid., p. 86.

20 Ibid.

21 Ibid., pp. 95–120.

22 David Hoddeson, Introduction to special issue of *American Imago* on 'Biography', 54(4), Winter 1997, pp. 324–25.

23 Elisabeth Young-Bruehl, *Hannah Arendt: For Love of the World* (New Haven, CT: Yale University Press, 1982); *Anna Freud: A Biography* (London: Macmillan, 1989); 'Profile of a Latency Woman: Development for Biographers', *American Imago*, 55(2), 1998, pp. 235–53.

24 Adam Phillips, *Becoming Freud: The Making of a Psychoanalyst* (New Haven, CT and London: Yale University Press, 2015) p. 22.

25 Ibid., p. 23.

26 Cited in Peter Gay, *Freud: A Life for Our Times* (London: Papermac, 1988), p. 268.

27 Sigmund Freud, *Leonardo da Vinci* (Harmondsworth: Penguin, 1963), p. 177.

28 Freud, *Leonardo da Vinci*, p. 117.

29 Richard Ellman, 'Freud and Literary Biography', *American Scholar*, 53, Fall 1984, pp. 465–78.

30 Malcolm Bowie, 'Freud and the Art of Biography', in Peter France and William St Clair (eds), *Mapping Lives: The Uses of Biography* (Oxford: published for the British Academy by Oxford University Press, 2002), pp. 178–84.

31 Mazlish, 'What is Psycho-history?', *Transactions of the Royal Historical Society*, Fifth Series, 21, 1971, p. 82.

32 Erik H. Erikson, *Young Man Luther: A Study in Psychoanalysis and History* (London: Faber and Faber, 1972), p. 18.

33 Erikson, *Young Man Luther*, p. 34.

34 See, for example, Fawn Brodie, *Thomas Jefferson: An Intimate History* (New York: Norton, 1974); *Richard Nixon: The Shaping of his Character* (New York: Norton, 1981); Bruce Mazlish, *James and John Stuart Mill: Father and Son in the Nineteenth Century* (London: Hutchinson, 1975).

35 Lawrence J. Friedman, *Identity's Architect: A Biography of Erik H. Erikson* (New York: Scribner, 1999); Kit Welchman, *Erik Erikson: His Life, Work, and Significance* (Buckingham: Open University Press, 2000).

36 Thomas A. Kohut, 'Psychohistory as History', *American Historical Review*, 91(2), April 1986, pp. 336–54.

37 Kohut, 'Psychohistory as History', pp. 348–54.

38 Thomas A. Kohut, 'Psychoanalysis as Psychohistory or Why Psychotherapists Cannot Afford to Ignore Culture', *The Annual of Psychoanalysis*, 31, 2003, p. 225.

39 Thomas Kohut, *A German Generation: An Experiential History of the Twentieth Century* (New Haven, CT: Yale University Press, 2012), pp. 1–2.

40 *Ibid.*, pp. 11–12.

41 Daniel Pick, '"*Roma o morte*": Garibaldi, Nationalism and the Problem of Psycho-biography', *History Workshop Journal*, 57(1), 2004, pp. 1–33.

42 Barbara Taylor, 'Separations of Soul: Solitude, Biography, History', *AHR* Roundtable: Historians and Biography, *American Historical Review*, 114(3), June 2009, p. 641.

43 *Ibid.*, p. 641.

44 Barbara Taylor, *Mary Wollstonecraft and the Feminist Imagination* (Cambridge: Cambridge University Press, 2003).

45 Lyndal Roper, *Martin Luther: Renegade and Prophet* (London: The Bodley Head, 2016).

46 *Ibid.*, pp. 6–8.

47 Garry Wills, *Cincinnatus: George Washington and the Enlightenment* (Garden City, NY: Doubleday, 1984).

48 Toril Moi, *Simone de Beauvoir: The Making of an Intellectual Woman* (Oxford: Blackwell, 1994), pp. 3–4.

49 *Ibid.*, p. 2.

50 Angela John, *Elizabeth Robbins: Staging a Life, 1862–1952* (London and New York: Routledge, 1995), pp. 4–9.

51 Lisa Merril, *When Romeo Was a Woman: Charlotte Cushman and Her Circle of Female Spectators* (Ann Arbor, MI: University of Michigan Press, 2000).

52 Margadant, *The New Biography*, pp. 4–10.

53 Susan Grogan, '"Playing the Princess": Flora Tristan, Performance and Female Moral Authority during the July Monarchy', in Margadant, *The New Biography*, pp. 72–98.

▶ 6 Changing Biographical Practices

1 Joe Law and Linda Hughes, 'And What Have *You* Done? Victorian Biography Today', in their edited collection *Biographical Passages, Essays in Victorian and Modernist Biography: Honoring Mary M. Lago* (Columbia: University of Missouri Press, 2000) pp. 3–4.

2 Richard Holmes, 'Biography: The Past Has a Great Future', *Australian Book Review*, November, 2008, p. 31.

3 Sidonie Smith, *A Poetics of Women's Autobiography: Marginality and the Fictions of Self-Representation* (Bloomington, IN: University Press, 1987); Carolyn G. Heilbrun, *Writing a Woman's Life* (New York: Norton, 1988); Linda Wagner-Martin, *Telling Women's Lives: The New Biography* (New Brunswick: Rutgers University Press, 1980); Paula Backscheider, *Reflections on Biography* (New York: Oxford University Press, 2001), Chapter 4. For Backscheider's sense of the changes in the past few years, see Paula Backscheider, *Reflections on Biography* (North Charleston, SC: Createspace Independent Publications, 2013), 'Introduction to the New Edition'.

4 Wagner-Martin, *Telling Women's Lives*, pp. 5–20.

5 Virginia Woolf, 'The Arts of Biography', in her *The Death of the Moth and Other Essays* (Harmondsworth: Penguin Books, 1965), p. 168.

6 Virginia Woolf, *Flush, a Biography* (London: Hogarth Press, 1933). Flush was the name of the dog belonging to the poet Elizabeth Barrett Browning.

7 Betty Boyd Caroli, *The Roosevelt Women* (New York: Basic Books, 1998).

8 Anne De Courcy, *The Viceroy's Daughters: The Lives of the Curzon Sisters* (London: Harper Collins, 2003); Lisa Appignanesi and John Forrester, *Freud's Women* (New York: Basic Books, 1992); see also Bernice Kert, *The Hemingway Women* (New York: W.W. Norton, 1983).

9 Norma Clarke, *Dr Johnson's Women* (London: Hambledon and London, 2000), p. 3.

10 Nigel Nicolson, *Portrait of a Marriage* (London: Weidenfeld & Nicolson, 1973).

11 Natania Rosenfeld, *Outsiders Together: Virginia and Leonard Woolf* (Princeton, NJ: Princeton University Press, 2000); James Covert, *A Victorian Marriage: Mandell and Louise Creighton* (London and New York: Hambledon and London, 2000).

12 Daniel Mark Epstein, *The Lincolns: Portrait of a Marriage* (New York: Ballantine Books, 2008); Joseph P. Lash, *Eleanor and Franklin. The Story of Their Relationship, Based on Eleanor Roosevelt's Private Papers* (London: Deutsch, 1972); Doris Kearns Goodwin, *No Ordinary Time: Franklin and Eleanor Roosevelt: The Home Front in World War II* (New York: Simon & Schuster, 1994).

13 Brenda Maddox, *D. H. Lawrence: The Story of a Marriage* (New York: Simon & Schuster, 1994); Geoffrey Skelton, *Richard and Cosima Wagner: Biography of a Marriage* (London: Gollancz, 1982); Rosemary Ashton, *Thomas and Jane Carlyle: Portrait of a Marriage* (London: Chatto & Windus, 2002).

14 Frederic William Maitland, *The Life and Letters of Leslie Stephen* (London: Duckworth & Co., 1906).

15 Virginia Woolf, 'Reminiscences', in Virginia Woolf, *Moments of Being: Unpublished Autobiographical Writings*, edited by Jeanne Schulkind (London: Chatto & Windus Ltd for Sussex University Press, 1976), p. 65.

16 Noel Annan, *Leslie Stephen: The Godless Victorian* (London: Weidenfeld and Nicolson, 1984).

17 Merrill D. Peterson, *Thomas Jefferson and the New Nation* (New York: Oxford University Press, 1970), p. 707.

18 Fawn Brodie, *Thomas Jefferson: An Intimate History* (New York: W.W. Norton, 1974), p. 32.

19 Annette Gordon-Reed, *Thomas Jefferson and Sally Hemings: An American Controversy* (Charlottesville, VA: University Press of Virginia, 1997).

20 Annette Gordon-Reed, *The Hemings of Monticello: An American Family* (New York: W.W. Norton, 2008).

21 See Jan Ellen Lewis and Peter S. Onuf (eds), *Sally Hemings &Thomas Jefferson* (Charlottesville, VA: University of Virginia Press, 1999).

22 Dumas Malone, *Thomas Jefferson, A Brief Biography* (Chapel Hill: University of North Carolina Press, 2002), p. 43.

23 Joyce Appleby, *Thomas Jefferson* (New York: Henry Holt, 2003) pp. 75–76, 120.

24 Seth Kovan, *The Match Girl and the Heiress* (Princeton, NJ, and Oxford: Princeton University Press, 2014), p. 1.

25 Shane White, *Prince of Darkness: The Untold Story of Jeremiah Hamilton, Wall Street's First Black Millionaire* (New York: St Martin's Press, 2015).

26 Kovan, *The Match Girl*, p.7.

27 Linda Colley *The Ordeal of Elizabeth Marsh: A Woman in World History* (London: Pantheon, 2007).

28 Natalie Zemon Davis, *The Return of Martin Guerre* (Cambridge, MA: Harvard University Press, 1983).

29 Martha Hanna, *Your Death Would Be Mine. Paul and Marie Pireaud in the Great War* (Cambridge, MA: Harvard University Press, 2006).

30 Emma Rothschild, *The Inner Life of Empires: An Eighteenth-Century History* (Princeton, NJ and Oxford: Princeton University Press, 2011).

31 Jill Lepore, 'Historians Who Love Too Much: Reflections on Microhistory and Biography', *Journal of American History*, 88, 2001, pp. 129–44.

32 Nina Rattner Gelbart, *The King's Midwife: A History and Mystery of Madame du Coudray* (Berkeley and Los Angeles, CA: University of California Press, 1998), pp. 14–15.

33 Gilbert, Olive. *Narrative of Sojourner Truth, a Bondswoman of Olden Time, Emancipated by the New York Legislature in the Early Part of the Present Century, with a History of Her Labors and Correspondence Drawn from Her Book of Life* (Chicago, IL: Johnson Pub. Co., 1970).

34 Nell Irvin Painter, 'Sojourner Truth in Life and Memory: Writing the Biography of an American Exotic', *Gender and History*, 2(1), Spring 1990, pp. 3–17; see also Nell Irvin Painter, *Sojourner Truth: A Life, A Symbol* (New York: W.W. Norton, 1997).

35 David Nasaw, 'Introduction', *AHR* Roundtable: Historians and Biography, *American Historical Review*, 114(3), June 2009, pp. 574–77.

36 Nasaw, 'Introduction', *AHR* Roundtable: Historians and Biography, pp. 578–79.

37 Kershaw's ideas and his approach were spelled out earlier in his two-volume biography *Hitler, 1889–1936: Hubris* (1999) and *Hitler, 1936–45: Nemesis* (2000). But the views expressed there are identical to those in the 'condensed' one-volume biography, which at more than 1,000 pages is still substantial. Much of the condensation involved cutting notes and other parts of the scholarly apparatus, rather than the content.

38 Alan Bullock, *Hitler: A Study in Tyranny* (London: Odham Books, 1964), p. 9.

39 Ian Kershaw, *Hitler: A Biography* (New York and London: W.W. Norton, 2008), pp. xxxiv–xxxviii.

40 R.J.B. Bosworth, *Mussolini* (London: Arnold, 2002), pp. 10–11.

41 Judith Brown, *Nehru: A Political Life* (New Haven, CT: Yale University Press, 2003), p. 3.

42 Lucy Riall, *Garibaldi: Invention of a Hero* (New Haven, CT: Yale University Press, 2007); see also Lucy Riall, 'The Shallow End of History: The Substance and Future of Political Biography', *Journal of Interdisciplinary History*, 40(3), pp. 381–92.

43 John Bew, *Citizen Clem: A Biography of Attlee* (London: Quercus Editions, 2016).. 216.

44 Bew, *Citizen Clem:* p. 16.

45 Leonard Huxley, *Charles Darwin* (London: Watts & Co, 1921).

46 Janet Browne, *Charles Darwin Voyaging* (Princeton, NJ: Princeton University Press, 1995), pp. xi.

▶ Conclusion

1 Kessler Harris, 'Why Biography?' *AHR* Roundtable: Historians and Biography, *The American Historical Review*, 114(3), June 2009, p. 625; Judith M. Brown, '"Life Histories" and the History of Modern South Asia', American Historical Review, 14(3), 1 June 2009, pp. 587–95.

2 Richard Holmes, 'Biography: The Past has a Great Future', *Australian Book Review*, November, 2008, p. 31.

3 Carlo Ginzburg, *The Cheese and the Worms: The Cosmos of a Sixteenth-Century Miller* (London: Routledge and Kegan Paul, 1980).

4 Natalie Zemon Davis, *The Return of Martin Guerre* (Cambridge, MA: Harvard University Press, 1983).

5 Natalie Zemon Davis, 'Decentering History: Local Stories and Cultural Crossings in a Global World', *History and Theory*, 50, May 2011, pp. 188–202.

6 Natalie Zemon Davis, *Trickster Travels: A Sixteenth-Century Muslim between Two Worlds* (New York: Farrar, Strauss and Geroux), p. 10.

7 Emma Rothschild, *The Inner Life of Empires: An Eighteenth-Century History* (Princeton, NJ: Princeton University Press, 2011), pp. 139–45.

8 Leonore Davidoff and Catherine Hall, *Family Fortunes: Men and Women of the English Middle Class 1780–1850* (London: Hutchinson, 1987), p. 13.

9 Eleanor Gordon and Gwyneth Nair. *Public Lives: Women, Family and Society in Victorian Britain* (New Haven, CT: Yale University Press, 2003).

10 Bill Schwarz, *^The White Man's World* (Oxford: Oxford University Press, 2011), p. 20.

11 Seth Koven, *Slumming: Sexual and Social Politics in Victorian London* (Princeton, NJ: Princeton University Press, 2006), p. 17.

12 Martha Hodes, *The Sea Captain's Wife: A True Story of Love, Race and War in the Nineteenth Century* (London and New York: W.W. Norton & Company, 2006).

13 Hodes, *The Sea Captain's Wife*, p. 5.

Further Reading

▶ **Chapter 1**

For an interesting discussion about the relationship between biography and history and about the differences between the ways in which historians write biography as compared with those who come from other disciplines, see the 'Roundtable: Historians and Biography', *American Historical Review*, 114 (June 2009). A rather stronger case for insisting on the importance of biography in history is evident in other roundtables: the two special issues of the *Journal of Women's History*, edited by Marilyn Booth and Antoinette Burton, entitled *Critical Feminist Biography*, 21(3 & 4), Autumn and Winter 2009, and in the special issue of *Journal of Interdisciplinary History*, edited by Robert I. Rotberg and titled 'Biography and History: Inextricably Interwoven', 40(3), Winter 2010. Another very useful collection of essays on this subject is Lloyd Ambrosius (ed.), *Writing Biography: Historians and their Craft* (Lincoln: University of Nebraska Press, 2004). A very strong statement of the importance of biography in history is provided in Ludmilla Jordanova, *History in Practice* (London: Arnold, 2000), and a rather more limited sense of its place can be seen in Ian Kershaw, 'Personality and Power: The Individual's Role in the History of Twentieth-Century Europe', *Historian* (Autumn 2004). Moving back in time, there is an excellent discussion of the status of biography in relation to history in eighteenth-century Britain in Mark Salber Phillips, *Society and Sentiment: Genres of Historical Writing in Britain, 1740–1820* (Princeton, NJ: Princeton University Press, 2000), pp. 103–40. Carlyle's approach to Cromwell is dealt with well in Blair Worden, 'Thomas Carlyle and Oliver Cromwell', 1999 Raleigh Lecture on History, *Proceedings of the British Academy*, vol. 105, published for the British Academy by Oxford University Press, 2000. For the establishment of university history in Britain, see Reba N. Soffer, *Discipline and Power: The University, History, and the Making of an English Elite, 1870–1930* (Stanford, CA: Stanford University Press, 1994). For the exclusion of women from university history, see Bonnie G. Smith, *The Gender of History: Men, Women, and Historical Practice* (Cambridge, MA: Harvard University Press, 1998).

▶ Chapter 2

Although there are some standard histories of literary biography, there are as yet no comprehensive histories of the subject – and few new general works. Ian Donaldson, Peter Read and James Walter's *Shaping Lives: Reflections on Biography* (Canberra: Humanities Research Centre, Australian National University, 1992) covers an extended period and contains several excellent essays; Mark Longaker's *English Biography in the Eighteenth Century* (Philadelphia: University of Pennsylvania, 1931) covers the eighteenth century, as does Donald A, Stauffer's *The Art of Biography in Eighteenth Century England* (Princeton, NJ: Princeton University Press, 1941), while Richard Altick's *Lives and Letters: A History of Literary Biography in England and America* (Westport, CT: Greenwood Press, 1979) offers a lively discussion of literary developments from the eighteenth century to the twentieth. There are a number of excellent studies of particular aspects of this subject. Mark Salber Phillips, *Society and Sentiment: Genres of Historical Writing in Britain, 1740–1820* (Princeton, NJ: Princeton University Press, 2000), offers an excellent discussion of the importance of biography in the eighteenth century. For Boswell and the way he wrote his biography of Johnson, see Adam Sisman, *Boswell's Presumptuous Task: The Making of the Life of Dr Johnson* (New York: Penguin Books, 2000). The general lines of development in the nineteenth century are set out in A.O.J. Cockshut's *Truth to Life: The Art of Biography in the Nineteenth Century* (New York: Collins, 1974). But for a very different view and an analysis of the gendered nature of biography and the problems that many faced in relation to it, see Trev Broughton, *Men of Letters, Writing Lives: Masculinity and Literary Auto/Biography in the Late-Victorian Period* (New York: Routledge, 1999). One of the best discussions of changing approaches to biography and of the 'new biography' is Laura Marcus, *Auto/Biographical Discourses: Theory, Criticism, Practice* (Manchester: Manchester University Press, 1994). For feminist approaches to biography, see Carolyn G. Heilbrun, *Writing a Woman's Life* (New York: Norton, 1988); and Linda Wagner-Martin, *Telling Women's Lives. The New Biography* (New Brunswick: Rutgers University Press, 1980), pp. 5–20.

▶ Chapter 3

As indicated in the chapter, as yet very little has been written on collective biography. Keith Thomas, *Changing Conceptions of National Biography: The Oxford DNB in Historical Perspective* (Cambridge: Cambridge University Press, 2005), provides a brief, elegant and informative introduction to the history of the *Dictionary of National Biography*. Rohan Maitzen, '"This Feminine Preserve": Historical Biographies by Victorian Women', *Victorian Studies*, 38(3), Spring 1995, offers an excellent account of the work of nineteenth-century women. The best introduction to prosopography is still Lawrence Stone, 'Prosopography', *Daedalus* 100(1), 1971.

▶ Chapter 4

There is a vast literature on autobiography and life writing. Amongst the best of the general works are James Olney, *Metaphors of the Self: The Meaning of Autobiography* (Princeton: Princeton University Press, 1980); Paul John Eakin, *Touching the World: Reference in Autobiography* (Princeton: Princeton University Press, 1992); and Laura Marcus, *Auto/biographical Discourses: Theory, Criticism, Practice* (Manchester: Manchester University Press, 1994). For earlier autobiographical writing, Felicity A. Nussbaum, *The Autobiographical Subject: Gender and Ideology in Eighteenth-Century England* (Baltimore: Johns Hopkins University Press, 1989) is excellent on the eighteenth century. For the nineteenth century, Regenia Gagnier, *Subjectivities: A History of Self-Representation in Britain, 1832–1920* (New York: Oxford University Press, 1991); and Trev Broughton's *Men of Letters, Writing Lives: Masculinity and Literary Auto/biography in the Late-Victorian Period* (New York: Routledge, 1999) are both excellent. The question of historians' autobiographies has become a subject of considerable interest. Jeremy D. Popkin's *History, Historians and Autobiography* (Chicago, IL: University of Chicago Press, 2005) offers the most comprehensive treatment of this subject, and Jaume Aurell, *Theoretical Perspectives on Historians' Autobiographies: From Documentation to Intervention* (Routledge, 2016), sees these autobiographies as an important part of contemporary historiography.

▶ Chapter 5

For a discussion of some current literary approaches to biography, see Paula R. Backscheider, *Reflections on Biography*, 1999 (2nd edn with a new Introduction, North Charleston, SC: Createspace Independent Publishers, 2013); Eric Homberger and John Charmley (eds), *The Troubled Face of Biography* (New York: St Martin's Press, 1988); David Ellis, *Literary Lives: Biography and the Search for Understanding* (New York: Routledge, 2000). For a discussion of psychobiography and psychohistory, George Moraitis and George Pollack (eds), *Psychoanalytic Studies of Biography* (Madison: International Universities Press, 1987), offer a good introduction to American approaches to the question of psychoanalysis and biography; see also Thomas A. Kohut, 'Psychohistory as History', *American Historical Review* 91(2), April 1986), pp. 336–54. The two special issues devoted to biography of the psychoanalytic journal *American Imago*, 54(4), Winter 1997, and 55(2), Summer 1998, provide a very good discussion of transference in biography writing. Adam Phillips looks at Freud's ambivalence about biography in his *Becoming Freud: The Making of a Psychoanalyst* (New Haven, CT: Yale University Press, 2015). For the question of literary theory and performativity in biography, see Jo Burr Margadant (ed.), *The New Biography: Performing Femininity in Nineteenth-Century France* (Berkeley, CA, 2000).

▶ Chapter 6

On the general question of continuity and change in biography, see Joe Law and Linda Hughes, 'And What Have *You* Done? Victorian Biography Today' in their *Biographical Passages: Essays in Victorian and Modernist Biography* (Columbia and London: University of Missouri Press, 2000); and Linda Wagner-Martin, *Telling Women's Lives. The New Biography* (New Brunswick: Rutgers University Press, 1980). On the question of Jefferson and the re-evaluation of his life in light of his relationship with Sally Hemings, see Annette Gordon-Reed, *Thomas Jefferson and Sally Hemings: An American Controversy* (Charlottesville: University Press of Virginia, 1997) and the excellent discussion in Jan Ellen Lewis and Peter S. Onuf (eds), *Sally Hemings & Thomas Jefferson* (Charlottesville: University of Virginia Press, 1999). For a later work incorporating Jefferson and the Hemings family, see Annette Gordon-Reed, *The Hemingses of Monticello: An American Family* (New York: W.W. Norton & Co., 2008). On the relationship between biography and microhistory, see Jill Lepore, 'Historians who Love Too Much: Reflections on Microhistory and Biography', *Journal of American History*, 88, 2001, pp. 129–44. Nell Irvin Painter provides an excellent discussion of the difficulties involved in her research in Nell Irvin Painter, 'Sojourner Truth in Life and Memory: Writing the Biography of an American Exotic', *Gender and History*, 2(1), Spring 1990, pp. 3–17. See also Nell Irvin Painter *Sojourner Truth: A Life, A Symbol* (New York: W.W. Norton & Co., 1997).

For Kershaw's approach, see 'Personality and Power: The Individual's Role in the History of Twentieth-Century Europe,' *Historian*, 83 (Autumn 2004), p. 8–19; and the Introduction in his *Hitler: A Biography* (New York and London: W.W. Norton & Company, 2008).

Janet Browne explains her views in the Preface to *Charles Darwin Voyaging* (Princeton, NJ: Princeton University Press, 1995).

Index

Druck:
Canon Deutschland Business Services GmbH
im Auftrag der KNV-Gruppe
Ferdinand-Jühlke-Str. 7
99095 Erfurt